Congress in Change

Congress in Change

Evolution and Reform

EDITED BY

NORMAN J. ORNSTEIN

PRAEGER PUBLISHERS
New York

Published in the United States of America in 1975
by Praeger Publishers, Inc.
111 Fourth Avenue, New York, N.Y. 10003

© 1975 by Praeger Publishers, Inc.

Library of Congress Cataloging in Publication Data

Ornstein, Norman J.
  Congress in change: evolution and reform.

  Bibliography: p.
  1. United States.   Congress—Addresses, essays,
lectures.   I. Title.
JK1096.074   328.73   73-10268
ISBN 0-275-10050-2
ISBN 0-275-85030-7 pbk.

Printed in the United States of America

CONTENTS

ACKNOWLEDGMENTS

Many people have earned thanks for assistance of various types in putting together this book; some are represented by their works within these pages. Herb Asher, Phil Brenner, Mike Robinson, Dave Rohde, Alan and Susan Wurtzel all deserve an additional word of thanks. Bob Peabody deserves even more, for he is in large part responsible for the very existence of the book. Finally, I would like to mention my family—Margaret, David, Andrea, Mitchell, and my parents.

INTRODUCTION

Just as American society has changed dramatically since the eighteenth century, so too has Congress, its first branch of government. Congress not only affects societal problems and directions, but in turn is also shaped by the society. By observing the ways in which Congress changes, we can gain a better understanding of how and why the institution responds to the society and, through its actions, shapes public policy.

Why focus on congressional change? The legislature has a real and historic position of importance in the American governmental system. Congress is the first branch of government, so designated by the Constitution. Congress is the law-making and law-non-making body; it can pass ground-breaking legislation (as it did, for example, with the Voting Rights Act of 1964) or fail to enact new policies with equally wide ramifications (as it did with the Nixon Family Assistance Plan of 1969 and 1970). And it can override a President's veto in order to make new policy (as it did with the War Powers Act in 1973). It can even undertake alteration of the Constitution by initiating the amendment process, as it did most recently with equal rights for women. As Congress changes internally, the directions it takes in making policy can change also.

Political scientists and journalists have focused particular attention on American legislative institutions in recent years, exploring many facets of their internal structures and operations. Congress has received more academic attention than our other branches of government for a variety of reasons. It is much more open than other political institutions. While citizens can walk freely through the halls of the Senate and the House, they are not allowed to wander about the White House or Executive Office Building. They can interview or observe important congressional actors, who are more easily identified than are bureaucrats or Presidential aides. For the would-be investigator, Congress provides 535 informants, plus several thousand professional staff, in contrast to the Supreme Court's nine justices with their small coterie of close-mouthed clerks, and one President, whose staff is much less accessible to the layman, though more accessible to the press. Furthermore, the legislative decision-making process, in the form of *Congressional Record* debate, committee hearing transcripts, and roll call votes, is easily available to scholars, and the size and diversity of Congress provide ample opportunity for varied and sophisticated analysis.

Congress is more than a branch of government; it is also a complex social system, a place where personalities can be the important determinants of policy directions and where people interact with institutions. Research on Congress in the 1950's and 1960's, influenced by scholars such as Ralph Huitt, David Truman, and Richard Fenno, tried to capture the factors which shaped congressional behavior by focusing on institutions such as the committees, political parties, and their caucuses, and on individuals like Lyndon Johnson and William Proxmire. The bulk of our knowledge about the contemporary legislative process comes from this research, which roughly encompasses the period 1957 to 1967. Much happened in this decade, including the enlargement of the House Rules Committee, several fascinating leadership battles, and much significant legislation. But in the past few years, scholars have begun to widen their focus, looking back historically to discern broader longitudinal patterns and looking forward as well at the internal and electoral shifts of the 1970's in terms of their impact on future Congresses.

In this book, we utilize both of these recent trends, by focusing directly on *change*, both historical and contemporary. We will not be concerned simply with congressional "reform"; change encompasses a broader range of behavior. It refers to both institutional and individual change; to change in personnel and in legislative structures. A movement from a Lyndon Johnson to a Mike Mansfield as the Senate Majority Leader fits our definition of change. So does the gradual alteration in regional makeup of the Democratic membership of the House brought about by electoral and societal trends. So too does evolution in accepted role for freshman legislators between the 1950's and contemporary Congresses.

This union of the historical and contemporary aspects of change deepens our understanding of legislative processes. By looking at the origins of a legislative structure, such as the seniority system, we can better understand how and why it operates as it does in the 1970's. By examining the turnover in congressional personnel, and its impact on legislative structures, we can better interpret the interaction between individuals and institutions that underlies the legislative process. Change in Congress can, of course, come about in many ways. It can be planned or accidental; brought about through institutional reform or individual personalities; be evolutionary or instantaneous.

Moreover, change in Congress can be either wholly internal or the result of outside pressures. We normally view Congress and legislative change in terms of its impact on the society; the legislative branch's policy outputs affect us all. But society and societal changes can also have a profound impact on Congress. Mass media, particularly the advent of television, have had a very significant effect on our governmental system and the role of Congress in it, as well as on the public's view of Congress and its members. Shifting political allegiances in the electorate, especially—but not exclusively—in the South, have affected turnover and thus the character of membership in both the House and Senate, which in turn has had repercussions for distributions of power within Congress.

Moreover, internal changes in congressional procedure can have spillover effects on other areas of legislative behavior. The institution of the recorded teller vote in the House of Representatives, as part of the 1970 Legislative Reorganization Act, dramatically changed vote turnout and is widely credited with changing the outcome of the House vote on the SST between 1970 and 1971. The implementation of the electronic voting system in the House has had other interesting, and unintentional, side effects.

These interrelationships, between change in the social system and the legislative system, between reforms and various facets of Congressional behavior, between personalities and structural characteristics within the House and the Senate, are our principal areas of interest here. Change in institutions, change in personnel, evolutionary change, structural reforms, and informal change are among the topics covered in the eighteen articles contained in the following pages. Taken together, they delineate the forces which have shaped, and continue to shape, our legislative branch, and suggest what impact future changes and reforms may have on Congress's internal operations and policy outputs.

I. Historical Perspective

Much of this volume focuses on changes in the contemporary Congress—the Congress of the 1960's and 1970's. But Congress has been evolving throughout our nation's 200-year history. And to comprehend the changes taking place today, it is essential that we understand the changes and the evolution which have gone on before.

The first section of this book examines the continual evolution of Congress in several important areas. What is most interesting is how past changes have helped to shape contemporary processes. Douglas Price examines the evolution of Congress into a professional institution whose members make long-term careers there; this has obvious implications for turnover patterns. What makes Price's article especially intriguing is his linking of this broad pattern of professionalization to the rise of the seniority system in the House and the Senate. Morris P. Fiorina, David Rohde, and Peter Wissel take on the enormous chore of examining personnel turnover in the House of Representatives from the 2d Congress to the present. They show, with quantitative evidence, that turnover in Congress has been affected by historical variations in party competition, by incumbency itself, and by historical events like reapportionments and economic disasters. The interesting implications of these past patterns on future turnover are also examined in a speculative concluding section.

The nature of congressional membership and patterns of turnover, and the role of the seniority system, topics given historical context here, are taken up with a contemporary focus in later sections of this book.

CONGRESS AND THE EVOLUTION OF LEGISLATIVE "PROFESSIONALISM"

H. Douglas Price

This paper seeks to explore a variety of approaches to such long-run changes in legislative bodies as the "professionalization" of careers and emergence of strict committee seniority systems. The data is drawn largely from records of the U.S. House and Senate, but some of the processes may well be relevant for state legislatures. The material lends itself to a wide variety of analytic techniques, including transition probabilities, the Mover-Stayer Markov model,[1] cohort analysis, evolutionary patterns of development, causal modeling, or even computer simulation. Since the total available data is so vast, this is simply an exploratory study.

The paper is organized into four main sections. The first section sets out various aspects of the general process of legislative "professionalization," and the second presents selected data relating to professionalization in the U.S. Senate and House. The third section examines the relevance of membership stability for the emergence of strict committee seniority systems in the Senate (last quarter of 19th century) and then the House (first quarter of 20th century). The last section presents some concluding comments, along with a comparative view of contemporary state legislatures.

This is a somewhat abbreviated version of the author's 1970 APSA paper on "Computer Simulation and Legislative 'Professionalism.' " H. Douglas Price is Professor of Government at Harvard University.

2

1. A General Model for Legislative "Professionalization"

The current tendency to view the national Congress as marked by professionalism and low turnover whereas state legislatures are marked by part-time amateurs and high turnover is remarkably lacking in time perspective. In the beginning, all American legislative bodies were quite nonprofessional. Very high turnover and frequent resignations were hallmarks of the national Senate and House of Representatives throughout the entire pre–Civil War period. The Senate emerged as a highly stable professional body only after the end of Reconstruction. The House remained fluid, both in membership and in committee structure, up to the massive realignment of 1896. We are interested in the causes and consequences of the radical change that occurred.[2]

In general, any legislature will have some mixture of career types, but one type may be numerically predominant. By taking as our criteria a long-run career perspective and a close to full-time career involvement, one perceives the following four individual types of legislators:

"Amateur": Part-time and short-run perspective
"Professional": Full-time and long-run perspective
"Notable": Part-time but long-run (often of high status)
"Marginal": Full-time but short-run (often of low status)

We are primarily interested in the shift from "amateur" to "professional," and in viewing the relative distribution of members within a legislative chamber as a macro-level characteristic of the legislature. This, in turn, may have "structural effects" on individual members.

The "professional" legislature is different. In it disparity of influence among members is generally less. And the professional legislature achieves substantial capability to oversee and influence the bureaucracies of the executive branch in a way that the amateurs never can. But this capability is achieved at the cost of reduced openness to shifting sentiments in the electorate (the motto of the professional legislature might well be, "The incumbent is always right."). In the professional legislature, "representation" is achieved largely by the shifting stands of sophisticated members rather than by physical turnover of members from presumably homogeneous constituencies. The member of a professional legislature faces complex problems of organizational theory, not the simple dilemmas of Edmund Burke.

The classic study of the "amateur" legislative body is Oliver Garceau and Corrine Silverman's account of the Vermont legislature.[3] Such legislative bodies are open to very substantial concentration of power by presiding officers and great disparity of influence. They also have little capability to deal with a sophisticated bureaucracy. But then, such bodies are most typical of the smaller, less industrial, less urban, and less bureaucratized states.

The professional legislator, though, has long-run career goals, and these are subject to the risks of the electoral process. But a member's career goals may also be subject to very substantial risks, at least to his influence, due to internal chamber (or leadership) practices. And in the long-run, the members have a way of affecting chamber practices and leadership.

Such a system may operate to produce a rather stable proportion of new members and stable distributions of prior service. In the twentieth century, however, both the Senate and House have shifted rather substantially in the direction of much more prior service. In the nineteenth century, sharp reductions in the proportion of new members were associated with major changes in the electoral module—thus the rate went up with the age of Jackson and came sharply down after the realignment of 1896. Deliberate efforts at intervention are difficult. Among sophisticated students of Congress, there is discussion of the need for compulsory retirement of congressmen or a limit on the number of terms or years served. This would dampen the system, but lack of congressional support for such changes may dampen the enthusiasm of advocates instead.

2. Professionalization of Careers: Senate and House

The so-called Clay Congresses (1811–25) mustered at no time more than twenty members who had served five terms each, while from 1789 to 1860 only forty exceeded six terms.

DeAlva S. Alexander[4]

We know that for the modern "professionalized" Senate and House, resignations from office are extremely rare, efforts at re-election are the norm, and successful re-election is overwhelmingly the case for the House and quite frequent for the Senate. But how frequent or infrequent were these during the formative period of this nation, and when did their rate of frequency begin to approach modern levels? We shall begin with the Senate.

The distinguished senators of the 1st Congress set the early career pattern for that chamber: They fled the Capitol—not yet located in Washington—almost as fast as was humanly possible. Five of the original twenty-six hastened to resign even before completing their initial terms, most of which were for only two or four years (they had drawn lots to determine who would serve two-, four-, or six-year terms). One chanced to die in office, and two who had been selected for short terms had the unusual misfortune to seek re-election and fail. Eight were re-elected, but six of these had been on short terms. The remaining ten managed to serve out their term (or sentence to obscurity), but did not seek another round. By the time the Capitol was moved from Philadelphia to the swamps of Washington, only two of the original twenty-six senators remained, and in two more years they were gone.

Career data on the early Senate is a morass of resignations, short-term appointees, elective replacements, and more resignations. There are *no* notable careers in terms of service. Rather, records are set by the same senator resigning the same seat in the same term twice (by coming back to it for a time after his initial replacement resigned), or by a single man's serving as a state's replacement for each of the state's two senate seats and quitting from each. From 1789 to 1801 the amazing total of ninety-four individuals (or ninety-five, if one counts Albert Gallatin, who was admitted but then held ineligible) had warmed senatorial seats for varying times.

Among the most distinguished of the initial Senators was Charles Carroll of Carrollton. He was a Maryland notable, a signer of the Declaration of Independence, and a delegate to the Continental Congress. He was re-elected in 1792, but resigned later that year since he preferred being a state senator, in which position he served from 1777–1800 (Maryland had passed a law preventing individuals from serving in both state and federal legislatures concurrently). Carroll lived to almost the end of Jackson's first administration, but had left the Senate at the end of Washington's first administration.

In its initial decades, of course, the Senate was an honorific nothing. Everyone was for a second chamber in theory, but no one could figure out what—if anything—it should do in actual practice. Some states used their senatorships as a sinecure for defeated House members, and ambitious young politicians—Madison or Clay—were unanimous in vowing that they intended to avoid being stuck in that "do-nothing" chamber. How and why this came to change is itself an exciting story, but cannot be pursued here. That it was a long time before it *did* change, however, is obvious from the careers of successive Senate cohorts.

Senate "cohorts" are a bit more awkward to define than are House "cohorts." There is the problem of the three classes of seats, with one-third coming up for election every two years. And there is the much greater role played by appointive or elective replacements. Many of the appointive replacements did not seek or expect election, and including them with the more regular senators tends to confuse the picture a bit. For exploratory purposes we have adopted the simple, though hardly ideal, expedient of taking as "cohorts" all those senators who were on hand at the beginning of a given Congress. We have then pursued their careers through to the end of their current terms, about one-third coming up for election every two years. This should not effect the probability of their seeking re-election or not, but it does somewhat reduce (to an average of about four years) the time in which they might resign from office. The advantage is that most of the very temporary interim appointees are thus eliminated, and we can concentrate on more or less "regular" senators. This also means that looking at such a "cohort" for a given Congress gives us data not just on the one-third elected to that Congress, but also on those (or their replacements) who were elected to the previous two Congresses. Conversely, data on Congresses less than six years apart include some overlap.

Up to about 1840 those who sought and won an additional term did not differ much from the original cohort. Thus of the eight Senators re-elected from the original twenty-six, no less than four (including Charles Carroll of Carrollton) resigned in the course of their new term. From the cohort of the 9th Congress (1805) fourteen are re-elected, but five of these resign. From the 11th Congress six are re-elected, but four of these resign. From the 24th Congress (1835) sixteen are re-elected, but nine resign. The Civil War intrudes to preclude this analysis for the 1850's, but a marked shift is evident in the 1840's. The cohorts of 1841, 1845, and 1849 show, with some overlap, a total of thirty-five members re-elected, but only three of these resign in their subsequent term. Here we have a glimmer of hope for the emergence of "stayers." Indeed, in the 1850's the dominant Southern Democrats dig in their heels and hang on for all they are worth. As a result even average terms of service shows a modest gain.[5]

Prior to the Civil War one just did not make a long-run "career" out of continuous Senate service, except perhaps as a fluke. Since no positions in the Senate rested on any form of seniority (in the chamber or on committees) major political figures drifted in and out of the Senate as convenience dictated. Cabinet posts were a major attraction, luring both Clay and Webster for a time. The less well known John J. Crittenden served *four* separate tours in the Senate off and on from 1817 to 1861, interspersing these with two stretches in the Cabinet (Attorney-General), a tour as governor of his state, an appointment to the Supreme Court (for which his former colleagues refused confirmation), and some other posts; at his death he was a member of the House of Representatives. Lateral movement from Senate to Cabinet and then *back* to the Senate was particularly important in the nineteenth century, but was a practice that could *not* easily be combined with a strict committee seniority system.

In the twentieth century one can pick almost any year and then turn to the Senate of a decade earlier and find at least one-fourth, sometimes one-third, and recently around one-half of the same individual members serving in a continuous stretch. Put another way, the political "half life" of a Senate cohort over the past decade has been close to ten years. But for the pre–Civil War Senate, it is rare to find more than two or three stray senators who might be on hand at points ten years apart. Thus the following table contrasts the number of such ten-year veterans for selected Congresses in both the nineteenth and twentieth centuries:

TABLE 1

SENATE VETERANS SERVING OVER TEN YEARS FOR
PARTICULAR CONGRESSES INDICATED

Period of Service	Number Surviving	From Total in Base Year
1st to 6th Congress:	3	26
6th to 11th Congress:	2	32
11th to 16th Congress:	3	34
16th to 21st Congress:	9	44
21st to 26th Congress:	4	48
26th to 31st Congress:	8	52
52d to 57th Congress:	22	88
62d to 67th Congress:	29	96
72d to 77th Congress:	28	95 (plus a vacancy)
82d to 87th Congress:	42	96
86th to 91st Congress:	52	100

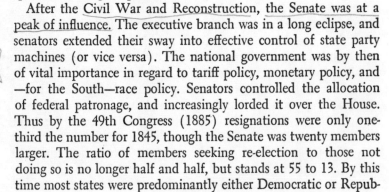

The long-term survivors in the earlier periods do include such historically important figures as Webster (from the 21st to 26th Congress, Clay and Calhoun (both from the 26th to the 31st), and Stephen A. Douglas (31st to 36th). But three of these four served "broken" Senate careers, the longer portion of which managed to span a five-Congress period.

After the Civil War and Reconstruction, the Senate was at a peak of influence. The executive branch was in a long eclipse, and senators extended their sway into effective control of state party machines (or vice versa). The national government was by then of vital importance in regard to tariff policy, monetary policy, and —for the South—race policy. Senators controlled the allocation of federal patronage, and increasingly lorded it over the House. Thus by the 49th Congress (1885) resignations were only one-third the number for 1845, though the Senate was twenty members larger. The ratio of members seeking re-election to those not doing so is no longer half and half, but stands at 55 to 13. By this time most states were predominantly either Democratic or Republican, so that electoral hazards were reduced. By this time also, Senate committee chairmanships were being quite rigorously handled in terms of continuous committee service. The Senate was a good place for a politician to be. And the longer he stayed there the better it would be. By the end of the century Thomas Hart Benton's record of thirty years service was beaten, and the Senate hailed its first six-term veteran.

But let us turn to the House of Representatives. It got off to a somewhat more impressive start than the Senate, but did not really shift into modern gear until the generation following the 1896 realignment. In an excellent senior honors thesis Richard Morningstar collected data on the careers of all members who left the House in three different periods.[6] The crucial importance of distinguishing between alternative reasons for turnover is evident in Morningstar's comparisons between the periods 1811–20 and 1887–96. Both are marked by very high turnover. But for the earlier period only 49 of 465 departures could be attributed to electoral defeat; for the latter period electoral defeat accounted for 309 of 750. What the early House lacked was not safe seats, but a desire and incentive to retain one's seat. In the late nineteenth century the desire for re-election was up somewhat, but re-election had become much more risky.

In 1964 I argued that changes in the structure of the House career were crucially linked to the massive political realignment of the 1890's.[7] This decade was marked by the emergence of the really solid Democratic South, by the rapid spread of ballot reform and registration systems, but above all by the collapse of the Democrats in the 1896 Bryan campaign. Democratic gains in the silver states and some farming states proved temporary, but massive Democratic losses in the Northeast and Midwest were to last until Al Smith and the Great Depression. As a result, re-election became more probable and more incumbents came to seek re-election. Successive new all-time records for amount of prior service in the House were set in 1900, then a higher record in 1904, then a yet higher record in 1906, and that one was broken in 1908. Successive new all-time low records for proportion of new members were set in 1898, again in 1900, again in 1904, and yet again in 1908.

Table 2 presents the career dispositions of five House cohorts. These include a Federalist Congress (2d), a Democratic-Republican Congress (12th), a Jacksonian Congress (24th), a post-Reconstruction Congress (49th), and a post-1896 Republican Congress (59th). The crucial point of what might be termed the Schattschneider-Price theory is that the realignment of 1896 sharply reduced the number of competitive House districts, leading to a steady increase in the number of committed "stayers" in the House. Thus the 1885 cohort of 325 House members produced only 193 who were re-elected to the following Congress; the slightly larger 1905 cohort produced 279 members re-elected to the following Congress. Of the 1885 group, 70 had not even sought re-election and 49 who did were defeated. Of the 1905 group only 44 did not seek re-election and only 42 were defeated.

There are at least three alternative theories that have been suggested more or less in lieu of the Schattschneider-Price emphasis on realignment leading to careerism. Nelson Polsby has sought to describe change in the House in terms of "institutionalization." There is some very useful literature relating to this process in various contexts, but the term is more useful for description than for historical explanation (it could, of course, be taken in the factor analysis sense of a single unobservable factor that underlies change in the observed variables).

A second alternative, frequently suggested, is of relatively steady incremental change in House careers. If this were the case then one might expect to pick up at least some trace of it from a simple linear regression over time. We ran this for both percentage of freshman members and for average terms prior service, using Stuart Rice's data, for all pre-1900 Congresses except for the very 1st Congress (i.e., for the 2nd through 56th). The results show no relationship whatsoever; the pre-1900 experience is *not* one of simple trend (though for the period after 1900, of course, there is a substantial trend).

A third alternative view is that the seeming change from nineteenth to twentieth century patterns is, in large measure, spurious. It simply rests on the admission of new states and creation of new seats. This raises a useful point; the new members due to

TABLE 2

HOUSE CAREERS FROM PRE-1800 TO POST-1896:
PERFORMANCE IN OFFICE OF FIVE HOUSE COHORTS CONSISTING
OF MEMBERS ON HAND AT OPENING OF CONGRESSES INDICATED

	Number of Cases from House Cohort Indicated:				
Congress:	2nd	12th	24th	49th	59th
Year:	1791	1811	1835	1885	1905
Entering Cohort	68	143	242	325	386
Serve Out Term:	65	136	224	311	365
Resign in Term:	2	5	13	5	8
Die during Term:	0	1	5	8	12
Unseated:	1	1	0	1	1
Seek Re-election:	43	92	137	242	321
Do not run for Re-election:	22	44	87	70	44
Re-elected:	43	80*	114	193*	279*
Defeated:	0	12	23	49	42

* Includes one or more who resigned *after* re-election but before opening of next Congress.

creation of new seats should indeed be considered. But doing this does not begin to account for the massive difference between nineteenth and twentieth century figures. With the exception of Oklahoma, no new state has begun its representation in the House with more than two members, and most received one. Seats were transferred between states in the nineteenth century— just as they still are in the twentieth century—but this only affects every fifth Congress. Following the 1970 census eleven new seats were created for the 1972 elections (including five in California and three in Florida), but turnover in 1972 was less than one-half of what one finds for nineteenth-century elections in which absolutely no new seats were involved.

As it happens, the House made a strenuous effort to hold the line on size from the 1843 figure (which was actually reduced from the previous decade) down to the 1870 census (at which time substantial expansion began again). This was the era of greatest turnover for the House, but at most elections there were no new seats at all and only for the post-census elections (for every fifth Congress) were the number of new seats of any real consequence.

Of the non-census related elections, only 1844 involved more than one or two new seats, and it included only four (for Texas, Florida, and Iowa). Thus the elections of 1854 through 1860 included *no* new seats, but two of these generated over 50 per cent freshmen and the other two more than 45 per cent freshmen. By contrast, the 1958 election was a partisan "landslide" and included new seats for Hawaii and Alaska, but generated well under 20 per cent freshmen.

The "new seats" hypothesis does explain the more or less regular "peaks" in which nineteenth-century turnover is up some 10 per cent, say from 40 to 50, but it does not begin to explain why the ordinary level in the absence of any new seats is at 40 per cent rather than the modern level of around 15 per cent. That shift, and not the mild peaking in the nineteenth century, is the big problem and "new seats" is simply *not* the main explanation. It is, however, a complication that needs to be considered in dealing with the data on turnover. For the Senate, incidentally, where the more-or-less uninhabited new states get 2 senators each right from the start, creation of new seats is more of a consideration.

Somewhat related to the "new seats" theory is the problem that overall national levels of turnover and careerism tend to conceal very marked state and sectional differences. The case for disaggregation, made in this volume by Fiorina, Rohde, and Wissel, is very strong and extremely interesting.

3. From Committee Stability to Committee Seniority: A Comparative View

My long service here and the custom which has obtained almost from the beginning of the Government entitles me to select from among the committees of which I am a member a chairmanship. I am senior Democrat on three important committees and can select the chairmanship of either one of them: Appropriations, Interstate Commerce, and Naval Affairs.

> Senator Benjamin R. Tillman (in
> personal letter to Woodrow Wilson,
> January 21, 1913) [8]

Congressional memories are often shorter than congressional careers. "Pitchfork" Ben Tillman was neither a good historian nor, in this case, a good prophet. Assigning committee chairmanships by seniority of committee service was not at all a practice obtaining "almost from the beginning of the Government." It had been more or less consciously adopted by the Democrats in the Senate when they found themselves in the majority, for the first time since the Civil War, in 1879. It clearly had not been followed by the Republicans in the decade of the 1870's, though after 1881 both parties seem to have abided by it with very few, usually minor, exceptions. By the time Tillman came to the Senate, in 1895, it was indeed the accepted norm. Seniority had not been visible in the Senate to Woodrow Wilson in 1885 (but then he did not bother to look). But it was accurately described in 1895 by Clara H. Kerr, and appears in even greater detail in McConachie's excellent 1898 book on *Congressional Committees*.[9]

Historians, apparently borrowing from each other, usually cite Stephen A. Douglas in 1859 and Charles Sumner in 1871 as the great "exceptions" to the general rule of Senate seniority. In fact, neither seems at the time to have been debated in those terms at all. But in 1913 Senator Tillman, then entering his fourth consecutive term, did become a sensational exception. In his letter to President-elect Wilson, quoted above, Tillman had gone on to indicate that he would take whichever chairmanship Wilson thought would make him most useful to the Administration. But Tillman's letter sounds most enthusiastic in discussing what he could do as chairman of the Appropriations Committee.

In fact, Tillman could probably have best served the Wilson Administration by just dropping dead. He was an eccentric, one of the few senators to be officially censured by that body, and certainly not the type to try and guide a complex legislative program. Wilson, caught in the throes of a Presidential transition, finally wrote back his thanks. Detecting Tillman's seeming preference for Appropriations, Wilson graciously endorsed the idea.

Six weeks later the Democratic caucus denied Tillman the chairmanship he desired, and the angry senator splashed his correspondence with Wilson in the *Congressional Record*. The

Democrats did very little other violence to the seniority rule,[10] finding it easier to put new members on so as to "pack" committees, or even to create new committees (as with Banking and Currency). Wilson's problem was that the official Democratic "leader" (a post not yet jelled into its modern form) was Thomas S. Martin, a conservative Virginian and anti-Wilson spokesman. The solution to Wilson's problem was to replace Martin with the progressive workhorse from Indiana, John W. Kern. But this needed to be done gracefully, and that could most easily be accomplished by easing Martin—who was number four on the Appropriations Committee—into its busy chairmanship. The second and third-ranking Democrats already held major chairmanships. Kern could replace Martin as leader, and Martin could be chairman, if only Tillman could be induced to take the chairmanship of Naval Affairs. But Wilson had thrown away the key to the situation by his letter of six weeks earlier. In a sense, however, Tillman had undermined his claim to Appropriations by offering to take any one of the three chairmanships. Armed with this knowledge the caucus voted the Appropriations post to Martin, Kern became floor leader (where he virtually created the modern role of majority leader), and Tillman was left with Naval Affairs.

For almost a century, violations of seniority in the Senate have been few and far between. What at first appears as a possible violation usually turns out to be a choice among chairmanships, a question of third-party status, or explained by a break in a senator's continuous service. The Senate seems almost fated to be the inventor of seniority: The chamber has a continuous existence, only one-third of the members come up for election every two years, and it lacks a powerful presiding officer who might dominate appointments or use them for bargaining (as in House speakership contests).

For the House there could be no question of modern-type "seniority" until membership turnover was reduced to a level such that there was substantial continuity of committee service. Such *de facto* stability tends to generate demands for *de jure* seniority. But members demands for seniority, or even for general stability, can still be frustrated by any one of several mechanisms. Thus in the Senate, open ballotting for committee positions precluded the emergence of much stability. For the House three obvious mechanisms worked against the establishment of seniority:

1. *Internal scramble for leadership.* So long as the Speaker made all appointments, both of members and committee chairmen, candidates within the majority party campaigned for the speakership nomination largely in terms of promises to make, or maintain, such appointments. This is still common in many state legislatures, and was the dominant pattern for the U.S. House of Representatives from the Civil War to the realignment of 1896. It is, of course, strengthened by relatively frequent alternation of majority control, and by relatively frequent change of Speakers. This was the case for pre-1896, but not the case after 1896, when the Republicans had a commanding lead until 1910.

2. *Executive interference.* This was common in the pre–Civil War House, and was blatant under Jefferson and Jackson. Subservient Speakers ran the risk of having the power of committee appointment removed. The House came within two votes of this in 1806, and in 1832 the Speaker had to break a tie vote to preserve his authority to appoint the select committee to investigate Nicholas Biddle and the National Bank (a subject of prime concern to Andrew Jackson).

3. *Cohesive legislative majority.* This has been the ideal of academic supporters of "responsible parties," but has only rarely developed in Congress. Thaddeus Stevens and the Radical Republicans are probably the best example of this, although the Democrats did rather well in 1911 and throughout most of Wilson's first term (during which the pattern became more one of executive interference via the legislative caucus).

Internal scrambles for leadership in which committee chairmanships are the pawns have not occurred since the 1890's; successful executive interference ended with Woodrow Wilson; party caucuses have done little to enforce cohesion since 1919. When the Republicans took over the House in that year they voted against former Speaker Cannon's protégé, James Mann, who had been minority leader, and for a mild-mannered nonentity. Just for insurance they also voted for Mann's proposal to lodge the power of recommending committee appointments to the House in a committee on committees.[11]

In the late nineteenth century House chairmanships were won or lost as a side product of the bargaining involved in the recurrent scrambles for the speakership. Often the same men hung on, but the dynamics of the process were such that each and every position was always available and might well be drawn into the bargaining game. This is clear in descriptions of the operation of every Speaker from the Civil War to the end of the century. Here we shall quote but two.

> Speaker Kerr in 1875: "He asked Marble [NYC Democratic editor and publisher] for help in the selection of chairmen for major committees and even 'peremptorily' insisted that Marble come to Washington to help draw up the slate. Kerr placed Randall [his rival for Speaker] at the head of Appropriations but was in a quandary as to Ways and Means since both Wood and Cox felt that their services to the party and to Kerr in the caucus merited the assignment. Eventually he made William H. Morrison of Illinois head of Ways and Means, Cox of Banking and Currency, and ignored Wood's claims to a position of honor."[12]

> Speaker Crisp in 1891: "On the first ballot in the caucus only a few votes separated Mills and Crisp, the leaders, and it was regarded as certain that one of them would be named. Then the dickering began among the managers of the candidates for high committee places, and the Crisp men outgeneraled the Mills' forces in that line of work. Judge Springer withdrew his name and voted for Crisp, and that settled it. Mr. Crisp was nominated, and Judge Springer secured the chairmanship of the Ways and Means Committee and, as the floor leadership went with it as usual, he was satisfied with the outcome. The other Crisp managers got important committee assignments."[13]

Alleged "seniority" simply had nothing to do with it. Some of the same chairmen might continue, but in principle every chairmanship was at stake every two years. As Polsby *et al.* show,[14] the percentage continuing or moving up tended to be high or low depending upon whether there was a change of parties and of party leaders, a change of leaders within same party, or simply an alternation of party.

This pattern continued so long as there was high membership turnover, rapid alternation of party control, and frequent change of party leaders (many preferring to trade the Speaker's post for a seat in the more stable Senate). But all three of these conditions were upset by the realignment of 1896. For 14 years the Republicans held the majority, more and more of the members sought a permanent career in the House, and soon "Czar" Joseph Cannon was embarked on his record tenure as Speaker.

Up to the turn of the century, House members quite literally did not understand what "seniority" was in the modern sense of continuous service on a party's list of committee members. Thus in 1895, after the Republicans recaptured the House, two leading Republican members (Nelson Dingley and Sereno Payne) *both* claimed the chairmanship of Ways and Means. Each claimed knowledge of the tariff *and* "seniority," though in fact Dingley was not even a member of the committee and had not been for the past four years. He had gone off the committee to make room for former Speaker Reed during the two Congresses the Republicans were in a minority (1891–95). Dingley, who had no continuous service on the committee, got the chairmanship.

Strict seniority, which had meant almost nothing in the House as of 1900, had come to mean almost everything in naming committee chairmen and ranking members by 1920. Michael Abram, in his excellent senior honors thesis on the subject, concludes that "after 1925 seniority stood as the sole criterion of committee advancement with only the insignificant exceptions we have noted,"[15] and sees the major shift as occurring between 1913 and 1919.

There are two broad classes of explanations for the emergence of seniority in the House between 1910 and 1920. The traditional one, more or less embraced by both Polsby *et al.* on the one hand and Joseph Cooper and Michael Abram on the other,[16] concentrates on the celebrated 1910 "revolt" against Speaker Cannon, and the reasons for the collision between the Republican "insurgents" and the Republican Speaker. The emphasis is on the tension and its causes. In my 1964 paper, I sought to minimize the importance attached to the strains of 1910, and instead argued that from 1896 on, career patterns and expectations had under-

gone basic structural change. Without this change a little conflict
in the House, a common thing in any decade, would have meant
little. Given the basic change, any old issue or conflict might
serve to challenge the old order.

Moreover, the 1910 revolt did *not* touch the Speaker's power
to make committee appointments. That more basic change was
carried out by the Democrats in 1911. They had denounced the
arbitrary power of the Speaker and promised changes in the 1908
Democratic platform. They had denounced Cannon for almost
a decade, and had denounced Reed for most of the decade before
that. Thus Cannon was operating on a very partisan Republican
interpretation of the speakership; any Democratic majority would
be expected to alter the rules of the game. And Cannon himself
was operating in a quite different House climate, where stability of
membership and of committee service had assumed unparalleled
proportions. As the years rolled by, there were no wide-open
speakership contests that invited and necessitated widespread
juggling of committee posts.

The extent of the stability which had settled on the House in
the Republican era of 1895–1910 is impressive. If one had asked
in 1910 who held the all-time record for longest service as chairmen of the fourteen most important substantive committees of
the House (DeAlva S. Alexander's list of fifteen, minus the
Elections Committee) in thirteen of the fourteen cases the all-
time record would have been set (or in two cases only tied) by
chairmen of the 1895–1910 era. Members were, as a matter of
plain observable fact, waiting in line for years. Increasingly, they
wanted their waiting recognized, and their positions on the
committee ladders protected. Around 1904 the *Congressional
Directory* shifted from its former alphabetical listing with prior
service indicated, to its modern-type listing in order of continuous
service. Cannon did not shift his style, and the *Congressional
Directory* goes on but Cannon was shunted aside.

The pressures for stability, continuity, and what amounted to
seniority were hard to resist. This was something new for the
House. Cannon's autocratic style reflected neither the fluidity of
the nineteenth-century House nor an appropriate response to the
stability of the modern House. "Cannonism" was an aberration

which could not last. It was ended not by the insurgents, but by a new Democratic majority that was committed to change. There were still the three major mechanisms that might prevent the emergence of Senate-style seniority in the House. But bargaining for committees as part of the scramble for leadership was over, as the power to appoint committees was removed from the Speaker and lodged with a plural body (by the Democrats in 1911, and by the Republicans at the end of World War I). Executive interference existed for a time with Wilson and the Democratic caucus, but this pattern was disrupted by war issues, and eventually led to disenchantments. After the war, one would not look for interference from the likes of Warren G. Harding. This left party cohesion, but the old party loyalty of post-Reconstruction days was fading, and was disrupted by new issues of progressivism and then war. McKinley had been a Civil War major, but Harding was born after Lee's surrender. For a time the Republicans put up a bold front against LaFollette and his outright party bolt, but by the mid-1920's the party found it easier to relax and embrace dissidents ranging from LaFollette, Jr., to the Non-Partisan League in North Dakota, Fiorello LaGuardia in Manhattan, and most of the agrarian radicals. Nothing was left to challenge the sway of seniority in the House or the Senate.

4. Conclusion

At the national level the triumph of legislative "professionalism" and of committee seniority are virtually complete. But the importance of seniority for its effect on policy outcomes has been diminishing. Within the Democratic Party, the South now has far fewer safe seats or even states, and an increasing number of quite safe seats are to be found outside the South. Moreover, the question of who has seniority is becoming less important as more and more congressional committees adopt internal rules and reforms which make the chairmanship a role of very limited importance. Seniority, like monarchy, may be preserved by being deprived of most of its power. When chairmen merely reign, in the fashion of constitutional monarchs, then the question of just who should hold the position, and by what criteria, ceases to be a burning issue.

For anyone interested in the variety of historical patterns of organization presented by the House and Senate in the nineteenth century, the current range of state legislative practices have a quite familiar look. One does not need to go, like Darwin, to the Galapagos Islands to rediscover long missing species of legislative operation. The Alabama legislature, for example, is still typically as executive-dominated as was the national House in the days of Jefferson or Jackson. Belle Zeller noted in 1950 that all fourteen Alabama House committees were headed by freshmen members.[17]

But state legislatures are changing. The New York legislature has long posted re-election rates that are quite comparable to the national House. Thus Charles Hyneman found for 1925–35 that the New York lower house averaged only 17.7 per cent freshmen. Freshmen members in California have dropped from the 40.7 per cent noted by Hyneman to the 17 per cent reported by John Wahlke and Heinz Eulau. For New Jersey the comparable figures are 37.2 for 1925–35 and 15 per cent for Wahlke-Eulau.[18]

One can make a direct comparison between turnover in the nineteenth-century House and the 1925–35 turnover rates found by Hyneman. A sustained effort is under way to "upgrade" state legislatures, largely by means of better pay, long (or unlimited) sessions, and other tangible benefits (staff, offices, etc.). A few years ago only three states had pay and allowances amounting to $10,000 per year; as of 1970 this is up to eleven states. For California—a leader in this trend—the biennial pay and allowances now come to $48,950 (a figure which compares well with the pay of most full professors).

In the 1960's the advance of professionalism at the state level has been slowed by recurring reapportionment crises. But when this settles down—beginning in 1972—many state chambers may find themselves in situations similar to the national House after 1896. The experience of both Senate and House suggests the strength of the drive for committee stability and then committee seniority once the membership of the chamber stabilizes. For the states, of course, there are the three counter-seniority mechanisms:

internal scramble for leadership, outside executive and party interference, and the possibility of strong legislative cohesion.

How important for a legislative body is a sharp drop in membership turnover, or a switch from a single authority appointing
committees to having this done by party committees? For a single
given legislative body this is a difficult question indeed. But the
American case affords us a rich body of varied experience both
over time and by making comparisons between Senate and House
and state legislatures. It is comparison between legislative bodies,
focusing on different time periods, that can give us significant
leverage on the tough questions. Hopefully, future research will
continue to move in these directions.

NOTES

1. Most of the discussion of this model has been omitted from this version
of the paper.

2. The best account of the 1896 realignment is E. E. Schattschneider,
"United States: The Functional Approach to Party Government," in Sigmund
Neumann, ed., *Modern Political Parties* (Chicago, Univ. of Chicago Press,
1956). The effects on Congress were first pointed out by myself in my 1964
working paper for the American Assembly on "The Congressional Career,"
reprinted in Nelson Polsby, ed., *Congressional Behavior* (New York, Random
House, 1971), pp. 14–27. See also the comments of Walter Dean Burnham
in his *Critical Elections and the Mainsprings of American Politics* (New
York, W. W. Norton, 1971).

3. Oliver Garceau and Corrine Silverman, "A Pressure Group and the
Pressured," *American Political Science Review* 48 (September 1954): 672–
91.

4. DeAlva S. Alexander, *History and Procedure of the House of Representatives* (Boston, Houghton Mifflin, 1916), p. 306.

5. See Figure II in Randall B. Ripley, *Power in the Senate* (New York,
St. Martin's Press, 1969), p. 46.

6. Richard Morningstar, "Congress as a Closed System: Its Characteristics
and Implications" (Senior honors thesis, Harvard, 1967). The author analyzes
House careers for the three periods 1811–20, 1887–96, and 1951–60.

7. See Price, "Congressional Career."

8. U.S., Congress, Senate, Senator Tillman, personal letter to Woodrow
Wilson, 63d Congress, special session, March 17, 1913, *Congressional Record*,
CI, Vol. 50, p. 31.

9. See Clara S. Kerr, *Origin and Development of U.S. Senate* (N.Y.,

Andrus & Church, 1895) and Lauroş G. McConachie, *Congressional Committees* (N.Y., Crowell, 1898).

10. Claude G. Bower's biography, *The Life of John Worth Kern* (Indianapolis, Hollenback Press, 1918), is helpful on many things, but distinctly superficial on the details of the 1913 Senate committee slating. Aside from the Tillman incident, Kern seems to have followed the modern tactic of accepting seniority but undermining its importance by means of committee "stacking" and emphasizing that a majority of committee members could take control away from the chairman. This latter step created some controversy at the time. But the pattern was often repeated in regard to chairmen opposed to Wilson's wartime policies. There remains an important substantive question of just when the Senate Republicans and Democrats adopted the practice of letting *chamber* seniority determine priority for *intercommittee* transfers (a norm ended for the Democrats by the "Johnson rule" of 1953, but only watered down by the Republicans in recent years).

11. From 1889 to 1919 the parties differed sharply on the role of the Speaker. Had the Republicans nominated Mann for Speaker in 1919 and given him the power of committee appointment, the old "autocratic" style of operation would have had a new lease on life. It is ironic that the Cannon-Mann wing of the Republicans, having lost the speakership nomination, made the final move to nail down the Democratic-style "syndication" of the speakership even for the Republicans. Polsby *et al.*, in "The Growth of the Seniority System," quote the *N.Y. Times* account, which emphasizes that the Mann proposal (for a committee on committees, with a member from each state electing a Republican but casting a weighted vote equal to the number of Republicans from the member's state) was a victory for long-term members who desired to protect their seniority. Poor Speaker Gillette was from the medium-sized state of Massachusetts, which would only cast 12 votes. Mann's Illinois got 20 votes, a number exceeded only by New York and Pennsylvania.

12. In Albert V. House, "The Speakership Contest of 1875: Democratic Response to Power," *Journal of American History* 52 (September 1965), p. 272.

13. O. O. Stealey, *Twenty Years in the Press Gallery* (New York, privately published, 1906), p. 106. This fascinating collection, by a variety of experienced Washington reporters, includes chapters on eleven Congresses, 48th to 58th, plus biographical studies of over a score of leading House members. There is not a single reference to committee seniority, although there is a great deal of discussion of the making of committee slates.

14. Nelson Polsby, Miriam Gallagher and Barry Rundquist, "The Growth of the Seniority System in the U.S. House of Representatives," *American Political Science Review* 63 (1969), pp. 787–807.

15. Michael E. Abram, "The Rise of the Modern Seniority System in the U.S. House of Representatives" (Harvard honors thesis, 1966).

16. Michael Abram and Joseph Cooper, "The Rise of Seniority in the House of Representatives." *Polity* 1 (1968): 52–85.

17. Belle Zeller, ed., *American State Legislatures* (New York, Thomas Y. Crowell, 1954).

18. Charles S. Hyneman, "Tenure and Turnover of Legislative Personnel," *Annals of the American Academy of Political and Social Science* 195 (1938), pp. 22–30. For the more recent figures for California and New Jersey see John Wahlke, Heinz Eulau *et al.*, *The Legislative System* (New York, John Wiley & Sons, 1962).

HISTORICAL CHANGE
IN HOUSE TURNOVER

MORRIS P. FIORINA, DAVID W. ROHDE,
and PETER WISSEL *

One of the most formidable barriers to change in contemporary Congresses lies in the very slight amount of change in the membership of those Congresses. According to popular stereotypes, few congressmen are defeated; few resign or retire; moreover, their longevity is legendary.[1] Thus, although the House is not a continuing body under the Constitution, the reality is far different. Representatives come to Washington, settle in, establish themselves within the congressional context, and eventually develop a vested interest in the status quo.[2] Only significant external shocks (particularly those which result in the political destruction of greater than normal numbers of congressmen) are sufficient to induce Congress to change its established rules, procedures, and behaviors.[3] And yet, as recent studies have noted, the petrification of Congress is a relatively new phenomenon.

Consider facts like these: In 1970 only 10 per cent of the members of the House had replaced incumbents of the previous

* We wish to thank Richard Fenno, Lance Davis, Robert Bates, and J. Morgan Kousser for their comments on an earlier version of this paper. Their remarks have clarified and improved our discussion, but all remaining deficiencies are ours. Morris P. Fiorina is Assistant Professor of Political Science at California Institute of Technology; David Rohde is Associate Professor of Political Science at Michigan State University; Peter Wisell is Assistant Professor of Political Science at Pennsylvania State University.

24

Congress. The average continuous service of representatives was more than eleven years. In 1870, however, 48 per cent of the House occupied seats that had been occupied by others in the preceding Congress. Average continuous service was less than four years. Even examining an intermediate time, 1920, one finds a turnover figure of 31 per cent and a tenure figure of somewhat less than seven years. By contemporary standards, nineteenth-century congressional turnover seems incredible. And even in the first third of the twentieth century congressional turnover varies between a fourth and a third of the total membership. Consider the implications for change if 150 representatives were replaced every two years. Providing that the same 150 districts were not producing all the change, the House might not now be known as a conservative body.[4] Rather, it might be living up to the Founding Fathers' fears that it would mirror swings in public opinion.

What accounts for the current low rate of congressional turnover? In this paper we will suggest some general answers to that question. We begin by reviewing the discussions of other scholars who have examined membership change in Congress. Then, after putting turnover data in more exact form, we will extend earlier discussions of House turnover. Our discussion is based on an analysis of subnational turnover patterns and on a preliminary statistical analysis.

Previous Studies

Much of the credit for reawakening congressional scholars to the historical dimension of legislative behavior must go to H. Douglas Price.[5] Among other things, Price pointed out the large differences in turnover and tenure between the nineteenth- and twentieth-century House. Price argues that during the nineteenth century, party competition was much more balanced than now. But he sees the 1896 election as a critical juncture that marks two different eras of electoral competition. One-party dominance became the rule in many areas after the Bryan debacle and its accompanying polarization of the electorate along various lines, chiefly sectional. One might recall that E. E. Schattschneider argued a similar thesis.[6] If such arguments are correct, the electoral risks faced by congressmen diminished sharply after 1896.

Perhaps most importantly, Price contends that much of the turnover in the nineteenth century appears to be *voluntary* turnover, or at least turnover not due to electoral defeat. This argument, of course, raises an important question. Why did congressmen choose not to seek re-election? Perhaps the threat of defeat deterred some. Or perhaps a congressional seat simply wasn't worth the costs of getting and holding it. Price suggests in addition that in some districts, tenure norms limited the service of members.

Soon after the reawakening of interest in the historical dimension of Congress, Nelson Polsby presented extensive time series data relating to congressional turnover and tenure.[7] Throughout much of the nineteenth century the percentage of new members hovers in the 40–60 per cent range. Interestingly, though, the downward trend in new members appears to have begun by 1860, thus raising some questions about the crucial significance of 1896. Similarly, average terms of congressional service hovers at about two until the time of the Civil War, then begins a general upward climb.

Polsby considers declining congressional turnover as an element in the institutionalization of the House of Representatives:

> As an organization institutionalizes, it stabilizes its membership, entry is more difficult, and turnover is less frequent. Its leadership professionalizes and persists. Recruitment to leadership is more likely to occur from within, and the apprenticeship period lengthens. Thus the organization establishes and "hardens" its outer boundaries.[8]

While Polsby considers declining congressional turnover as both a defining characteristic and a contributing factor to the process of institutionalization, for the most part he does not treat turnover as a dependent variable. One important exception is Polsby's suggestion that institutionalization might increase the worth of a position in the organization.[9] Thus, a feedback situation may exist: Increased membership stability helps to produce a more stable and attractive organization which, in turn, diminishes the rate of voluntary turnover.

A third study which focuses on the changing congressional career is provided by T. Richard Witmer.[10] Like Polsby, Witmer concentrates primarily on the consequences of the rising seniority of House members. But he speculates that increasing terms served may be due to such *apolitical* factors as rising life expectancy, *recruitment* factors such as earlier age at entry and greater willingness to serve, and *electoral* factors such as increased information about constituencies available to incumbents and the trend for incumbents to perform valuable constituency casework.

In sum, there has been a large-scale secular change in an important feature of Congress: the turnover and tenure of its members. According to several authors, this change has contributed to the development of the seniority system, increased the power of the House in the federal system, and facilitated the development of professional norms of conduct in the House. In short, it is argued that increased membership stability is one of the most important factors shaping the nature of the contemporary House of Representatives. Evidently, an attempt to isolate the reasons for that membership stability is a matter of high priority. For, if low congressional turnover and high tenure really have had the claimed effects, then any change in these variables should produce correspondingly large changes in the House.

Congressional Turnover 1789–1973

Obviously, to analyze possible influences on secular changes in Congressional turnover, one first must settle on a measure of turnover. The most straightforward measure is that used by Polsby: per cent first term. There is a small problem with this measure, however. The House did not reach its present size until 1917. Prior to that date, the House periodically added new seats, most usually at the decennial reapportionments. These new members were unsocialized, unattached, and a potential source of change, yet not turnover in the strict sense, i.e., replacements for members of the previous Congress. Thus, we believe it advisable that a measure of turnover not reflect membership change via the creation of new seats.[11] We have employed the following measure dubbed "percentage replacements" [12]:

$$PR = \frac{(\text{Number new members}) - (\text{Number new seats})}{(\text{Number seats}) - (\text{Number new seats})}$$

In a year when no seats are new, PR = percentage of first-term members. But for a Congress in which some seats are newly created, PR controls out membership change from that source. The correlation between the percentage of new seats and the percentage of new members is a nontrivial 0.4. But when PR is substituted for the percentage of new members, the correlation drops to 0.18. This remaining positive correlation no doubt stems from the fact that reapportionments usually "shake" the boundaries of some existing districts at the same time that they create new seats.

Adopting PR as a measure of turnover leads to one further difference between our consideration of congressional turnover and that of most previous authors. Under our procedure, a representative who enters and leaves Congress several times over a number of years is counted as a replacement each time he returns to Congress following an interruption in service. In contrast, scholars who used the measure "percentage first-term" have counted as first-term members only those representatives with no prior service in Congress. While one should distinguish between "new representatives with prior service" and "genuine freshmen" for some purposes, e.g., to study the growth of internal norms, we see no reason to distinguish them for the purpose of studying turnover. If a new man replaces an incumbent congressman, turnover has occurred regardless of whether the replacement has had some prior service or is enjoying his first congressional experience. A representative who serves six terms in twelve Congresses may illustrate something quite different from one who serves six terms consecutively. As mentioned earlier, several state delegations during the nineteenth century turned over at a very high rate. Yet some of the turnover seemed to arise from the repeated exchange of a seat between two or three individuals. Thus, we compute higher turnover for these states than have others, but failure to consider these representatives with interrupted service as turnover each time they re-entered the House after an absence both underestimates House turnover and obscures the nature of the political processes in these states.

In Table 1 we list several time series for comparative purposes. As is evident, treating new members with prior service as turnover leads to a "percentage first-term" series which is almost invariably higher than the Polsby-Rice series, sometimes very noticeably so.[13] In fact, PR is typically higher than the Polsby-Rice percent first-term data.

TABLE 1

1		2	3	4	
			Polsby-Rice	Percentage	
		Percentage	Percentage	Replace-	
Congress	2 minus 3	First-Term	First-Term	ments	4 minus 3
01	0.0	100.0	100.0		
(1791) 02	—.9	45.6	46.5	42.2	—4.3
03	3.5	60.0	56.5	37.3	—19.2
04	2.6	41.5	38.9	41.0	2.1
05	2.2	45.3	43.1	45.3	2.2
06	10.2	46.2	36.0	46.2	10.2
(1801) 07	11.3	53.8	42.5	53.8	11.3
08	8.0	54.9	46.9	39.6	—7.3
09	—6.8	33.1	39.9	33.1	—6.8
10	1.8	38.0	36.2	38.0	1.8
11	5.0	40.9	35.9	40.9	5.0
(1811) 12	7.0	45.5	38.5	45.1	6.6
13	5.1	57.7	52.6	46.2	—6.4
14	7.4	50.3	42.9	50.0	7.1
15	6.2	65.4	59.2	65.0	5.8
16	10.5	51.3	40.8	50.8	10.0
(1821) 17	10.4	55.6	45.2	53.9	8.7
18	11.3	54.5	43.2	47.0	3.8
19	0.0	39.4	39.4	39.4	0.0
20	6.7	39.9	33.2	39.9	6.7
21	7.4	48.4	41.0	48.4	7.4
(1831) 22	3.8	41.8	38.0	41.8	3.8
23	3.8	57.5	53.7	51.2	—2.5
24	6.3	46.3	40.0	45.8	5.8
25	3.9	52.5	48.6	52.5	3.9
26	8.7	55.0	46.3	55.0	8.7
(1841) 27	13.1	50.8	37.7	50.8	13.1
28	8.2	74.9	66.7	72.6	5.9
29	6.5	55.5	49.0	54.5	5.5

1		2	3	4	
			Polsby-Rice	Percentage	
		Percentage	Percentage	Replace-	
Congress	2 minus 3	First-Term	First-Term	ments	4 minus 3
30	7.0	57.4	50.4	56.8	6.4
31	6.0	59.1	53.1	58.5	5.4
(1851) 32	5.5	58.8	53.3	58.6	5.3
33	3.2	63.7	60.5	62.1	1.6
34	4.5	62.0	57.5	62.0	4.5
35	10.0	50.2	40.2	49.6	9.4
36	8.7	53.8	45.1	53.6	8.5
(1861) 37	1.4	55.3	53.9	55.0	1.1
38	8.9	67.0	58.1	63.0	4.9
39	5.4	49.7	44.3	47.3	3.0
40	5.6	51.6	46.0	43.5	−2.5
41	2.7	51.9	49.2	48.0	−1.2
(1871) 42	7.0	53.5	46.5	53.5	7.0
43	6.6	58.6	52.0	50.2	−1.8
44	5.8	63.8	58.0	63.7	5.7
45	2.9	49.5	46.6	49.5	2.9
46	4.1	46.4	42.3	46.4	4.1
(1881) 47	6.8	38.6	31.8	38.6	6.8
48	8.8	60.3	51.5	55.5	4.0
49	6.3	44.3	38.0	44.3	6.3
50	5.9	41.5	35.6	41.5	5.9
51	1.9	40.0	38.1	38.8	.7
(1891) 52	5.9	49.7	43.8	49.7	5.9
53	5.4	43.5	38.1	39.5	1.4
54	5.2	53.8	48.6	53.7	5.1
55	4.7	42.6	37.9	42.6	4.7
56	3.2	33.3	30.1	33.3	3.2
(1901) 57	4.2	28.6	24.4	28.6	4.2
58	4.7	36.0	31.3	30.8	−.5
59	3.6	24.6	21.0	24.6	3.6
60	6.7	29.2	22.5	28.2	5.7
61	3.1	23.0	19.9	23.0	3.1
(1911) 62	3.0	33.5	30.5	33.0	2.5
63	4.2	38.6	34.4	32.8	−1.6
64	7.6	34.8	27.2	34.2	7.0
65	4.7	20.7	16.0	20.5	4.5
66	5.1	27.8	22.7	27.8	5.1
(1921) 67	7.4	31.0	23.6	31.0	7.4
68	6.0	33.1	27.1	33.1	4.0
69	5.3	21.6	16.3	21.6	5.3
70	1.0	14.3	13.3	14.3	1.0
71	1.6	19.3	17.7	19.3	2.2
(1931) 72	4.9	23.9	19.0	23.9	4.9
73	3.4	40.6	37.2	36.8	−.4
74	4.2	27.6	23.4	27.4	4.0
75	−.6	22.1	22.7	22.1	−.6

1		2	3	4	
			Polsby-Rice	Percentage	
		Percentage	Percentage	Replace-	
Congress	2 minus 3	First-Term	First-Term	ments	4 minus 3
76	4.5	30.0	25.5	29.7	4.2
(1941) 77	3.9	20.9	17.0	20.9	3.9
78	5.1	28.0	22.9	26.5	3.6
79	6.4	22.2	15.8	21.2	5.4
80	2.8	26.9	24.1	26.9	2.8
81	7.8	30.1	22.3	30.1	7.8
(1951) 82	2.8	17.7	14.9	17.7	2.8
83	2.1	21.6	19.5	19.0	−.5
84	2.8	14.5	11.7	14.5	2.8
85	.9	10.8	9.9	10.8	.9
86	2.6	20.8	18.2	20.5	2.3
(1961) 87	2.3	14.9	12.6	14.9	2.3
88	2.9	18.1	15.2	14.4	−.8
89	1.2	22.1	20.9	22.1	1.2
90		17.5		17.5	
91		9.9		9.9	
(1971) 92		12.6		12.6	

SOURCES: Data for "percentage first-term" and "percentage replacements" are drawn from the *Biographical Directory of the American Congress, 1774–1949* for the 1st to 80th Congresses, and from *Congressional Directory* for the 81st to 91st Congresses. The Polsby-Rice "percentage first-term" is from Nelson Polsby, "The Institutionalization of the U.S. House of Representatives," *American Political Science Review* 62 (1968): 144–68.

Thus, even after eliminating the effects of newly created seats, it appears that nineteenth-century House turnover is somewhat higher than previously thought.

To describe the shape of congressional turnover more accurately, one must examine its historical trends. One should not assume that turnover either has been declining monotonically since 1800, or that it dropped suddenly from a high to a low level at the end of the nineteenth century. Rather, the data show evidence of a set of occurrences richer than either of the preceding two suggestions.

Figure 1 shows the trend in PR both by each Congress and for ten Congress periods. Clearly the graph shows evidence of several changes in congressional turnover trends.

In the beginning, turnover increases (albeit with considerable fluctuation) until about the 17th Congress (election of 1820).[14] Then turnover takes a sharp drop in level (nearly 15 per cent),

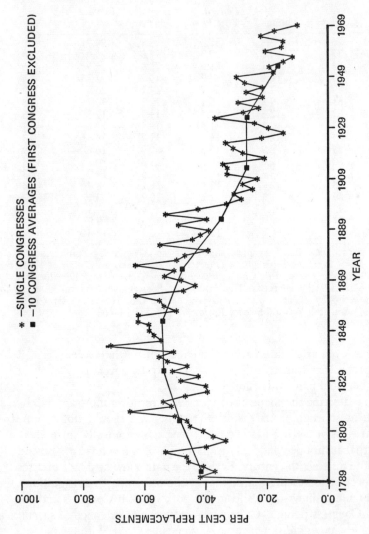

Figure 1. Per Cent Replaced in All 50 States

but resumes its upward trend.[15] Somewhere about the time of the 33d and 34th Congresses (elections of 1852 and 1854) turnover levels off and begins a quite ragged decline. After the peak for the 54th Congress (election of 1894), the turnover level suddenly drops and continues to decline gradually for some years. Turnover rises a bit during the Wilson years, falls to a local minimum in the 70th Congress (election of 1926), then shoots up with the Great Depression and the election of 1932. Since then, turnover has fluctuated a bit from election to election while declining still further overall.

What we find most interesting about these gross changes in congressional turnover is the degree to which they appear to coincide with what political historians have come to call the American party systems.[16] For example, the first party system had deteriorated after Madison's administration and had died by 1824.[17] The Jacksonian system which took its place crumpled with the rise of the Republican Party in the elections of 1854 and 1856. The Civil War system which next arose persisted until the Bryan faction captured the Democratic Party and polarized the country along sectional lines in the 1890's. The era of Republican industrialism which followed came crashing down with the Great Depression and the election of 1932. And since that time we have had our present party system, which may or may not be giving way, depending on one's reading of the evidence.

Naturally, it would be no surprise to find American political history reflected in congressional turnover. But what aspect of that history might the turnover data reflect? Differences in the degree and nature of party competition define the various party systems. Perhaps that is what one sees reflected in the turnover data, although it is too early to tell. One should keep in mind, too, that despite five different party systems, there are only two different *trends* in turnover: upward until the 1850's and downward since then. Although *levels* appear to change in fairly close correspondence with changes in the party systems, pre-existing upward or downward trends appear to continue after changes in levels.

Turning from a gross examination of Figure 1 to a more specific perusal, one sees indications of the effects of factors more localized in time than party systems. For example, James Young refers to the ill-fated 14th Congress which raised its pay and promptly suffered an outraged voter reaction.[18] Note that turnover for the 15th Congress exceeds turnover in the 14th and 16th Congresses by 15 per cent, breaking up what would have been an 18-year upward trend in turnover. As mentioned previously, one finds peaks in turnover for the elections of 1932 and 1894, elections following major economic setbacks. The peak in turnover for the 44th Congress similarly follows the panic of 1873. Even the 1958 recession is followed by a sizable (10 per cent) rise in turnover. Seemingly, the economic health of the country affects the political health of congressmen.[19]

Eyeball analysis can take us only so far, of course. Later in this paper we will examine more formally the suggestions made in this section. First, though, we wish to develop one further hypothesis about the historical changes in House turnover. That hypothesis concerns the expected benefits of holding a seat in the U.S. House of Representatives. Following Joseph Schlesinger, Gordon Black has analyzed candidates' decisions to seek office.[20] He argues that such decisions are consistent with a simple calculus which incorporates the costs of running, the probability of winning, and the benefits of winning. We are unable to examine the first factor; we have referred briefly to the second. What of the third? Can one measure the benefits of holding a seat in the House? If so, how have these benefits changed over time? A striking difference in subnational turnover patterns suggests the importance of this set of questions.

Subnational Variations in House Turnover

Throughout the past three decades liberal commentators have decried the power of Southern Democrats in the committee system of Congress. The Southern chairmen were there for all to see; however, the explanation for their power was less self-evident. Some have simply pointed to the fact that the South was a one-party area: safe seats=seniority=power. Others posited a more complex theory. According to their argument, Southerners are more likely to be dedicated House careerists than are their non-

Southern counterparts. The Southerners enter Congress at an earlier age,[21] accumulate committee seniority by retaining their early committee assignments, and do not leave Congress for other political positions. Political scientists who have examined the question conclude that the safe-seats explanation is sufficient.[22]

Still, even if we do not need to posit a dedicated, careerist, Southern congressman to account for Southern congressional *influence* in the New Deal era, we may need to do so to explain lower Southern *turnover* in past and present. Throughout our history the Southern congressman has been less likely to be replaced than the Easterner. Eastern turnover exceeds Southern in 73 of 89 Congresses (excluding, of course, the first Congress in which no one was a replacement, and the Civil War 38th and 39th Congresses); historically, average Southern turnover falls 9.7 per cent below average Eastern turnover. Table 2 shows the average excess of Eastern over Southern turnover for each of the five party systems.

TABLE 2

AVERAGE AMOUNT BY WHICH EASTERN TURNOVER EXCEEDS
SOUTHERN TURNOVER IN FIVE PARTY SYSTEMS

Party-System	Average (Eastern PR minus Southern PR)
1789–1822	10.2%
1824–1852	14.4%
1854–1894	6.6%
1896–1930	11.4%
1932–1970	6.9%

Even during the turmoil of the Civil War, party system Southern representatives showed more staying power than Easterners. The data presented in Table 2 cannot be explained by party competition alone. If one wishes to attribute low Southern turnover to a relative lack of party competition, one must assert that this has been the case since 1800. Is such an assertion accurate? Certainly the South has not always had a monopoly on safe seats. The East had numerous safe, machine-controlled districts following the Civil War and especially after the 1896 election. Even when parties did compete in the South, turnover remained relatively low. For example, by general agreement, the second party system (Whigs versus Democrats) was the most competitive in our history. All regions and most states supported relatively balanced party competition.[23] Yet, during this period the disparity between Eastern and Southern turnover was greatest.

If party competition is not a sufficient explanation for the data in Table 2, what other factors are operating? Recruitment practices are one likely answer. If the Northern urban machines parceled out congressional nominations as political payoffs, turnover might be unrelated to party competition—or anything else except the processes of local political organizations. How suggestive is the lament of a Northern representative in 1863:

> Under our Northern miserable system of representation, every two or four years, after a man has been educated to a place in this body, after he has come to know its rules and understand its duties, after he has been trained and educated as a statesman, then at that hour the political wheel rolls him out, and a green man comes here to meet the representatives of the South who have been here ten, twenty, thirty and even forty years.[24]

Are there any plausible reasons why recruitment practices might differ systematically between North and South? One possibility is that Southern political leaders saw a value in congressional experience that Northern leaders did not. Consider some suggestive data produced by economic historians and shown in Table 3.

Unfortunately, the South Atlantic classification includes several border states as well as the older Confederate states. But despite the imprecision of the classification, the striking regional disparities in federal spending clearly stand out. In the antebellum period the federal government appears to have spent more than twice as much per capita in the South Atlantic states as in New England and the Middle Atlantic states. Even after losing the Civil War, the South Atlantic states did slightly better than New England and much better than the Middle Atlantic states.[25] (Of course, the figures for 1870 and 1875 include moneys spent on reconstruction, which can't be described as beneficial to the South.)

Moreover, Table 3 tells only half the story. Not only are the

TABLE 3

PER CAPITA FEDERAL EXPENDITURES BY REGION, 1815–1900

Year	New England	Middle Atlantic	South Atlantic
1815	$ 3.28	$ 3.51	$ 5.03
1820	1.76	1.83	2.59
1825	1.20	1.52	2.07
1830	1.49	2.17	1.75
1835	1.31	.77	2.20
1840	1.45	.98	3.84
1845	1.76	1.26	3.00
1850	1.56	1.03	4.61
1855	1.79	1.67	6.88
1860	1.46	1.04	5.41
. . .	. . .	. . .	. . .
1870	14.28	10.30	12.98
1875	7.55	5.62	11.48
1880	21.13	14.70	9.78
1885	9.29	6.80	11.09
1890	11.11	8.45	13.44
1895	6.54	5.18	12.21
1900	11.05	10.65	15.45

New England: Conn., Me., Mass., N.H., R.I., Vt.
Middle Atlantic: N.J., N.Y., Pa.
South Atlantic: Del., Fla., Ga., Md., N.C., S.C., Va., W.Va.
SOURCE: Adapted from Table 1 in Lance Davis and John Legler, "The Government in the American Economy, 1815–1902: A Quantitative Study," *Journal of Economic History* 26 (1966): 514–52.

Northeastern states absolutely disadvantaged in terms of federal expenditures, we find them even more relatively disadvantaged when considering the ratio of federal expenditure to receipts. At least in the coastal Southern states, a congressional seat apparently was a profit-making enterprise in the nineteenth century.[26] To some extent, of course, this state of affairs may have been a *result* of more experienced representation in Congress. Yet at the same time Southern leaders must have seen that they would contribute little to federal revenues (chiefly tariffs) while they could gain considerably from federal expenditures (prior to 1860 mainly military expenditure and civil expenditures).[27] If Southern leaders saw their opportunity and began to return their representatives to Congress, the success of the latter in bringing home the bacon could only have reinforced the practice. When one also considers that Congress regularly made decisions about slavery we believe it reasonable to surmise that Southern leaders saw greater potential payoffs from congressional experience than did their Northern counterparts.

Moreover, there exist plausible reasons why Southern incumbents might have been more reluctant to give up their seats voluntarily than Northern incumbents. Many have suggested that the agrarian South had fewer nonpolitical career opportunities than the commercial (later industrial) North. Additionally, Lance Davis and John Legler comment that local government activity in the South lagged behind that in the North.[28] Ergo, Southern congressmen may not have had as varied a menu of local political alternatives as did, say the New York City congressman. Finally, if the congressional seat were valued more highly in the South, then holding one carried more prestige, and, given the suggested reasons for the seat's higher value, a greater opportunity to serve one's district and state.

To sum up, we believe that more than regional differences in party competition underlie the data in Table 3. Although our discussion is highly speculative, we hypothesize that the value of a congressional seat is an important variable. One would expect the value of an office to affect both an incumbent's willingness to continue holding it, and thereby the rate of voluntary turnover, and also the attitudes of political influentials toward the office, thus affecting the recruiting practices used to fill it. The recruiting practice which kept Abraham Lincoln from seeking a second term as an Illinois congressman evidently differed considerably from that prevailing south of the Mason-Dixon line.[29] As yet there has been no systematic effort to measure the changing value of a congressional seat. In the next section of this article, we will take the first tentative step in that direction.

A Quantitative Analysis of House Turnover

In the preceding sections we have described historical variations in congressional turnover, and indulged in a considerable amount of speculation about the factors underlying such variations. Now we turn to a more ambitious task. Can one go beyond speculation to a more precise specification of variables influencing congressional turnover? We believe so. In this section we report the results of a preliminary statistical analysis. The particulars of the analysis are described in detail in the appendix.

In any Congress, turnover is due to a combination of three factors: defeats, voluntary retirements, and involuntary retirements (e.g., death, being deprived of a nomination by party leaders, and so on). We have confined our attention to the first two factors.

A member's decision on whether or not voluntarily to retire would seem to depend on (1) the value of the House seat to him and (2) the likelihood of defeat if he chooses to run again. The lower the value and the higher the likelihood of defeat, the higher is the probability of voluntary retirement. The percentage of defeats will depend on the proportion of House seats that are safe for the competing parties. Thus, for our statistical analysis we need to select real world indicators for the value of a House seat and for the proportion of House seats that are safe.

One of the things that makes the House of Representatives important in our political system is that it controls the federal government's purse strings. We have chosen, therefore, to measure the value of a House seat by federal government expenditures as a proportion of the nation's gross national product.

We use a number of variables to indicate the proportion of safe seats:

1. A *variable for each of the party systems during the nation's history*. The degree of party competition, and thus the proportion of safe seats, varied substantially from one party system to another.

2. A *variable for reapportionments*. The reallocation of House seats among the states and the subsequent redistricting can alter the safeness of districts.

3. A *variable for the percentage of freshmen*. We assume that a newly elected member is more vulnerable to defeat than are his more senior colleagues.

4. A *variable for economic panics*. Serious economic setbacks within the nation can render a usually safe seat unsafe, because citizens may decide to blame incumbents for the problems.

The analysis indicates that the measure of the value of a seat has little impact on House turnover. We believe this result may be due to either a weakness of the measure or to possible counteracting effects. (See Appendix.) Each of the measures of the proportion of safe seats, on the other hand, have a strong relationship to turnover. The instability of the earlier party systems appears to have led to higher turnover. Reapportionments, panics, and the proportion of freshmen each have a clear effect on the level of turnover in the House. Taken together, this small set of variables explains (in a statistical sense) a large proportion of the historical variation in the stability of membership in the House.

What Does the Future Hold?

Any speculation about the future impact of the component causes of turnover we have discussed is risky, but there appear to be a number of possibilities which are more or less plausible.

Reapportionment and Redistricting

The statistical analysis demonstrates that the decennial reapportionment of House seats has a substantial impact on turnover. Some states are given new seats, others are deprived of old ones, thus forcing a redrawing of district lines. Additionally, due to Supreme Court redistricting decisions, most other states must draw new lines in accord with population shifts documented by the new census statistics. The reapportionment and consequent redistricting can be a substantial "shock" to the system, leading to the termination of a number of House careers. In 1972, for example, redistricting was the direct cause of eight incumbents' failure to return—five were forced to run against other incumbents in primaries and three were opposed by other incumbents in general elections.[30] In addition redistricting contributed to a number of other 1972 incumbent defeats.

No doubt, we will not see again the orgy of redistricting which followed the Supreme Court decisions of the 1960's. Probably most future redistricting will be confined to the two years following a new census. One interesting possibility, however, could lead to even more turnover from redistricting than we would predict from past reapportionments. In the future those who redraw district lines might show less concern for the protection of incumbents of either party than has been the case in the past. In 1972, for example, the new California redistricting was declared unconstitutional by the California Supreme Court. The following year a new plan was prepared for the court by a group of special masters, a plan the court accepted on November 28. In drawing the lines, the masters explicitly rejected the protection of incumbents as a consideration. Their report states:

> While protection of incumbents may be desirable to assure a core of experienced legislators, the objective of reapportionment should not be the political survival or comfort of those already in office. It is best if an incumbent's continuation in office depended upon effectiveness and responsiveness to constituents rather than upon the design of district boundaries.[31]

As a result of the plan one district will disappear, divided among three others, three incumbents will each be put in the district of another incumbent, and four other members will have their districts substantially and unfavorably altered.[32] The new plan prompted one affected member (William Mailliard, a Republican) to announce his retirement almost immediately. Should such an approach to redistricting become more widespread, one could expect markedly greater turnover after reapportionments.

Retirements

Earlier we specified that the rate of voluntary retirement depends on the relative value of a House seat and the risk of running for re-election. Interestingly, in recent years the relative value of a seat may have declined, because Congress has consciously raised the value of not holding a seat. In 1969, the Congress liberalized its pension benefits.[33] Twenty-nine incumbents retired in 1972, their first year of eligibility for the increased benefits. Only eight had retired in 1970, and thirteen in 1968.[34] Many of the 1972 retirees were among the more senior members, including two committee chairmen and nine ranking minority members. As of March 1, 1974, nineteen members had already announced their retirements.[35] While retirements will probably decline again in a few years, the temporary impact is quite substantial.

Party Realignments

In recent years numerous observers have speculated about the possibility of a major party realignment.[36] Only time will tell whether such speculations are correct, and if they are, the new pattern of party competition. Clearly, though, a sixth party system which resembled the second could drastically change the shape of congressional turnover. Unfortunately, we are not seers.

Somewhat less speculative is a second possibility. Some scholars argue that we actually may be undergoing a "dealignment," a general weakening of party loyalties.[37] Consider the rise in ticket-splitting and self-identified independents, for example.[38] If party loyalties are weak or nonexistent, we could have an era of extremely fluid politics. Voters might overwhelmingly support one party in one election and just as overwhelmingly desert them in the next. "Safe" seats would cease to exist.

Whether it is realignment or dealignment (or neither) that is happening, it is clear that in at least one region of the country—the South—partisan attachments have changed sharply in the past two decades. In 1953 the Republicans held only 5 per cent of the House seats from the South; by 1973 their share of Southern seats had risen to 24 per cent. Probably this trend will continue, at least in the short run, thereby producing higher Southern turnover than in the recent past.[39]

Primaries

Another factor which has implications for the amount of House turnover is the recent slight increase in primary defeats. Table 4 compares the electoral fortunes of incumbents in the periods 1956 to 1968 and 1970 to 1972.[40] While the frequency of incumbent defeat in general elections declined, the frequency of defeat in

TABLE 4

HOUSE INCUMBENTS AND ELECTORAL SUCCESS, 1956–68 AND 1970–72

Period	Incumbents Seeking Re-election	Incumbents Defeated in Primaries	Incumbents Defeated in General Elections	Incumbents Re-elected
1956–68	2814	42 (1.5%)	186 (6.6%)	2586 (91.9%)
1970–72	793	23 (2.9%)	25 (3.2%)	745 (93.9%)

primaries almost doubled. As we have already noted some of the primary defeats in the later period were due to two incumbents opposing each other. But many of the others were a result of relatively conservative Northern Democrats losing to more liberal opponents.[41] Thus, we are reminded that electoral risk and therefore turnover depends on intraparty competition as well as interparty competition.

Election Financing and the Advantages of Incumbency

One clear implication of Table 4 is that incumbents are seldom beaten. Indeed, from 1956 through 1972, the average rate of success for incumbents who sought re-election was over 90 per cent. Two of the advantages of incumbency are (1) an incumbent is almost always better known to the voters than his opponent and (2) he is more successful at raising money. Prior to 1972 data on money raised and spent by House candidates were notoriously unreliable. As a result of new campaign financing legislation, however, we now have some relatively sound data on the subject. An analysis of the data from 1972 by Common Cause shows that in races where incumbents had major party challengers, the challengers raised an average of $31,355, while incumbents raised an average of $58,359. The corresponding expenditure figures are $50,873 for incumbents and $32,127 for their challengers.[42]

In 1973, the Congress considered two different approaches to the question of campaign financing. One approach placed additional limitations on the amounts of contributions and total expenditures, and established tighter reporting requirements. The other approach proposed the financing of federal election cam-

paigns with public funds. By the end of 1973, the Senate had
passed bills containing both approaches but the House had accepted neither.[43]

While we do not think that this is the place for a general discussion of the merits or demerits of campaign finance reform, one
point is most germane to our subject: Alterations in the structure
of campaign financing could have a substantial impact on the
level of congressional turnover. But the reforms could lead either
to increased or decreased turnover, depending on the particular
system chosen.

On the one hand, if low limits on contributions were combined
with low limits on total campaign expenditures, challengers would
find it even more difficult to defeat incumbents. Wayne Hays
(D.-Ohio), chairman of the House Administration Committee
(which has jurisdiction over election legislation) has advocated
such a system, proposing a spending limitation of $40,000 in
House races.[44] An idea of the impact of such a limitation can be
gained from the 1972 Common Cause campaign spending study
which shows that those nonincumbent challengers who were successful in defeating their incumbent opponents spent an average
of $125,521.

On the other hand, if a system of public financing were combined with a higher spending limit (the Senate bill proposed a
limit of $90,000), some of the natural advantages of incumbency
could be overcome and increased turnover might result. For the
first time in their careers, many entrenched incumbents would
face adequately financed opponents. Moreover, such a prospect
might also increase the rate of retirement since it would increase
the electoral risks faced by incumbents.

Conclusion

While the analysis in earlier sections of this article demonstrates
a declining level of congressional turnover during this century, we
have discussed in this section a number of factors which could
produce increased turnover, at least in the short run. We would
hesitate to predict, however, that we will see a recurrence of turn-

over levels even as high as that of the 1930's. Events have created a situation which makes the future of most incumbents quite secure, and we see no great likelihood that the situation will change drastically in the foreseeable future. During the present era an examination of membership change in the House impresses one most by the picture of membership stability which emerges.

NOTES

1. For evidence bearing on this popular stereotype see Charles Bullock, "House Careerists: Changing Patterns of Longevity and Attrition," *American Political Science Review* 66 (1972): 1295–1300.

2. For example, political observers felt that a major obstacle to congressional approval of President Nixon's 1970 executive branch reorganization plan was that the reorganization would upset existing patterns of congressional committee jurisdictions.

3. Recall the Republican leadership changes following the 1958 and 1964 electoral disasters, and the adoption of the 21-day rule following the 1964 election.

4. Lewis Froman, *The Congressional Process* (Boston: Little, Brown, 1967), pp. 6–15.

5. H. Douglas Price, "The Congressional Career—Then and Now," in Nelson Polsby, ed., *Congressional Behavior* (New York: Random House, 1971), pp. 14–27. An earlier version of this paper circulated privately among congressional scholars.

6. E. E. Schattschneider, "United States: The Functional Approach to Party Government," in Sigmund Neumann, ed., *Modern Political Parties* (Chicago: University of Chicago Press, 1956), pp. 194–215.

7. Nelson Polsby, "The Institutionalization of the U.S. House of Representatives," *American Political Science Review* 62 (1968): 144–68.

8. *Ibid.*, 145–46.

9. *Ibid.*, 166.

10. T. Richard Witmer, "The Aging of the House," *Political Science Quarterly* 79 (1964): 526–41.

11. Of course, one should keep in mind that if one's goal simply is to put new blood in Congress, creating a couple of hundred new seats would serve that goal nicely.

12. This measure appears to be the same as that used by James Young. See his *The Washington Community: 1800–1928* (New York: Columbia University Press, 1966), p. 90.

13. Although tenure data is not discussed in this paper, coding members with noncontinuous prior service as new gives us a slightly different tenure measure from those which now exist. Witmer and Polsby consider data on

average terms served by the members of each Congress. Our data comprise average *continuous* terms served by the members of each Congress. The reason we present turnover data rather than tenure data lies in our failure to formulate a measure which can correct tenure figures for the effects of new seats. Until a seat has existed at least as long as the mean terms served for a Congress the incumbent of that seat has no chance to attain the mean. Thus, there is a slight downward bias in all data on congressional tenure. Actually, not much is lost by considering turnover data alone. The correlation between percentage first-term and mean tenure is −.91, and between percentage replaced and mean tenure, −.90.

14. Note the exceptionally high turnover for the 15th Congress. Young suggests this increase resulted from public outrage at a pay raise passed by the 14th Congress. See Young, p. 59.

15. The 28th Congress (election of 1842) is a deviant case in this period. The 28th Congress was a reapportioned Congress in which the size of the House was *reduced* from 242 to 223. Moreover, 1842 was an off-year election following the first Democratic Presidential defeat in the nineteenth century. Following Harrison's death Tyler became President. In the next election his party lost 51 seats, 39 of them to the Democrats.

16. William Chambers and Walter Burnham, eds., *The American Party Systems* (New York: Oxford University Press, 1967).

17. Richard McCormick, "Political Development and the Second Party System," in Chambers and Burnham, eds., *American Party*, p. 91.

18. See Note 14.

19. Although the proposition seems very plausible, a number of studies have cast doubt on its empirical validity. See for example, George Stigler, "General Economic Conditions and National Elections," *American Economic Review* 63 (1973): 160–67. Francisco Ancelus and Allan Meltzer, "The Effect of Aggregate Economic Variables on Congressional Elections," 1973 American Political Science Association Paper. For conflicting evidence see Gerald Kramer, "Short-Term Fluctuations in U.S. Voting Behavior, 1896–1964," *American Political Science Review* 65 (1971): 131–43.

20. Gordon S. Black, "A Theory of Political Ambition: Career Choices and the Role of Structural Incentives," *American Political Science Review* 66 (1972): 144–59.

21. Probably the variable age at entry deserves more serious consideration than it has received thus far. Schlesinger's data for the period 1900–1958 show that over 50 per cent of Southern congressmen entered Congress before age 40. By contrast, just over 30 per cent of Middle Atlantic congressmen, just over 40 per cent of New England congressmen, and approximately 35 per cent of Midwestern congressmen entered Congress before age 40. Thus, other things being equal, we would expect less turnover from deaths and retirement among Southern congressmen. See Joseph Schlesinger, *Ambition in Politics* (Chicago: Rand McNally, 1966), p. 189.

22. Raymond Wolfinger and Joan Hollinger, "Safe Seats, Seniority, and Power in Congress," in Robert Peabody and Nelson Polsby, eds., *New Per-*

spectives on the House of Representatives (Chicago: Rand McNally, 2d ed., 1969), pp. 55–77.

23. McCormick, "Second Party System." See also Everett Ladd, *American Political Parties* (New York: Norton, 1970), pp. 93–103.

24. This is a statement by Representative James Brooks, quoted in W. R. Brock, *An American Crisis* (New York: Harper, 1963), p. 55. Such relations are fairly common in the congressional literature. In 1820 Edward Dowse of Massachusetts commented that the Southern representatives "have a great preponderancy of talent against us." And in 1897 James G. Blaine commented that the "best and most talented" men in the South enter politics. Why did the South elect and re-elect a higher caliber of man than did the North? See Edmund Quincy, *Life of Josiah Quincy of Massachusetts*, 1867, p. 387, and Theron Crawford, *James G. Blaine*, 1893, p. 161. Neil MacNeil draws attention to these comments. See his *Forge of Democracy* (New York: David McKay, 1963), p. 287.

25. The regional differences suggested in Table 3 are somewhat inflated by the inclusion of the District of Columbia in the South Atlantic region. During the nineteenth century federal civil and miscellaneous expenditures accounted for approximately 25 per cent of all federal expenditures. Half or more of this 25 per cent typically resulted from expenditures in and around the District of Columbia. Still, this fact would not seem to account for all the South Atlantic region's advantage, particularly the pronounced pre–Civil War advantage. Moreover, whatever the influence of D.C. on the regional distribution of federal expenditures, it had no comparable influence on the regional distribution of receipts: the South Atlantic region's advantage is real. See John Legler, "Regional Distribution of Federal Receipts and Expenditures in the Nineteenth Century: A Quantitative Study," (Ph.D. diss., Purdue University, 1967).

26. The interior Southern states did not receive nearly as much federal money per capita as the Eastern states, let alone the South Atlantic states. But the interior Southern states gave very little to the federal government. On balance they were nearly even or a little in the red in their total financial interaction with the federal government. See Legler, "Regional Distribution," Table 52, p. 190.

27. To elaborate, prior to the Civil War customs brought in 80 per cent of all federal revenues. After the war internal revenue increased in importance, finally overtaking customs by the turn of the century. As for federal expenditures, civil and miscellaneous accounted for about 25 per cent during the nineteenth century. Military expenditures accounted for 40–60 per cent prior to the Civil War, but only 20–25 per cent thereafter. During the first and last thirds of the century interest on the public debt came to nearly one-third of all federal expenditures, but required only a small amount from 1835 to 1870. After the Civil War, pensions reached a high of 40 per cent of all federal expenditures, but before the war they were 10 per cent or less. The regional allocations of expenditures are interesting. The Eastern states (particularly New England) received the highest per capita federal expenditures

for debt retirement and pensions. They received a lower per capita federal expenditure for civil expenses and military operations. The South fared better in the latter two categories. Apparently, the presence of hostile Indians stimulated federal spending: the Mountain states received huge per capita military expenditures. See Legler, "Regional Distribution."

28. Lance Davis and John Legler, "The Government in the American Economy, 1815–1902: A Quantitative Study," *Journal of Economic History* 26 (1966): 514–52.

29. Further observations on the nature of the Southern recruitment process have been offered by a historian friend. Briefly, he suggests that the nonurban South was tightly controlled by a relatively small social hierarchy extremely fearful of conflict on major issues. Even personal, intraparty competition has the potential to broaden into issue conflict and thus was squelched by the power structure. Once in office, even demonstrable incompetents could count on solid local support in many areas.

30. The five defeated in primaries were Jack McDonald (R.-Mich.), James Byrne (D.-Pa.), James Scheuer (D.-N.Y.), Cornelius Gallagher (D.-N.J.), and James Kee (D.-W. Va.). Those defeated in the general election were John Kyl (R.-Ia.), Graham Purcell (D.-Tex.) and Alvin O'Konski (R.-Wis.).

31. Quoted in *Congressional Quarterly Weekly Report*, November 3, 1973, p. 2912.

32. *Ibid.*

33. See *Guide to the Congress of the United States* (Washington, D.C.: Congressional Quarterly, Inc., 1971), p. 411.

34. These figures do not include members who sought other offices.

35. See David S. Broder, "Six Senior House Republicans to Retire," *The Washington Post*, January 1, 1974, p. A2. More congressmen have announced their retirements since Broder wrote.

36. See, for example, Kevin Philips, *The Emerging Republican Majority* (New York: Arlington House, 1969).

37. Walter Burnham notes this process. See his *Critical Elections and the Mainsprings of American Politics* (New York: Norton, 1970), Ch. 5.

38. See Walter DeVries and V. Lance Tarrance, *The Ticket-Splitters* (Grand Rapids, Michigan: William B. Erdmans, 1972).

39. This shift in control of Southern House seats, along with a similar change in regard to Senate seats, has important implications for the distribution of power within each house. See Norman J. Ornstein and David W. Rohde, "Seniority and Future Power in Congress," pp. 72–87 in this volume.

40. The data on the years 1956 to 1966 were taken from Charles O. Jones, *Every Second Year* (Washington: The Brookings Institution, 1967), Table 9, p. 68. The data on the years 1968 to 1972 were gathered from the appropriate volumes of *Congressional Quarterly Almanac*.

41. For example, Philip Philbin of Massachusetts was defeated in 1970 by Father Robert Drinan, an antiwar Jesuit priest.

42. We wish to thank Fred Wertheimer of Common Cause for making

their analysis available to us. Some results of the Common Cause study, and data on contributions and expenditures for all House races in 1972, are reported in *Congressional Quarterly Weekly Report*, Dec. 1, 1973, pp. 3130–37.

43. For provisions of the bill containing the former approach, see *Congressional Quarterly Weekly Report*, August 4, 1973, pp. 2152–55. Public financing of elections was passed as an amendment to a debt ceiling bill. See *Congressional Weekly Report*, December 1, 1973, pp. 3163–64.

44. See *Congressional Quarterly Weekly Report*, October 6, 1973, pp. 2666–67.

APPENDIX

Details of the Statistical Analysis of Turnover

House turnover poses certain problems as a dependent variable. Turnover in the 2d Congress (1791) is based on thirteen states, but turnover in the 36th Congress (1859) reflects data from thirty-four states. Two Congresses later (1863) only twenty-three states are represented in House turnover, whereas turnover for the 92d Congress (1971) includes data from fifty states. Thus, one must be aware of the possibility that changes in "House turnover" might partially reflect the differing composition of the House over time. Moreover, we already have shown that regional subsamples of the House data differ considerably. Such differences are obscured in an analysis of aggregate House turnover. Nevertheless, one has to begin somewhere. We will ignore the changing data base and subnational differences in this preliminary analysis. But a more thorough analysis should take account of such facts.

We will work from a basic identity. Per cent replacements in the tth Congress is the sum of three components from the $(t-1)^{th}$ Congress: percentage defeated (PD), percentage of voluntary retirements (PVR) and percentage of involuntary retirements (PIR) not due to electoral defeat (e.g., being canned by the local party leaders, dying, etc.). Systematic study of the third component appears to be all but impossible. For example, how can one gather data on local recruitment practices over a 180-year period? Therefore, we are forced to consider involuntary turnover not due to electoral defeat as an error term. The other two components are more amenable to analysis. The percentage of voluntary retirements by incumbents of the $(t - 1)^{th}$ Congress would appear to depend primarily on two variables: the anticipated relative value of a congressional seat and the electoral risks they face. Specifically, we hypothesize that

$$PVR_{t-1} = a_1 + b_1V_t + b_2ER_{t-1} + \varepsilon_1$$

Equation (1)

where V_t = relative value of a seat in the next Congress, i.e. vis-à-vis other public and private positions, and ER_{t-1} = electoral risk of running for the next Congress. Presumably $b_1 < 0$, $b_2 > 0$: Voluntary turnover varies directly with electoral risk and inversely with the expected relative value of the congressional seat. The error term, ε_1, represents retirements due to ill health and other personal reasons which we assume occur more or less randomly.

Moving on, the percentage defeated depends on the electoral risk present during a congressional campaign:

$$PD_{t-1} = a_2 + b_3ER_{t-1} + \varepsilon_2 \qquad \text{Equation (2)}$$

where b_3 is hypothesized to be positive. At this point, of course, we must come to grips with what we mean by "electoral risk." Earlier we mentioned several factors which heighten the risks faced by congressmen during a campaign. These include reapportionments, which alter district boundaries, and economic setbacks, which may provoke citizens to retaliate against incumbents. Of course, in the long run other less discrete factors no doubt affect congressional turnover more than sudden shocks like economic setbacks or reapportionments. As H. Douglas Price notes, the level of party competition no doubt strongly influences turnover. Put another way, the proportion of safe seats should strongly affect House turnover. Political scientists have expended considerable effort in attempting to operationalize concepts like party competition and electoral safety.[a] Major difficulties exist in the present usage of both concepts, but estimates of the number of safe seats are available for recent Congresses, and, in principle, one could obtain rough measures of party competition, safe seats, or the like back to 1789.[b] We have not embarked on such a tremendous data collection project, however; rather, we will employ some crude but more available surrogates for party competition and safe seats.

As we have seen, congressional turnover appears to vary across the American party systems—political eras in which the degree and nature of party competition differed one from the others. The first and fourth party systems, for instance, had a pronounced regional basis. In parts of the East and most of the South, two-party competition was nonexistent. In contrast, during the second party system balanced two-party competition occurred in all regions and most states. Thus, we include in our analysis a set of dummy variables for the party systems. With these we may capture the gross effects of variations in party competition. The fifth party system is taken as a baseline. Then we interpret the coefficients of the dummy variables for the other party systems as estimates of greater or lesser (depending on whether they are positive or negative) competition during those periods.

Some political scientists have suggested that safe seats are not solely a function of party competition. They hypothesize in addition an "incumbency effect," a tendency for voters to support incumbents over challengers whether on the basis of name recognition, established political credit, or voter conservatism.[c] We will allow for such an effect by introducing a lagged variable into the analysis. Namely, we hypothesize that the electoral risk facing the incumbents of a Congress is proportional to the percentage of freshmen in that Congress. Thus, the percentage of replacements in each Congress will be proportional to the percentage of freshmen (PF) in the preceding Congress. Note that this reasoning is incorrect if the incumbency effect occurs all at once, i.e., for first-term incumbents just as strongly as for ten-termers. We are assuming that first-term incumbents face greater electoral risks than more senior incumbents.[d]

Finally, we recognize that a variable already introduced—the relative value of a House seat—also probably affects electoral risk. The greater the anticipated value of a seat, the greater the likelihood that congressmen will be challenged, *ceteris paribus*.

The upshot of this discussion, then, is the following estimate of the electoral risk faced by the incumbents of the $(t-1)^{th}$ Congress:[e]

$$ER_{t-1} = a_3 + b_4R_{t-1} + b_5P_{t-1} + b_6PS_1 + b_7PS_2 + b_8PS_3$$
$$+ b_9PS_4 + b_{10}(PF_{t-1}) + b_{11}V_t + \varepsilon_3 \qquad \text{Equation (3)}$$

where R = Reapportionment
     P = Panic
     PS_i = Party System i, i = 1, 2, 3, 4
     PF = Percentage of freshmen
     V = relative value of a seat, as previously.

Coefficients b_4 to b_8, b_{10}, b_{11} are all expected to be positive. Now we may substitute equation (3) into (1) and (2), then substitute the result into our basic identity, letting ε_4 signify PIR. These substitutions yield:

$$PR_t = (a_1 + a_2 + b_2a_3 + b_3a_3) + (b_2 + b_3) b_4 (R_{t-1}) +$$
$$(b_2 + b_3) b_5 (P_{t-1}) + (b_2 + b_3) (b_6PS_1 + b_7PS_2 + b_8PS_3$$
$$+ b_9PS_4) + (b_2 + b_3) b_{10} (PF_{t-1}) + (b_1 + b_2b_{11} + b_3b_{11})$$
$$V_t + (b_2 + b_3) \varepsilon_3 + \varepsilon_1 + \varepsilon_2 + \varepsilon_4 \qquad \text{Equation (4)}$$

Based on earlier discussion one would expect the estimated coefficients of reapportionment, panic, the first three-party systems and percentage of freshmen all to be positive. But the coefficient of the value of a seat presents a problem in interpretation. On the one hand, a high value makes incumbents less likely to quit voluntarily; thus we hypothesize that $b_1 < 0$. But on the other hand a high value should make the race more attractive to challengers, thus increasing the incumbents' electoral risk $(b_{11} > 0)$. Increased electoral risk in turn should increase both the defeat rate of incumbents $(b_3 > 0)$ and their voluntary retirement rate $(b_2 > 0)$. Perhaps b_1 clearly outweighs $[(b_2 + b_3) b_{11}]$ or vice versa. But should the estimated coefficient of value in equation (4) be 0, we do not know whether we have two significant but opposing effects, or no important effects at all.

A mixture of dummy and real variables has been used to estimate equation (4). Reapportionments occur every ten years following the census. Thus, we use a dummy variable which takes on a value of 1 for every Congress elected in a year ending in 2 (excepting 1922, when Congress ignored its constitutional charge.) Similarly, for panics, we use a dummy variable which takes on a value of 1 for every Congress elected following the more noteworthy financial crises in our history.[f] Finally, as mentioned, we use dummy variables to represent the American party systems. Table 1 contains the dates used in our classification.

The figures for percentage of freshmen are straightforward. These data were gathered while compiling our turnover data. We hypothesize that the percentage of replacements in each Congress is related to the percentage of freshmen (including those from new seats) in the preceding Congress.

The relative value of a congressional seat is the most difficult variable to measure. Because the House holds the power of the purse, we decided to use an indicator of the importance of the federal government in the national economy. Presumably, the power and prestige of the House varies directly with the power and prestige of the federal government. And while federal power does not necessarily entail federal spending, we could come up with no better measure of the former. Estimates of GNP are available back to the 1840's, and estimates of federal expenditures back to 1789.[g] For want of a better indicator, then, we will use federal expenditures as a proportion of GNP as an indicator of the relative value of a seat in the House. Because of the truncated nature of the GNP series we have no measure of value for the 1st to 24th Congresses. Thus, listwise deletion of observations with missing data has the effect of eliminating the first party system from the analysis.

Table 1A presents the estimates of the equation specified by equation (4):

Equation (4) yields a reasonably good fit, although high R^2 are common with aggregated time series data. The estimated coefficients are rather interesting. The party system dummies turn in an impressive performance, particularly that for the very competitive second party system. The coefficient for the fourth party system is smaller than its standard error. Thus, to the extent that the party system dummies are surrogates for the level of party competition for congressional seats, one might conclude that the big

TABLE 1A
ESTIMATED COEFFICIENTS FOR EQUATION (4).

Variable	B	σB	
Reapportionment	6.25	2.01	
Panic	4.99	2.60	
Party System 2	21.20	4.76	$R^2 =$ .87
Party System 3	14.96	4.03	s.e.e. = 6.15
Party System 4	2.66*	2.82	
			$\alpha = 12.18$
% Freshmen	0.40	0.10	
Value	0.08*	0.14	
* p > .05			

change occurs between the third and fourth systems, as Schatt-schneider and Price have suggested.

Proceeding further, we see that a reapportionment is expected to result in a 6 per cent incumbent replacement rate, and a financial disaster will add another 5 per cent to that.[h] Thus, the incumbents of the 72d Congress (1931–32), in which the two events coincided, were particularly unlucky. PR in the 73d Congress was up 12.9 per cent, fairly close to the *ceteris paribus* prediction of 11.24 per cent.

Evidently, the effects of electoral shocks like reapportionments will last more than one election. For, we see that the percentage of freshmen in a Congress bears a significant positive relationship to PR in the next Congress. Turnover begets turnover, so to speak. Thus, the aggregate model does produce results consistent with an incumbency effect.

Finally, we see that the coefficient of value is not significant. Whether the indicator is too weak, the arguments are incorrect, or the hypothesized effects are counteracting (see p. 53) is impossible to say. If the latter, and if we put any credence into the negative sign of the coefficient, then we might suggest that the effect of value on the voluntary retirement calculation (1) is most important. But this would be an extremely tenuous conclusion.

In sum, a statistical analysis of congressional replacement suggests the importance of historical variations in party competition, incumbency effects, and sudden shocks like reapportionments and economic disasters. The importance of career calculations involving the value of the congressional seat remains unclear. None of these conclusions are startlingly new, of course. But at the least they support the more speculative conclusions of others, and they illustrate the possibility of explaining membership stability in the House on the basis of a small number of variables.

NOTES TO APPENDIX

a. For a critical survey of attempts to measure party competition see David Pfeiffer, "The Measurement of Inter-Party Competition and Systemic Stability," *American Political Science Review* 61 (1967): 457–67. For one measurement of the safety of congressional seats see Raymond Wolfinger and Joan Hollinger, "Safe Seats, Seniority, and Power in Congress," *American Political Science Review* 59 (1965).

b. Charles Jones provides data for the period 1914–60. See his "Inter-Party Competition for Congressional Seats, *Western Political Quarterly* 17 (1964): 461–76.

c. See Robert Erickson, "Malapportionment, Gerrymandering, and Party Fortunes in Congressional Elections," *American Political Science Review* 66 (1972): 1234–45. Also Andrew Cowart, "Electoral Choices in the American States: Incumbency Effects, Partisan Forces, and Divergent Partisan Majorities, *American Political Science Review* 67 (1973): 835–53.

d. Jones's data support such an assumption. From 1956 to 1966 the average rate of defeat of freshmen members of the House was more than twice as great as the average rate of defeat of non-freshmen. See Charles Jones, *Every Second Year* (Washington, D.C.: Brookings, 1967), pp. 67–70.

e. Note that dummy variables for only four of the five party systems are included in the analysis. Regression analysis necessitates this practice. If all five dummies are included, the data matrix is singular and cannot be inverted.

f. Our procedure for constructing this variable was very simple. We took an introductory American history text and looked in the index under "panics." Our presumption was that any financial setback severe enough to make it into the history books carried the potential for affecting the political fortunes of incumbent Congressmen. The book used was John Garrity, *The American Nation* (New York: Harper and Row, 1966). One should note, incidentally, that panics are not the same phenomenon as depressions. The former are financial in nature and thus affect primarily the financial community, whereas the latter are more universal in impact. Naturally, one would expect both panics and depressions to affect turnover—hurting a few big money men can do as much damage as hurting a much larger number of ordinary citizens. Unfortunately, we could not procure the data to measure depressions during the nineteenth century.

g. Data on federal expenditures are drawn from *Historical Statistics of the United States, 1789–1957,* series Y255, and from *Statistical Abstract of the United States,* annual volumes from 1958 to the present. The data are direct general expenditures which correspond to the pre-1969 Federal Administrative Budget. The GNP data are more scattered. After 1958 we used the *Statistical Abstract.* From 1920–57 we used *Historical Statistics.* The latter reference also contains five-year estimates by the Department of Commerce for the period 1894–1919 and by Simon Kuznets for the period 1871–94. Finally, we pushed the series back to 1840 by using decadal estimates by Robert Gallman. The latter are contained in Table 3 of Charles Holt, "The Role of State Government in the Nineteenth-Century American Economy, 1820–1902: A Quantitative Study, "(Ph.D. Diss., Purdue University, 1970). Where five- or ten-year averages were available, we assigned the average to the mid-point of the period and used simple linear interpolation between the midpoints.

h. Note that the latter conclusion conflicts with the conclusion of several studies cited earlier (Note 20) to the effect that variations in economic conditions do not affect the incumbents' electoral welfare. We suspect the conflict stems from the different measures of economic conditions employed. The studies which report negative evidence rely on continuous measures of mass economic conditions, i.e., a 1 per cent rise in real income or fall in unemployment affects the vote proportionately. In contrast, our use of a dummy variable for major financial setbacks reflects our belief that only "big" economic shifts matter.

II. Change and the Committee System

From its earliest days Congress found that a division of its workload into committees was a necessary way of handling legislative business. Starting with four permanent (standing) committees in the House in 1800, including Appropriations and Interstate Commerce, the number of committees burgeoned as the country grew economically and geographically. By 1909, there were sixty-one House committees, with mostly narrow (sometimes nonexistent) jurisdictions, such as the Committee on Ventilation and Acoustics. At that point, the number of committees began to drop, for classic congressional reasons. The Cannon Office Building was erected, and for the first time, every member, not just committee chairmen, could have his own private office.[1] Nearly twenty committees were dropped during the next two decades, and in the 1946 Legislative Reorganization Act the number of standing committees was reduced to nineteen in the House (now twenty-one) and fifteen in the Senate (now seventeen).

Committees were always important, but they were eclipsed in power by the autocratic party leaders of the 1890–1910 era. Following the famous 1910 House revolt against "Czar" Speaker Joseph Cannon, this power relationship was reversed, making committees pre-eminent and strengthening their chairmen. Cannon had derived considerable power from his ability to handpick committee chairmen and also to control committee jurisdictions. After his fall in 1910, Congress began to adopt a more objective selection process: the seniority system.[2] The custom of selecting as committee chairmen the members with the longest continuous service on each committee has prevailed into the 1970's.

Senator Robert Packwood (R-Ore.), speaking on the Senate floor in 1970, mustered a series of arguments in favor of abolishing the Senate seniority system for selecting committee chairmen, arguments which had been echoed for several years by Congressional liberals who were frustrated by the predominance of Southern conservatives in senior positions. Packwood also gives us an interesting look at the serendipitous origins of the seniority system in the Senate, which builds on the description in Price's article in Section I. David W. Rohde and I demonstrate that recent electoral trends will soon change the seniority system's outcomes, in both the House and the Senate—in future years, ironically, it may be the conservatives who will be calling for the abolition of seniority.

Interestingly, until 1973, the seniority rule did not apply to House subcommittees; prior to that, committee chairmen could for the most part define subcommittee jurisdictions, assign or withhold bills from them, and name subcommittee chairmen. These enormous powers were cut down by the Democratic Party Caucus (as majority party, they control all chairmanships) at the beginning of the 93d Congress.[3] In "Causes and Consequences of Congressional Change," I discuss the implementation of these reforms and examine their present and future impact on power and policy in the House of Representatives.

NOTES

1. Neil MacNeil, *Forge of Democracy*. (New York: David McKay, 1963), p. 61.

2. For a more detailed look at the seniority system in the House, see Nelson Polsby, Miriam Gallagher, and Barry Rundquist, "The Growth of the Seniority System in the House of Representatives," *American Political Science Review* 63 (September 1969): 787–807. For a different interpretation, see Price's article in this volume.

3. These rules changes would become moot if the Republicans gained a majority in the House; in the near future, this is very unlikely.

THE SENATE SENIORITY SYSTEM

SENATOR ROBERT W. PACKWOOD

I am today circulating for cosponsorship, and will later introduce as an amendment to one of the two legislative reorganization bills presently before the Congress, [a measure] to abolish the Senate seniority system.

Under the provisions of this amendment, the chairman of each standing committee of the Senate will be elected by the members of that committee who are of [the] majority party. The ranking minority member will be elected by the members of that committee who are of the minority party.

I know it is going to be alleged that this is a startling and abrupt change in our Senate procedures and it should not be done hastily. But for 125 years we have lived under the seniority system, and most fair evaluators of it have found it wanting. The seniority system as we presently use it has caused Congress to be a laughing-stock among the public. I am merely asking that we experiment with something new. If it does not work we can alter it, or if the Senate desires, we can go back to the seniority system. Nothing will be lost by trying something new.

Defenders of the seniority system assert that in spite of its

Excerpted from a speech delivered on the Senate floor by Senator Robert Packwood, R.-Ore. Reprinted from the *Congressional Record*, August 24, 1970, pp. S14006–10. Senator Packwood was first elected in 1968, unseating incumbent Senator Wayne Morse.

frailties, it is the best system that has yet been devised to select committee chairmen. I cannot agree.

In this age of crisis, Government must be flexible to meet new challenges. The world is moving at a dizzy pace. Emergencies are omnipresent. Everything is changing. . . .

At a time when other American institutions are turning over the reins of leadership to younger men, the chairmen of Senate committees are more deeply entrenched than ever before.

One hundred years ago, the average age of a Senator was 50.6; today the average age is 56.6. Not really so great a difference. But 100 years ago the average age of a committee chairman was 53.7 and today it is 65.4

One hundred years ago, a committee chairman had served an average of 6.8 years in the Senate. Today the average Senate committee chairman has served 20.9 years. . . .

AGE DISTRIBUTION OF SENATE COMMITTEE CHAIRMEN
IN 1870 AND 1970

Age range	Number	Per cent
1870		
40 to 49	9	34.6
50 to 59	13	50.0
60 to 69	3	11.5
70 to 79	1	3.9
1970		
40 to 49	1	6.25
50 to 59	3	18.75
60 to 69	6	37.50
70 to 70	6	37.50

SOURCE: Congressional Directory 1870; Congressional Directory 1970; and Biographical Directory of the American Congress.

This table shows that while 84.6 per cent—or twenty-two—of the Senate's committee chairmen were between 40 and 60 years old in 1870, only 25 per cent—or four—were between 40 and 60 in 1970. Instead, in 1970, 75 per cent—or twelve—committee chairmen were between 60 and 80 years old; while in 1870 only 15.5 per cent—or four—committee chairmen were between 60 and 80 years old.

As I indicated, the average age of Senate committee leaders is 65.4. In private business the usual age for retirement is 65. If the retirement rules of private business were followed by the Senate, all but four of the sixteen Senate committee chairmen would be forced to retire.

Congress has itself passed rules requiring civil servants to step down at age 70. But if the Senate followed the rules it laid down for others, six committee chairmen would have to retire. Only Congress has institutionalized age and length of service

Let us look at the executive branch for a moment. In the executive branch, the average age of Cabinet members on taking office under President Nixon was 55.7 years. . . . Under President Johnson, it was 50. And under President Kennedy it was 48. While in the Senate, the average age of committee chairmen is 65.4.

The Senate's seniority system allows some States which regularly re-elect Senators to be overrepresented as far as actual power and influence in national affairs are concerned. On the other hand, States which are more sensitive to political change and switch from one party to the other may not elect members to a sufficient number of consecutive terms for them to receive chairmanships.

Implicit in this analysis is the fact that those states where the two parties are more closely matched politically—as New York, Illinois, California, Pennsylvania—have not held major Senate committee chairmanships for a considerable number of years, despite their vast populations and their importance to the nation's economy. I can think of no more compelling reason for modifying the seniority rule than the manner in which seniority must inevitably discriminate against great two-party states such as these.

Admittedly, my knowledge of the seniority system was slight when I first came to this Congress. My only previous legislative experience had been that of serving in the Oregon Legislature. In the Oregon Legislature, committee chairmen are picked by the majority leader on the basis of merit and ability rather than seniority. This system worked well in Oregon. I was resolved, however, to say nothing about the seniority system until I had had a chance to both study it and serve under it. Unfortunately, studying it was easier said than done because there has always been more heat than light spread upon this problem in the past.

I shall limit my comments to the Senate, although I feel the pros and cons of the seniority system would apply equally to either House. Now, regardless of the merits or demerits of the seniority system, one thing is obvious: The seniority system favors those who are elected to Congress at a young age and continue to be re-elected. The chairmen of the standing committees in the Senate today served an average of over two terms before obtaining their chairmanship. That is an average, and many able men had to wait much longer to achieve chairmanships. . . .

Therefore, those who are elected to the Senate at the age of 50 or over are playing hide-and-seek with the standard insurance mortality tables as to whether or not they will ever chair a significant committee in this body. On the other hand, those elected at age 50 or under may have the good fortune to chair a committee. Certainly those elected in their thirties or early forties can, by virtue of the simple fact that they were first elected to the Senate at a young age, propel themselves to power by the sole expedient of being re-elected. Having been elected myself to the Senate at the age of 36, I will, if the voters of Oregon re-elect me, by virtue of seniority alone, find myself eventually elevated to a committee chairmanship at a younger age than that at which many of my distinguished colleagues are elected for the first time.

The obligation of a U.S. Senator, however, runs deeper than personal advantage. As U.S. Senators, our obligations run to all of the people of this country. It is incumbent upon us to attempt to govern, with their consent, in the most expedient and intelligent way possible. Thus, with some misgivings about even questioning this system that would favor me, I started to look into the background and antecedents of the seniority system.

The first place to look, of course, was at Congress in its days of infancy. How did the Founding Fathers of this country view the seniority system? After all, the early leaders of the Congress of this country were the very people who had carried us through a revolution with Britain and fashioned the American Constitution, which Gladstone called "the most wonderful work ever struck off at a given time by the brain and purpose of man." These were indeed the giants of our history. If they could fashion a U.S. Constitution that has governed us well for so many years, would there be anything we could learn from their method of organizing the Senate of the United States?

SELECTION OF SENATE COMMITTEE CHAIRMEN FROM 1789 TO 1846

1789–1823.—The Senator having the greatest number of votes is first named and, as such, is Chairman.

1823–1826: Presiding Officer named Chairman.

1826–1828: Elected by separate ballot of the Senate (Ezekiel Chambers Rule).

1828–1833: President *pro tempore* appointed Chairman. (President *pro tempore* specifically designated so as to insure that the Vice-President—as Presiding Officer—would not appoint committee chairmen.)

1833–1837: Elected by separate ballot of the Senate as in 1826.

1837–1841: Appointed by the Presiding Officer.

1841–1845: Appointed by the President *pro tempore*, as Presiding Officer (Because of the death of President William Henry Harrison, Vice-President John Tyler succeeded to the Presidency, leaving the Vice Presidency vacant from 1841 to 1845.)

1845: Appointed by Vice President or Presiding Officer in March; elected in December.

1846: Selected by caucus. (Beginning of the seniority system.)

Before even considering, however, how committee chairmen were selected, the first thing we learn is that from the time of the first Congress in 1789 until 1816 there were no standing legislative committees at all in the Senate. Pending legislation was scrutinized instead by select committees named as the occasion for such service arose. These select committees were abolished after finishing work on the problem or legislation submitted to them.

One of the first 19 rules adopted by the Senate in 1789 provided:

All committees shall be appointed by ballot, and a plurality of votes should make a choice.

However, during this entire period of select committees, the rules made no specific provision for committee chairmen.

In his monumental study of the Senate, the distinguished historian George Haynes noted that in the tentative draft apparently prepared by Senator William Maclay of Pennsylvania for the consideration of the committee which framed the Senate's first code of rules, adopted in April, 1789, it was stipulated that each committee's chairman "shall be the senator from the most northerly state of those from which the committee is taken." Fortunately, this outlandish proposal never found its way into the rules.

My study of the early Senate Journals has revealed that while no specific method for selecting committee chairmen was mentioned in the rules, it was the practice when the committees were elected to designate as chairman the man receiving the most votes. This is confirmed by John Quincy Adams, who served in the Senate from 1803 to 1808 and was later Secretary of State and President, when he said of the practice of the Senate while he served in it:

> The member having the greatest number of votes is first named, and as such is chairman. (*Memoirs* 1, page 482).

For example, on November 3, 1803, a committee was appointed to study an appropriations bill to effect the Treaty of Amity and Commerce between the United States and England. John Quincy Adams, whose Senate service began in 1803, was chairman. The two other members of the committee were Uriah Tracy of Connecticut, who had been a senator since 1796, and Abraham Baldwin, who had served since 1799. By the standard of seniority, John Quincy Adams would not have been chairman. . . .

Even after the Senate changed from its system of select committees to standing committees, the early Senate Journals reveal that seniority was not a factor in the selection of committee chairmen.

For example, in 1823, when chairmen were appointed by the President *Pro Tempore*—as the Presiding Officer—a freshman senator was named chairman of the powerful Military Affairs Committee. This freshman senator had less seniority than every other member of the committee, but his unique background and ability were considered more important. His name was Andrew Jackson.

In 1834, when committee chairmen were elected by ballot of the Senate, Henry Clay became chairman of the prestigious

Committee on Foreign Relations, though he was only the third-ranking member of the committee.

In 1841, when the committee chairmen were appointed by the President *pro tempore*—as presiding officer—out of the sixteen standing committee chairmen, seven were freshmen Senators, four had been in the Senate only one year and two had been Senators for only two years. Only two committee chairmen had served more than four years.

As I have previously indicated, the Senate abandoned the system of select committees in 1816 and went instead to a system of standing committees. However, the Senate continued to elect its committee chairmen and members until December 9, 1823. On that day Senator John Eaton of Tennessee proposed that the chairmen of the five most important committees be chosen by ballot and that these five men be given the power to fill up their own committees and to select the members of all remaining committees. However, the Senate rejected Eaton's proposal and adopted instead an amendment to the rules that all committees "shall be appointed by the presiding officer"—who was [almost] always the President *pro tempore*—"of this House, unless otherwise ordered by the Senate. . . ."

The next Vice-President, though, was John Calhoun. Contrary to precedent, Calhoun took the chair on the opening day of the 19th Congress and—as Presiding Officer—appointed the committee chairmen and members with such blatant bias that four months later, on April 14, 1826, the Senate, with hardly a dissenting vote, took the appointment of committee chairmen and members away from the Presiding Officer, be he the Vice-President or the President *pro tempore*, and restored choice by Senate ballot as it had existed from 1789 to 1823.

In 1826 the Senate again slightly changed its procedure. On December 8 of that year, on the motion of Senator Ezekiel Chambers of Maryland, the Senate divided the election of chairmen from the election of members. It was provided that the chairman of each committee would be selected on a separate ballot by majority vote and the other members of the committee would be selected on another ballot by plurality vote.

On December 24, 1828, the rule regarding the appointment of

committees was changed again, this time to provide for the appointment of committee chairmen and members by the President *pro tempore*. It was further provided, if there should be no President *pro tempore*, that appointment should be made by ballot, in accordance with the rule of 1826.

The 1830's were marked by the birth of two dynamic political parties. Early in the decade a cleavage developed in the Senate based on these two parties. While there had been factions and loose coalitions in the Senate prior to this time, this period ushered in the two-party system as we know it today. And, though the cleavage was not completed until the end of Andrew Jackson's administration in 1837, it was unmistakable by 1833, and in that year an unforeseen contingency arose.

Under the rule, as it had stood for the previous five years, the committees would be appointed by Senator Hugh White of Tennessee, elected President *pro tempore* at the previous session. But, the November election had placed his party in the minority in the Senate. Hence, the 1826 rule by which committee chairmen and members were selected by separate ballot was restored, and so remained until 1837.

Between 1833 and 1837, however, a difficulty that frequently arose from the election of members by plurality balloting was that the senator heading the list might be of the party opposed to that of the chairman who had just been elected by majority vote on a separate ballot. To remedy this situation, after all committee chairmen and members had been elected by ballot in compliance with the rules, it was frequently voted that the committee members be "arranged" in accordance with a schedule presented by the mover, the object being to secure succession to the chairmanship of the committee on the basis of party in case of the chairman's absence or withdrawal.

By 1837 frequent and continual balloting was becoming a nuisance and an inconvenience. Thus, in that year, after four chairmen had been elected, Henry Clay moved, and it was agreed to by unanimous consent, that the other appointments be made by the Presiding Officer. This gave the task to Vice-President Richard M. Johnson. At the beginning of the regular session three months later the power to appoint committee chairmen and members was again placed in his hands. It thereafter became customary, by unanimous consent, to suspend the rule requiring the ballot and to authorize the appointment of the committees by the presiding officer. Therefore Vice-President Johnson continued this task until 1841.

In 1841, William Henry Harrison, who had been elected President in 1840, died and John Tyler became President. Therefore, there was no Vice-President from 1841 to 1845 and committee appointments were made by the President *pro tempore*. . . .

It was not until the first ten days of the second session of the 29th Congress, December 7 to 17, 1846, that the seniority system in the U.S. Senate was born. After defeating a motion to entrust the appointment of committees to the Vice-President, the Senate began balloting for chairmen—in accordance with the rule of 1826. After the chairmen of six committees had been elected, there developed a long debate over the method of choosing the other chairmen and all committee members.

The Democratic floor leader then presented motions which arranged by seniority the names of committee members and safeguarded the majority's succession to chairmanships which might become vacant. After several committees had been filled by this method, the Senate proceeded to elect upon one ballot a list of candidates to fill the vacancies on all of the remaining committees. This list gave to each committee thus filled its chairman and the majority of its members from the same party which held a majority in the Senate.

The Senate in 1846 did not "back into" the seniority system for any of the high-sounding reasons advanced by its defenders today for its retention. Instead, the Senate turned to the seniority system over a century and a quarter ago in desperation. The Senate was tired of balloting for weeks to choose chairmen and fill the committees. It distrusted the Vice-President. It wanted to assure that members of the majority party would be in line for succession to the chairmanship in case of the chairman's absence or withdrawal. The seniority system enabled the parties to rapidly organize the Senate and assured succession to the chairmanship on the basis of party loyalty.

From that day to this, the appointment of Senate committees—

in most cases—has been a perfunctory affair. By unanimous consent the rules requiring election of the chairmen on one ballot and the committee members on another ballot have been suspended and the election has taken place by acceptance of a resolution for the adoption of a list of committee assignments which has been drawn up by the Republican and Democratic caucuses. The general rule is that the Senator of the majority party with the longest continuous service on each committee is named chairman.

It will thus be seen that from 1789 to 1846 committee chairmen were selected in a variety of ways. Sometimes they were elected by ballot. At other times they were picked by the presiding officer, be he the Vice-President or the President *pro tempore*. Regardless of whether the chairman was elected or appointed, however, there was always one striking consistency: The committee chairmen were not picked on the basis of seniority. In addition, the committee members themselves, no matter whether they were elected by their fellow members or selected or appointed in some other method, were selected on some basis other than seniority. It is obvious, then, that our forefathers eschewed the seniority system and instead preferred electing or appointing their committee chairmen and committee members on a basis other than that of seniority. . . .

Not only did they reject the seniority system as a method of picking committee chairmen and committee members; they also rejected it as a method of picking their party leaders and presiding officers. No better example of this can be found than Henry Clay.

Clay was elected to the U.S. Senate on January 4, 1810, to fill the vacancy caused by the resignation of Senator Buckner Thruston. He found the Senate, however, to be a moribund and dull place and in the election of 1810 he ran for the U.S. House of Representatives and was elected. In 1811, Henry Clay was elected Speaker of the House of Representatives on his first day as a Representative.

By the standard of seniority the 34-year-old Clay would have gone unnoticed for decades, but because of his towering prestige and limitless ability his colleagues chose him immediately upon election as their leader in the House of Representatives.

One of Clay's biographers later wrote:

So unexpected was this upset of precedent that the new speaker was at first confused with Matthew Clay (his distant relative), the veteran Virginia Representative. But the country was soon informed that the man selected was young Mr. Clay of Kentucky, formerly of the Senate; a new man but capable and accustomed to legislation; a proper man at this crisis to conduct public business with dignity and dispatch. (*Henry Clay* by Bernard Mayo, p. 403).

Clay became Speaker because, though he was short on seniority, he was long on ability. And, far from being a failure—because of his youth and lack of seniority—history records that

Henry Clay . . . became one of the best and most powerful Speakers that the House of Representatives has ever had. When he assumed the office in 1811 the Speaker was little more than a presiding officer. But Clay made the position one of party leadership and by his precedents immeasurably strengthened the office. Six times he was elected Speaker and never was his election seriously contested.

He was the boldest and most decisive, perhaps, of the long line of Speakers of the House of Representatives. (*Henry Clay and the Art of American Politics* by Clement Eaton, pp. 22–23.)

Although Henry Clay was elected as Speaker of the House, all evidence indicates that in the election of Senate leadership, seniority has never been a factor in the selection of Senate leaders. Reviewing just the last half century, it will be noted that there has not been a single majority or minority leader or majority or minority whip who was the ranking member of his party at the time of his election, with the exception of Styles Bridges, who was elected as minority leader in 1952. This is stark and clear evidence that in the selection of party leaders we in the Senate pay no attention to seniority but instead pick our leaders on the basis of ability. Why do we adhere to the wisdom of our forefathers in rejecting the criteria of seniority in picking our party and floor leaders, and yet persist in selecting committee chairmen on the basis of seniority, a method which our forefathers so assiduously avoided?

As I have previously detailed, the birth of the seniority system in 1846 in the Senate was a matter of convenience because of the exigencies of the time. It obviously was not intended by the proponents in 1846 as the be-all and the end-all of congressional organization. One would think that there must be some stronger force binding the supporters of seniority than historical accident.

SENIORITY AND FUTURE
POWER IN CONGRESS

NORMAN J. ORNSTEIN and DAVID W. ROHDE

Over the past several years, a surprisingly large and varied group of people—journalists, congressmen, lobbyists, and citizens—have vigorously and vocally opposed the seniority system of selecting committee chairmen in the House of Representatives and the Senate. Perhaps no other nonpolicy issue has ever generated as much public discussion and concern, most of it directed toward overturning not a formal rule but an informal, party-based custom created in 1910 by an earlier generation of congressional reformers.[1] Because of the public focus, and the concerted lobbying efforts of Common Cause and other groups, some alterations in the rigidity of the system were accomplished in 1971 and again in January, 1973, in both the House and the Senate. The automatic aspect of the custom was abolished, and each chairman is now voted upon by the caucus of the majority party, the Democrats. The revisions, while significant, remain technical—every chairman selected in January in both houses was the senior member of his committee. So, the seniority system continues basically unchanged.

Most of the evidence and rhetoric generated in the heated seniority debate have centered on the inherently "evil" aspects of the system; opponents have argued that it ranks senility ahead

Norman J. Ornstein is Assistant Professor of Political Science at The Catholic University of America; David W. Rohde is Associate Professor of Political Science at Michigan State University.

of competence. There has, however, always been an underlying—but rarely publically mentioned—ideological division. The opponents of seniority have been mainly liberals, who have been upset not only by the illogic of the system but also by the fact that a disproportionate number of committee chairmen are Southern conservatives who have used their powers to continually thwart liberal policy objectives. Former Senator Paul Douglas (D-Ill.) noted pessimistically in 1971:

> Joe Clark used to say that we Northern liberals would outlast the Southerners and would ultimately take over even under the seniority rule. . . . But the elections of 1966, 1968, and 1970 have in fact reduced the relative strength of the Northern Democrats.   . . The Southerners, therefore, still hold the citadels of power. They still control the Committee on Committees, and up to now no one has been elected majority leader or secretary without their approval. The committees are almost as much under their control as formerly. Indeed, in 1967–68, they seemed to be slightly more so; no Northerner was chairman of any committee.[2]

Douglas's statements may be true; whether they can be applied indefinitely to the future is another question entirely.

Largely because of the one-party nature of most Southern congressional districts after World War II and the competitiveness of the Northern ones, the congressmen and senators with the greatest longevity today are overwhelmingly Southern and mainly conservative. But times have changed since the late 1940's; the South has become increasingly competitive, while in many areas of the North and West, especially in the cities, party control has solidified.[3] The South's overall role in the Democratic congressional parties in both the House and the Senate has dramatically declined: 49 per cent of the Democrats in the 1947 Senate were Southerners, but in 1973 only 26 per cent were. The figures for the House are just as striking: from 55 per cent in 1947 to 31 per cent twenty-six years later. Figure 1 clearly illustrates the continuous decline of the proportion of Southerners in the Democratic Party in Congress.[4]

Because of the time lag inherent in the seniority system, these changes in the composition of congressional ranks are not yet wholly reflected in committee chairmanships. But in assessing

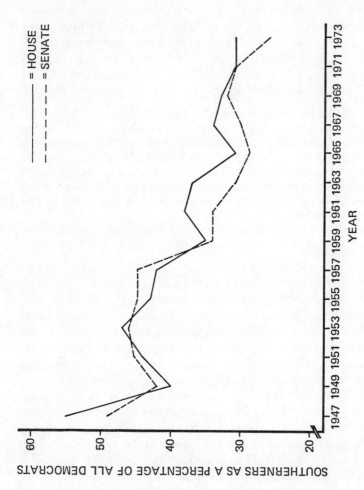

Figure 1. Southern Shares of Democratic Delegations in the House and Senate, 1947–1973

the implications of abolishing the seniority system, it is important to have a rough map of the future terrain of congressional power.

Table 1 shows a breakdown of House and Senate Democrats by age and geographical region and provides clues to where congressional power will lie in the years to come.[5] The 65-and-over group includes the current chairmen of most of the major committees. Assuming that the seniority system continues, the next tier, those 55 to 65, will inherit the reins of congressional power when the older group departs.

Of course, region does not reflect ideology perfectly. There are in the House Southern liberals like Bob Eckhardt (D-Tex.) and Northern conservatives like James J. Delaney (D-N.Y.). This is especially true for the House, where many senior Northerners are machine Democrats who are often quite compatible ideologically with their Southern colleagues. Nevertheless, the broad

TABLE 1

AGE AND REGIONAL DISTRIBUTION
HOUSE AND SENATE DEMOCRATS, 93d CONGRESS*

	under 45	45–54	55–64	65 and over
Senate				
South	23%	23%	15%	55%
	(3)	(3)	(3)	(6)
Border	8%	15%	0	18%
	(1)	(2)	0	(2)
Other	69%	62%	85%	27%
	(9)	(8)	(17)	(3)
Total				
Number	13	13	20	11
House				
South	34%	23%	35%	34%
	(16)	(21)	(26)	(10)
Border	15%	6%	15%	14%
	(7)	(5)	(11)	(4)
Other	51%	71%	50%	52%
	(24)	(64)	(37)	(15)
Total				
Number	47	90	74	29

* Percentages are ratios of the number of Democrats for each region (in parentheses) to the total number for each house, by age group.

pattern of regional ideology exists, with important implications for the distribution of congressional power in the years ahead.

While Southern and border-state legislators have dominated committee chairmanships in the postwar years, their declining membership, especially at the upper levels of seniority, means that their share of power, *ceteris paribus*, will continue to decline as well. Let us assume, to project ahead six and ten years, an age limit of 70 for chairmen[6] and continuity in service among the other senior members who would be below that age at these time periods. Table 2 shows past, present, and future distributions of committee chairmanships under these assumptions. The overall (and projected) decline in Southern hegemony is strikingly evident. In the House, committee chairmen from Southern states went from 55 per cent in 1963 to 40 per cent in 1973, and would go to 35 per cent by 1979, and to 20 per cent by 1983. In the Senate, the proportions of Southern standing committee chairmen declined from 63 per cent to 47 per cent between 1963 and 1973, are projected to plummet to 12 per cent in 1979, and rebound somewhat to 24 per cent by 1983.

The numbers alone do not reflect the qualitative change in the making. Consider Tables 3 and 4 which list present committee chairmen and those members who would be chairmen in six and ten years under our assumptions, with their conservative coalition support ratios for the 92d Congress.[7]

Many of the changes are complete ideological reversals: John Sparkman, whose 1972 re-election was a top priority for the banking lobby, would be replaced as chairman of the Senate Banking Committee by William Proxmire, an outspoken ally of the consumer. Arch-conservative Mississippi Senator James O. Eastland would relinquish his Judiciary Committee chair to Ted Kennedy. Even the less dramatic changes would be largely in a liberal direction—on Senate Armed Services, for instance, Thomas McIntyre, who sometimes votes to trim defense spending, would replace current chairman John Stennis (D-Miss.), who almost never does.

A look at the conservative coalition support ratios for all the committee chairmen more clearly indicates the extent of projected change. For the Senate, the projected ten-year changes show eleven of sixteen chairmanships moving in a more liberal direction, with

TABLE 2
COMMITTEE CHAIRMANSHIPS*

	1953	1963	1973	1979**	1983**
House					
South	53%	55%	40%	35%	20%
	(10)	(11)	(8)	(7)	(4)
Border	11%	5%	20%	15%	15%
	(2)	(1)	(4)	(3)	(3)
Other	37%	40%	40%	50%	65%
	(7)	(8)	(8)	(10)	(13)
Total Number	19	20	20	20	20
Senate					
South	46.5%	63.5%	47%	12%	23.5%
	(7)	(10)	(8)	(2)	(4)
Border	7%	0	12%	6%	12%
	(1)	0	(2)	(1)	(2)
Other	46.5%	37.5%	41%	82%	64.5%
	(7)	(6)	(7)	(14)	(11)
Total Number	15	16	17	17	17

* Percentages are ratios of the number of committee chairmanships for each region (in parentheses) to the total number for that year in each house.
** Projected

none following the reverse pattern, while for the House, eleven of twenty chairmanships become more liberal, with only five becoming more conservative. Figure 2 gives the average conservative coalition support ratios for all standing committee chairmen, for the years indicated, in the House and the Senate.[8] The figure shows a steady decline of conservative as well as Southern power in both bodies, though more markedly for the Senate.

Subcommittee Power

It is possible that these changes might not be particularly meaningful in showing distributions of power, especially in light of the reforms by the House in the 92d and 93d Congresses that have limited the powers of committee chairmen and strengthened those of subcommittee chairmen.[9] Perhaps, in acquiescing to re-

TABLE 3

Senate Committee Chairmen Projected to 96th and 98th Congresses with Conservative Coalition Support Ratios

COMMITTEE	93rd (1973) Chairman	96th (1979) Chairman	98th (1983) Chairman
Aeronautical and Space Sciences	Moss (Utah) (19)*	Moss (Utah) (19)	Abourezk (S.D.) (9)
Agriculture and Forestry	Talmadge (Ga.) (92)	Talmadge (Ga.) (92)	Talmadge (Ga.) (92)
Appropriations	McClellan (Ark.) (86)	Byrd (W.Va.) (58)	Byrd (W.Va.) (58)
Armed Services	Stennis (Miss.) (100)	Jackson (Wash.) (48)	McIntyre (N.H.) (43)
Banking and Currency	Sparkman (Ala.) (92)	Proxmire (Wis.) (15)	Proxmire (Wis.) (15)
Commerce	Magnuson (Wash.) (34)	Hartke (Ind.) (11)	Hartke (Ind.) (11)
District of Columbia	Eagleton (Mo.) (16)	Eagleton (Mo.) (16)	Eagleton (Mo.) (16)
Finance	Long (La.) (83)	Long (La.) (83)	Long (La.) (83)
Foreign Relations	Fulbright (Ark.) (25)	Church (Idaho) (15)	Church (Idaho) (15)
Government Operations	Ervin (N.C.) (91)	Ribicoff (Conn.) (10)	Chiles (Fla.) (57)
Interior and Insular Affairs	Jackson (Wash.) (48)	Metcalf (Mont.) (15)	Johnston (La.)**
Judiciary	Eastland (Miss.) (98)	Hart (Mich.) (4)	Kennedy (Mass.) (9)
Labor and Public Welfare	Williams (N.J.) (9)	Williams (N.J.) (9)	McGee (Wyo.) (49)
Post Office and Civil Service	McGee (Wyo.) (49)	McGee (Wyo.) (49)	McGee (Wyo.) (49)
Public Works	Randolph (W.Va.) (47)	Muskie (Maine) (6)	Muskie (Maine) (6)
Rules and Administration	Cannon (Nev.) (69)	Cannon (Nev.) (69)	Pell (R.I.) (13)
Veterans' Affairs	Hartke (Ind.) (11)	Cranston (Calif.) (8)	Cranston (Calif.) (8)

* Conservative coalition support ratio. (See footnote 7 for explanation)
** Senator Johnston was not a member of the 92d Congress, therefore no score is available.

TABLE 4

House Committee Chairmen Projected to 96th and 98th Congresses with Conservative Coalition Support Ratios

COMMITTEE	93rd (1973) Chairman	96th (1979) Chairman	98th (1983) Chairman
Agriculture	Poage (Tex.) (85) *	Foley (Wash.) (23)	Foley (Wash.) (23)
Appropriations	Mahon (Tex.) (90)	Whitten (Miss.) (89)	Shipley (Ill.) (52)
Armed Services	Hebert (La.) (94)	Bennett (Fla.) (69)	Stratton (N.Y.) (53)
Banking and Currency	Patman (Tex.) (63)	Reuss (Wis.) (5)	Ashley (Ohio) (18)
District of Columbia	Diggs (Mich.) (4)	Diggs (Mich.) (4)	Diggs (Mich.) (4)
Education and Labor	Perkins (Ky.) (38)	Perkins (Ky.) (38)	Thompson (N.J.) (7)
Foreign Affairs	Morgan (Pa.) (41)	Zablocki (Wis.) (51)	Fountain (N.C.) (96)
Government Operations	Holifield (Calif.) (37)	Brooks (Tex.) (59)	Moss (Calif.) (7)
House Administration	Hays (Ohio) (55)	Hays (Ohio) (55)	Nedzi (Mich.) (29)
Interior and Insular Affairs	Haley (Fla.) (94)	Taylor (N.C.) (86)	Udall (Ariz.) (6)
Internal Security	Ichord (Mo.) (87)	Ichord (Mo.) (87)	Ichord (Mo.) (87)
Interstate and Foreign Commerce	Staggers (W.Va.) (51)	Macdonald (Mass.) (25)	Macdonald (Mass.) (25)
Judiciary	Rodino (N.J.) (5)	Rodino (N.J.) (5)	Brooks (Tex.) (59)
Merchant Marine and Fisheries	Sullivan (Mo.) (34)	Clark (Pa.) (58)	Clark (Pa.) (58)
Post Office and Civil Service	Dulski (N.Y.) (41)	Dulski (N.Y.) (41)	Dulski (N.Y.) (41)
Public Works	Blatnik (Minn.) (19)	Blatnik (Minn.) (19)	Wright (Tex.) (62)
Rules	Madden (Ind.) (9)	Bolling (Mo.) (22)	Bolling (Mo.) (22)
Science and Astronautics	Teague (Tex.) (85)	Teague (Tex.) (85)	Hechler (W.Va.) (8)
Veterans' Affairs	Dorn (S.C.) (82)	Dorn (S.C.) (82)	Dorn (S.C.) (82)
Ways and Means	Mills (Ark.) (65)	Mills (Ark.) (65)	Ullman (Ore.) (37)

* Conservative Coalition Support Ratio.

Figure 2. Mean Conservative Coalition Support Ratio for House and Senate Committee Chairmen, Selected Years 1959 – 1973 and Projected

forms in seniority and committee chairmanship power, Southerners cleverly recognized that soon committee chairmen will largely be liberals, and this would curtail their influence more, over the long run. It makes sense, then, to extend our analysis to the subcommittee level. If power has been diffused to subcommittee chairmen, who holds and will hold these positions? As Table 5 demonstrates, the regional patterns we have described hold even more strikingly for subcommittee chairmen, in both the House and the Senate. The *non*-Southern proportion of subcommittee chairmen goes from 42 per cent in 1963 to 72 per cent in 1973 for the House, and from 59 per cent to 75 per cent for the Senate. Because subcommittee chairs encompass a greater proportion of members in the two legislative bodies, they are more sensitive to changes in the makeup of the membership, and so already reflect the regional and ideological evolution more closely than committee chairmanships.

TABLE 5

REGIONAL DISTRIBUTIONS OF SUBCOMMITTEE CHAIRMANSHIPS,
HOUSE AND SENATE, 1955–1973*

	1955	1963	1973
House			
South	58%	58%	29%
	(48)	(65)	(36)
Border	12%	14%	10%
	(10)	(16)	(12)
Other	30%	28%	62%
	(25)	(32)	(77)
Total			
Number	83	113	125
Senate			
South	42%	41%	25%
	(33)	(37)	(32)
Border	17.5%	12%	6%
	(14)	(11)	(8)
Other	40.5%	47%	69%
	(32)	(42)	(88)
Total			
Number	79	90	128

* Percentages are ratios of the number of subcommittee chairmanships for each region (in parentheses) to the total number for that year in each house.

Other Patterns of Change

The changes which are, and will be, occurring are not simply because senior conservative Southern Democrats are being replaced by liberal Northerners. Contrasts occur within the regional groupings as well. The newer Southern members of Congress, as a group, are more liberal than their senior colleagues. Just as interestingly, the younger Northern Democrats are a considerably more liberal group than *their* senior counterparts. Overall, of course, Southern Democrats remain much more conservative than Northern Democrats, but the mean for the entire congressional party is shifting in a more liberal direction. As Table 6 shows, the most senior group of House and Senate Democrats (19 years or more in seniority) are relatively conservative legislators (with conservative coalition support ratios of 63.1 and 60.8, respectively) while the youngest groups of members (1 to 6 years seniority) average only 35.4 and 43.1. These contrasts hold for *both* North and South.

TABLE 6

MEAN CONSERVATIVE COALITION SUPPORT RATIOS FOR
DEMOCRATS IN 92d CONGRESS BY SENIORITY AND REGION

	SENATE			HOUSE		
Years	Southern Democrats	Northern Democrats	All Democrats	Southern Democrats	Northern Democrats	All Democrats
19+	81.4% (7)*	35.0% (6)	60.0% (13)	83.8% (26)	40.0% (30)	60.4% (56)
13–18	90.3% (3)	28.9% (13)	40.4% (16)	74.5% (8)	35.2% (40)	41.7% (48)
7–12	0 (0)	15.5% (12)	15.5% (12)	71.9% (21)	20.4% (51)	35.4% (72)
1–6	75.6% (7)	10.6% (7)	43.1% (14)	75.0% (23)	18.8% (55)	35.4% (78)
Total	80.6 (17)	22.3 (38)	40.3 (55)	77.1 (78)	26.6 (176)	42.1 (254)

* Number of members in parentheses

Several patterns appear to be emerging at once. The South has shifted to a two-party Congressional arena, and that has brought about an increase in the number of Republican congressmen from that region at the expense of the Democrats. Moreover, the heavy overrepresentation of Southern conservative Democrats at the highest levels of seniority has been declining steadily in recent years, as a result of a number of factors: age; the growth in importance of primaries and the defeat of a number of incumbents in that electoral arena; and retirements encouraged by an increasingly heavy congressional workload and higher pensions.

The growing urbanization and industrialization in the South, and the reduction in importance of the racial issue have in turn encouraged the recruitment of less conservative candidates for Congress, who no longer have to run with the sole objective of "out-segging" their opponents. One need only contrast Florida's Senator Lawton Chiles with his predecessor Spessard Holland, or Louisiana's Bennett Johnston with Allen Ellender, to see this change.

The continuing decline in urban political machines in the North and the increasing "clout" of minority voting power have given liberals better electoral chances in the North; issues such as the Kennedy and King assassinations and the Vietnam war may have spurred more liberals to run for Congress. Certainly, Congress did not, through the 1950's, have legislators like Ron Dellums, Father Robert Drinan, or Bella Abzug populating its committee rooms.

In a fascinating way, electoral and demographic patterns in the society have interacted with the internal structural changes in Congress to provide a congressional power structure which will soon be virtually unrecognizable in contrast to the one described by journalists and political scientists in the 1950's and 1960's.

Liberals and the Seniority System

In the Senate, it is clear, the balance of power will soon shift—and shift dramatically—to the North. Southerners make up six of the seven most senior Senate Democrats—but only two of the next thirty. In five years, the leading Senate opponents of the "undemocratic" seniority system will probably be the Southerners. In the House, however, the picture is somewhat different. It will probably take a bit longer for power at the very top to shift, either regionally or ideologically, especially given the extraordinary survival patterns shown by many committee chairmen.

These regional and ideological changes in congressional power have not escaped House liberals, despite the intensity of their rhetoric about the evils of the seniority system. In 1971, as we have indicated, liberals included in their reform package provisions to expand the number of House Democrats chairing subcommittees. Nearly half the House Democrats now have their own subcommittees, and the passage of time has already shifted subcommittee power into the hands of Northern liberals.[10] In 1973 House liberals, while simultaneously pushing for reform of the seniority system for selecting committee chairmen, also manuevered through a *strengthened* seniority system for selecting subcommittee chairmen. To further safeguard the power of these subcommittee chairmen, House Democrats also approved a "Subcommittee Bill of Rights." All these moves are designed to give liberals a greater share of congressional power as they wait for attrition in the ranks of Southern conservatives to give them the committee chairmanships they have long coveted.

Like so many battles over seemingly great principles, the fight over the seniority system has been as much rooted in political self-interest as genuine moral outrage. While its operation is admittedly arbitrary and often inequitable, the seniority system would probably not have emerged as a standard liberal issue if congressional liberals had been getting a fair share of choice committee chairmanships. As Southern congressional hegemony steadily wanes, it is ironically the "evil" seniority system that will give Northern liberals more power in Congress than any other envisioned system of selecting committee chairmen.

Conclusion

Several words of caution are in order at this point. We should not forget Lord Acton's principle that "power tends to corrupt"; it is entirely conceivable that many liberals will not be quite so liberal, activist, or adventuresome when they hold the reins of power. All of these great demographic changes may prove illusory. All of our statistics cannot help us predict the likelihood of that occurrence. Even the fact that voting scores seem to remain quite stable throughout congressional careers (that is, members' voting seldom becomes more conservative as they get older or more senior), is not convincing proof to the contrary, for floor voting is a basically different phenomenon. However, the fact that a large number of liberal congressmen actively fought against committee reform in the 93rd Congress is disturbing confirming evidence.

Nevertheless, intuitively, and armed with the examples of numerous current reform-oriented and activist liberal subcommittee chairmen, such as Don Fraser, Brock Adams, and Jerome Waldie in the House, and William Proxmire, Walter Mondale, and Birch Bayh in the Senate, we do not think that these projected changes are meaningless, or even less significant than the figures indicate they will be. Rather, we are convinced that Congress is evolving into two legislative institutions that will be markedly different from the House and Senate of today, let alone the 1960's.

Whether this means more "power" in Congress vis-à-vis the executive branch remains to be seen. The ever increasing congressional workload makes it more and more difficult for legislators to cope effectively with their decision-making burden, a problem that increased staff assistance can only partially alleviate. The abundance of personnel and resources in the executive branch may give them an insurmountable edge in setting the agenda and working out the details of most intricate policy decisions.

The liberal Congress's reaction to a liberal Democratic President cannot be confidently predicted either. They might be obedient and quiescent, as was the 89th Congress under Lyndon Johnson, or they might be active overseers of the executive branch and independent formulators of policy. Most likely they would be more vigorous watchdogs than they are now, but no more willing to draw up detailed congressional alternatives for major social policy initiatives. Future liberal congressional power over policy is likely to be more greatly exercised in foreign and defense policy questions, a legacy of Vietnam. Though Presidents will doubtless remain pre-eminent in foreign affairs, their judgments will in future be more suspect and open to question by a liberal activist Congress.

NOTES

1. For a history of the seniority system in the House of Representatives see Nelson W. Polsby, Miriam Gallagher, and Barry Spencer Rundquist, "The Growth of the Seniority System in the U.S. House of Representatives," *American Political Science Review* 63 (September, 1969), 787–807.

2. Paul H. Douglas, *In the Fullness of Time* (N.Y.: Harcourt, Brace, Jovanovich, 1971), p. 212.

3. This trend was noted some time ago by Raymond E. Wolfinger and Joan Heifetz in "Safe Seats, Seniority, and Power in Congress," *American Political Science Review* 59 (June, 1965), 337–49. We should also note that they anticipated a number of the consequences which we discuss below.

4. We define the South as the eleven states of the Confederacy. Border states are Kentucky, Maryland, Missouri, Oklahoma, and West Virginia.

5. We limit our discussion here and in the remainder of the article to Democrats because they have been the majority party in both houses for all but a few years in the postwar period, and are likely to remain so for the foreseeable future.

6. While a formal age limit on chairmen is unlikely, this is not an unreasonable assumption in practice. At the beginning of the 93d Congress, only 6 of 20 chairmen in the House were 70 or over, while the corresponding number in the Senate was 5 of 17. (Here and throughout the remainder of the article, we omit Standards of Official Conduct when counting House committees.)

7. The conservative coalition support ratio is a measure of how conservative or liberal a member is in his floor voting, and is derived from the conservative coalition support and opposition scores published by Congressional Quarterly, Inc. Congressional Quarterly defines a conservative coalition vote as one on which a majority of Republicans and a majority of Southern Democrats vote together in opposition to a majority of Northern Democrats. They then calculate the percentage of votes on which each member voted with or against each group. If, however, a member fails to vote, both support and opposition scores are lowered. Since the amount of nonvoting varies across members, the scores can be misleading. Therefore, to eliminate this problem we calculated for each member a conservative coalition support ratio, which is simply the support score divided by the sum of the support score and the opposition score.

8. The ratios for 1959, 1963, and 1969 are derived from votes taken in the 86th, 88th, and 91st Congresses respectively. The ratios for 1973, 1979, and 1983 are derived from votes taken in the 92d Congress. The ratios were

calculated from conservative coalition support and opposition scores taken from the appropriate volumes of *Congressional Quarterly Almanac*.

9. For a discussion of these reforms see Norman J. Ornstein, "Causes and Consequences of Congressional Change: Subcommittee Reforms in the House of Representatives, 1970–73," published in this volume, and David W. Rohde, "Committee Reform in the House of Representatives and the Subcommittee Bill of Rights," *The Annals* (January, 1974).

10. *Ibid.*

CAUSES AND CONSEQUENCES OF CONGRESSIONAL CHANGE: SUBCOMMITTEE REFORMS IN THE HOUSE OF REPRESENTATIVES, 1970-73

NORMAN J. ORNSTEIN

Since the 1960's, students of Congress have come to look more and more at the nature and origins of institutional change.[1] Such a focus is useful, in particular, for two reasons: It illuminates the impact of long-range patterns, electorally or institutionally based, on more immediate outcomes (and vice versa); and it characterizes the interaction between legislative actions and legislative structures that is at the crux of the congressional process.

This paper traces the causes, nature, and consequences, individually and institutionally, of a series of subcommittee reforms enacted by the Democratic Caucus in the U.S. House of Representatives in January of 1971 and January of 1973 at the beginnings of the 92d and 93d Congresses. We will look initially at the extent to which the successful implementation of these reforms was due to broad institutional and electoral patterns and to the strategic input and activity of individual legislative actors—that is, why and how structural changes in Congress are generated. Second, the impact of these seemingly minor reforms on subsequent legislative actions will be examined; and third, we will speculate

Presented in an earlier version at the 1973 Annual Meeting of the American Political Science Association, September 4-8, New Orleans, Louisiana.

about possible future patterns of behavior and change in the House, in the context of the preceding two sections.

Institutional Change in the House

Where does reform come from? In a complex, ongoing institution formal structural change is not spontaneously generated, and the House of Representatives is no exception. Congressmen have great demands on their time, and there are seemingly few rewards for spending scarce resources like time and staff on internal reform. Such effort achieves little outside publicity, garners far fewer constituent votes than casework, and is not likely to enhance one's prestige within the institutional power structure.

For legislators to devote time and effort to reform, they must see a possible payoff. Thus structural reform in Congress is generally a product of those who feel shortchanged of power. The feeling of deprivation can cross ideological and party lines; for instance, House Republicans as a group have for the past several years consistently argued for more minority committee staffing. Though this paper deals largely with liberal-initiated proposals and strategies, liberals are not invariably against the status quo and for reform; indeed, as we shall see, several prominent liberals, whose positions would be adversely affected by the proposed subcommittee changes in 1971, vehemently opposed them. And the liberals who fought the evils of the seniority system for committee chairmen through the 1960's, in turn attempted (successfully) in 1973 to implement stricter seniority guidelines for the selection of subcommittee chairmen. The reason major reform efforts of the 1960's and 1970's have emanated from the liberal Democrats is simply that they were most in need of payoffs. There are other, related reasons as well for liberal initiatives: their ready access to institutional machinery for considering and analyzing proposals for change, and for coordinating the massive efforts necessary to make them part of the decision agenda; and, just as importantly, the inclination to view the House and its structures analytically in terms of power and outcome—an inclination not shared by the vast majority of House members. We will discuss these reasons in detail shortly. It should be emphasized, though, that the necessity for developing this institutional machinery (the Democratic Study Group) and this way of thinking exists when one is losing, not winning, one's legislative battles. The beginnings in 1973 of a Southern counterpart to the Democratic Study Group underscore this point.[2]

Reform in the 1970's: From Frustration to Fulfillment

Most reforms proposed in the House since 1946 have been closely and bitterly fought, and sometimes reversed soon after enactment.[3] Reform efforts of the late 1950's and early 1960's centered on neutralizing some of the initiative-blocking strongholds of the House; they were proposed by liberals trying to push through new legislation, who were frustrated in their efforts by the fabled "conservative coalition" of Republicans and Southern Democrats. The main focus was Judge Smith's Rules Committee, and reformers tried both to bypass it (via the 21-day rule), and to pack it.[4] Success at the latter shifted liberal attention to more direct substantive concerns, especially legislative committee leadership (the seniority system). Push for institutional reform remained largely dormant in the mid-1960's, with the ascendance of Lyndon Johnson to the Presidency and the 1964 Democratic landslide. It was brought to the fore again about 1967 as the Vietnam war dragged on and Johnson's success in promoting domestic programs waned. The period of 1967–70 was one of maximum frustration, both substantive and procedural, for Democratic liberals; much was tried and little was accomplished. Principal reasons for this were their drop in numbers from the peak years 1965–66 and the intra-party split created by the war.

Beginning in late 1970, a series of reforms initiated by liberals were enacted by the Democratic Caucus or by the whole House. Unlike the previous efforts, these reforms were not preceded by deep divisions, and in fact were passed in many instances without major opposition. Why did reform efforts, which met with earlier failure, succeed in the post-1970 period?

THE ROLE OF THE DEMOCRATIC STUDY GROUP

From 1959 on, reform efforts were centralized and channeled through the newly formed Democratic Study Group,[5] with early reform leaders including Lee Metcalf (Mont.), Frank Thompson, Jr. (N.J.), John Blatnik (Minn.), and James G. O'Hara (Mich.). The DSG was formed out of a liberal frustration and dissatisfaction with the information and initiatives provided by the formal party structure in the House. It was the first "informal" group to employ separate staff personnel, it is the largest and most institutionalized group of its type, and it is still the principal vehicle for reform ideas and strategies.

The DSG is highly regarded on Capitol Hill for its excellent research and information capability. The institutionalization of the Democratic Study Group and its staff, and especially the accession in 1968 of Richard P. Conlon as staff director, have given the liberals the necessary machinery to initiate and deal with structural reform while still actively pursuing substantive issues.

The first major reason for positive movement in the direction of reform after 1968 was a change in liberal strategy initiated through the executive leadership of the DSG. Early reform efforts, centering as they did on the Rules Committee, meant that success had to be ratified by the entire House, Democrats and Republicans alike. When attention shifted to the substantive committee leadership and the seniority system, the relevant group became the Democrats alone, as the majority party selects all committee and subcommittee chairmen. The only available forum was the organizational caucus at the beginning of each new Congress, when committee memberships, chairmanships, and party leaders are selected. This forum proved singularly unsuccessful. As one liberal noted in an interview with the author,

> The organizational caucus was really limited to one issue—after that, Members were too exhausted or impatient to deal with anything else. Our attention spans aren't very great.

The key change in strategy was a push for regular monthly caucuses, an idea originated by James O'Hara and Donald Fraser

(Minn.), DSG chairmen in the 90th and 91st Congresses, and adopted by the Democrats in 1969. On the surface, the idea appears to have been an abject failure—the vast majority of the caucuses called under the new rule failed to produce the necessary 50 per cent attendance and so were never held. In the first two and a half years of this practice (through June 1971), twenty-seven nonorganizational caucuses were held; of these, nineteen were adjourned for lack of a quorum. But the other eight caucuses did meet and the most common topic on the agenda was House reform.[6] Most importantly, as *Congressional Quarterly* recently pointed out, these meetings "established the caucus as an available tool for liberal Democrats."[7]

At the same time, Fraser and O'Hara moved the reformers away from an "all-or-nothing" confrontation mentality. Fraser comments,

> Our first major step was to break the link of funneling reform through the organizational meeting of the caucus. Re-establishing the precedent of monthly caucuses was the beginning of the incremental approach to reform—the first step. The second step was to have the *caucus* appoint a committee to deal with reform issues. This also wasn't too threatening to anybody.[8]

On March 18, 1970, the Caucus was convened with 137 members (56 per cent) present, and a resolution calling for creation of a seniority-study committee, initiated by the DSG, was passed.

The idea for a *caucus-selected* committee probably came from Dick Conlon, the DSG staff director, as an "inoffensive way to maneuver for change in the seniority system."[9] The major thrust of the reformers was the selection of committee chairmen; subcommittee reform was at most a secondary issue at this stage. At any rate, the DSG executive leadership—Fraser, O'Hara, John Brademas (Ind.), and James Corman (Calif.)—immediately adopted the idea, and sent a notice ("a very innocuous one"[10]) to the caucus chairman to put the topic on the March agenda.

This idea had two immediate effects. First, it changed the agenda from the seniority system itself to whether or not to form a study committee (which had a much greater chance of passage among 90th Congress Democrats). Secondly, it diffused the ideological conflict by having the eventual reform proposal come from the caucus committee, not the DSG ultra-liberals.

THE HANSEN COMMITTEE

The Committee on Organization, Study, and Review was named one week later, on March 26, 1970, by Daniel Rostenkowski of Chicago, chairman of the Democratic Caucus. The eleven-member committee was to be chaired by Julia Butler Hansen, a five-term Appropriations subcommittee chairman from Washington State. The makeup of this Hansen Committee, as it is usually called, was a key element in the eventual success of its recommendations; in a virtually unprecedented fashion, the committee membership has been universally praised as being "representative".[11] Controversy occurred soon after its formation, but it was controversy over the committee reporting date, not over the committee makeup.[12]

While Rostenkowski named the committee, he clearly consulted with a large number of party leaders, including Majority Leader Hale Boggs, Ways and Means Committee chairman Wilbur Mills, Southern Democratic leader Joe Waggoner, and others. Table 1, below, lists the names of the Hansen Committee members, along with their seniority, committees, and 1970 Americans for Democratic Action (ADA) Scores.

As the table makes clear, the group is extraordinarily well-balanced regionally, ideologically, and in seniority. The ADA ratings define three rough groupings, which jibe with interview comments on the committee's internal interactions. The Southern conservatives, the major factor in party policymaking in the past, were represented on the Hansen Committee by Landrum, Teague, and Jones. The moderates included Hays, Annunzio, Smith, and Hansen, with Hays having close ties to the Southerners. The liberals were Burton, O'Hara, Thompson, and Chisholm.

The Hansen Committee first met on May 12, 1970, a mainly organizational meeting, and set up three subcommittees, first on the selection of standing committee chairmen, second on the organization of the Democratic Committee on Committees, and finally on other seniority matters. The subcommittees themselves were not subsequently important *per se*, but the topics they considered

TABLE 1
CHARACTERISTICS OF HANSEN COMMITTEE MEMBERSHIP

Members	State	Years of Service (as of March 1970)	Standing Committees	ADA Scores* 1970
Phil Landrum	Georgia	17	Ways and Means	8
Olin Teague	Texas	24	Science and Astronautics; Veterans' Affairs	8
Ed Jones	Tennessee	1	Agriculture; House Administration	24
Wayne Hays	Ohio	21	House Administration; Foreign Affairs	32
Neal Smith	Iowa	11	Appropriations	48
Frank Annunzio	Illinois	5	Banking and Currency; House Administration	60
Julia B. Hansen	Washington	10	Appropriations	68
Shirley Chisholm	New York	1	Veterans' Affairs	80
James G. O'Hara	Michigan	11	Education and Labor; Interior	92
Frank Thompson	New Jersey	15	Education and Labor; House Administration	92
Phil Burton	California	5	Education and Labor; Interior	96

* Based on an evaluation of selected roll call votes on a scale from 0 (most conservative) to 100 (most liberal).

indicate the impetus behind the formation of the Committee. In other words, their primary focus was the mode of selection of committee chairmen, the seniority system. Other matters, especially subcommittee reform, were secondary.

Over the next several months, the committee members' major activity was to consider suggestions and recommendations of Democratic members of the House, solicited by a "Dear Colleague" letter from Julia Hansen. The replies varied greatly in length and subject matter, and undoubtedly served to broaden the scope of the committee.

The second formal meeting of the committee was on November 24, 1970, six months after the first meeting, with only some informal meetings and discussions among members held in the interim period. It was at this meeting that reforms relating to subcommittees were first formally raised, by Frank Thompson, Jr., (N.J.). Thompson suggested limiting subcommittee chairmanships to one per member. Discussion ensued, but apparently, according to interview reports of the meeting, little vocal opposition was raised. One major reason for this is that only one member of the Hansen Committee, Teague (Tex.) chaired two subcommittees and thus would be directly affected. (Moreover, because Teague also chaired a full committee, the impact on him would be limited.) Another important reason is that the basis of argument was "give the younger members a chance; spread the action." The younger members, as liberals on the Committee pointed out, included Dawson Mathis and Walter Flowers, conservative young Southerners. Such concrete examples of the balanced ideological impact of this reform apparently satisfied Landrum, Jones, Teague, and Hays, the most conservative members of the Hansen Committee. Of the four liberals on the committee, Burton and Thompson were the major proponents of this reform, with Burton particularly active. O'Hara was much more concerned with the selection process for committee chairmen; Shirley Chisholm's participation in any of the Committee's deliberations was virtually nil.

There is little question that the liberals and the DSG were well aware of the quantitative nature of potential change inherent in the subcommittee reform—that, while its greatest impact might be delayed, on balance, it would advance more liberals to chairmanships than conservatives. Moreover, the positive effect would multiply in the years to come, for the liberals dominate the lower-middle seniority levels. It is just as apparent, from interviews with several Southern Democrats, that they were far less analytic or broadly power-oriented in coping with reform proposals; for them, one or two or three concrete counterexamples sufficed. Here again is an example of the presence of institutional machinery—the DSG and staff, which had the inclination and resources to analyze the power-related impact of reform proposals. The nonliberals lacked both the machinery and the inclination, and, in common with most legislators, tend to view things in a more personalized light. Said one member:

Around here, we respond to change proposals with, "What's in it for me?" It's only natural—we're politicians, and ego-oriented. With the subcommittee reform, the potential "positive" answers to that question far outnumbered the "negatives" and even where the answer was indifference, the impact appeared to be balanced. After all, we were helping Dawson Mathis as well as Ben Rosenthal, and we were hurting John Moss as well as Teague. Making that clear was enough for most members.

Thus the subcommittee chairmanship reform proposal occurred in an atmosphere where primary attention was given to committee chairmen, was proposed by liberals expecting to gain through it, and accepted by other members because it seemed to spread the action to the younger members, *not* give more power to the liberals.

This is not a definitive interpretation. It has also been suggested that this reform was part of a compromise involving seniority reform—that the conservatives, aware of the implications, were willing to accept the subcommittee change in order to limit change in the mode of selection of committee chairmen. There is some evidence in support of this interpretation. First, some liberals had initial misgivings about spreading subcommittee chairmanships, and not just those directly hurt by it. As one perceptive reform-oriented liberal commented,

> I originally had reservations about the subcommittee reform. I said, "My God, you'll bring another thirty or forty guys into the status quo and we won't get *any* change in the future!"

Second, Phil Burton, the most vocal supporter of the subcommittee reform on the Hansen Committee, was also the only liberal on the Committee to limit his support for committee seniority change. Other liberals pushed for an automatic vote by the Caucus on each committee chairman; the compromise achieved permitted a vote only if ten members demanded it. One member noted this fact:

> The limitation of subcommittee chairmanships to one per member was Burton's thing. He pushed it vigorously, and he, for whatever reason, opposed the automatic election of chairmen. Whether the two were tied together, I don't honestly know. But Burton, of course, will deal and politick with anybody, if it suits his purpose.

Burton vigorously denies that he was party to a compromise, and most (but not all) of the members involved agree with him.

Regardless, Burton's role in the Hansen Committee is a peculiar and interesting one. Unquestionably a moving force in the Committee's activities, Burton also managed to bring about a major change in the attitudes of non-DSG members towards him. Previously considered to be an "ultra-liberal," Burton was highly praised by moderates and conservatives for his open-mindedness, ability to compromise, and integrity on the Committee. Burton's desire to become part of the leadership was no secret, and his participation on the Hansen Committee figured in his overall "plan," as Bob Peabody documents in his incisive analysis of the 1973 leadership struggle.[13] More than likely, this desire to be recognized by conservatives as a flexible and pragmatic politician was a consideration of Burton's as early as 1970.

The weight of evidence would suggest, however, that subcommittee reform and committee reform were separate issues in the Hansen Committee, not tied together by Burton or other members. Burton forcefully countered the "enlarging the status quo" argument by his fellow liberals and was ultimately both successful and correct in his interpretation of its impact.

The Hansen Committee met several more times in December, 1970, to tie together their reform proposals in order to meet the deadline for consideration by the organizational caucus in January. The major reforms were worded and confirmed on December 2 and December 3, including the subcommittee chairmanship limitation. In the fifth and sixth meetings of the committee, on December 8 and December 9, Frank Thompson brought up a further refinement of the subcommittee reform, to allow subcommittee chairman to each hire one professional staff member. Once the chairmanship limitation had been accepted, this reform's passage was much easier—especially since the benefits were even more widespread, hurting only committee chairman who had authority over all staff hiring and firing. A compromise with the Southern members of the Hansen Committee did become necessary here, however; they asked for, and got, the provision that staff must be approved by the full committee caucus. As we shall see, this reform ultimately also aided the liberals. In the House, it is mainly the urban Northern liberals who utilize fully their staff resources, and are in need of more[14] and who, with positive legislative goals to achieve, could best make use of professional staff assistance. Two final meetings were held December 15 and 16. No recommendations were made on the composition of the Committee on Committees, discussed at the first of the two meetings. The final twelve recommendations were written and ratified by the Committee at the last meeting, on December 16.

Why did the Hansen Committee succeed, where prior reform efforts had failed? There are several reasons. One is the nature of the Committee itself—its diverse character, and its determination to reach internal unanimity by compromise on its recommendations. Its members had credibility and respect from the broad Democratic membership—Phil Burton could explain the recommendations to DSG liberals (whose suspicions would be allayed by the endorsements of O'Hara and Thompson); Neal Smith's and Wayne Hays's agreement on the substance of the proposals satisfied the moderate and conservative non-Southerners; and Phil Landrum could reassure the Southern contingent that the compromise achieved was the best they could hope for under the circumstances—that he and "Tiger" Teague had held the line against drastic change. The internal dynamics of the Committee which permitted it to achieve unanimity in its recommendations are more difficult to explain. As one bemused member of the Committee exclaimed:

> You'd have to attend one of the meetings to believe it—a real circus! You had ———, who's like a bull in a china shop . . . ———, who's a high-strung, hypersensitive nitwit, ———, who can't hear too well and was always misunderstanding and getting upset, and ———, who would sometimes have had a few before the meeting . . . It's utterly amazing that anything got accomplished—but it did! And its strength was its motley character.

Once the Committee's program reached the Caucus floor, they were helped by Julia Butler Hansen's floor leadership. Hansen is highly regarded by her colleagues, and worked diligently as chairman. A chauvinist Committee member described her as "the most highly respected of the women members . . . She doesn't pull that 'woman' bullshit; she really knows her stuff and doesn't pull any punches."

What was perhaps more helpful to the Committee's credibility at that point was the vehement vocal opposition to some of the reforms by a few well-known liberals. This was especially true of the subcommittee chairmanship limitation. John Moss (Calif.) chaired two powerful subcommittees, the Government Information Subcommittee on Government Operations, and Commerce and Finance on the Interstate and Foreign Commerce Committee; John Dingell of Michigan chaired the Fisheries and Wildlife Conservation Subcommittee on Merchant Marine and Fisheries, and was due to inherit the Transportation and Aeronautics subcommittee on Commerce, with the defeat of Sam Friedel (Md.) in the 1970 election. Thus, each would be forced to relinquish one of his two power bases, and they both opposed the reform proposal vigorously on the caucus floor. A liberal member of the Hansen Committee noted:

> There is no question that Moss and Dingell screaming on the floor strengthened our case. It made our proposals seem reasonable and balanced to the conservatives.[15]

Further objections to the subcommittee reform were raised by Chet Holifield (Calif.), who as chairman of the Government Operations Committee was upset over the limitations imposed on his power as chairman. The 67-year-old Holifield, once a liberal champion and founder of the DSG, but increasingly conservative in recent years, also probably helped the reform cause.

While all of these internal factors helped to contribute to the Hansen Committee's unanimity and to the caucus's acceptance of their proposals, one important external factor remains to be mentioned. This is the character of turnover among Democrats that occurred with the 1970 election. The 91st Congress lost twenty-seven Democrats who were defeated or chose not to run; thirty-eight new Democrats were elected to the 92d Congress, taking their seats in 1971 when the Committee's report was ratified. In this net gain of eleven Democrats, it is more the character than the amount of change that is important.

While it is difficult (and perhaps foolhardy) to label members as "reform-oriented" or "anti-reform" when it comes to seniority or committees, a rough categorization would divide the outgoing twenty-seven Democrats as split quite evenly on seniority reform. Thus, losses from the caucus neither helped nor hurt reform. However, we can label the overwhelming majority of the thirty-eight new members, at least thirty, as being pro-reform. The new Caucus, which decided on the Hansen Committee proposals, thus contained at least twenty-five more reform-oriented members than its predecessor—a factor which had a greater impact on reform success than any of the prior internal machinations.

Finally, it should again be emphasized that the major focus of the Hansen Committee, the Caucus, and the press reports was on reform of the selection of committee chairmen, and subsequently on challenges raised by liberal members of the District of Columbia Committee to incumbent chairman John MacMillan (S.C.). Subcommittee reforms were *secondary* issues in the Caucus, despite the protestations of the subcommittee chairmen mentioned above. Subcommittee chairmanships were limited to one per member and professional staff members allowed, but these reforms were "second thoughts," and received scant public attention in the aftermath of the first significant changes in the seniority system.

Short-Term Consequences of the 1971 Changes

Partly because of the secondary aspect of the subcommittee reforms, and partly because of the hurried nature of the last few 1970 Hansen Committee meetings, the language of the reforms was loose, and open to interpretation. Controversy arose soon after the January Caucus. The reform read, in part:

> No Member shall be chairman of more than one legislative subcommittee . . . The following committees shall be exempt from the foregoing rule(s): House Administration; Ethics; House Restaurant; Parking; Recording Studios; House Beauty Shop; Joint Committees.

Chairman Chet Holifield of the Government Operations Committee, who had unsuccessfully opposed these reforms on the Caucus floor, reconstructed five of his subcommittees as "investigative," their chairmen all holding other subcommittee chairmanships on other committees. Holifield claimed that since the caucus retained the word "legislative" in the reform provision, it implied that there could be other kinds of subcommittees.[16]

Along with sloppy language, no enforcement mechanisms had been provided for. The Hansen Committee was hastily reconstituted in February 1971 and redefined a legislative subcommittee as any subcommittee whose parent committee reports legislation, with the given exceptions. Holifield then backed down, causing five subcommittee chairs to open up, one on Government Operations, two on Foreign Affairs, one on Judiciary, and one on Banking and Currency.[17]

In the Science and Astronautics Committee, Representative Ken Hechler (D-W.Va.) at the beginning of the 92d Congress, offered an amendment to the committee rules to make them conform to the Hansen Committee reforms regarding the hiring of staff by subcommittee chairmen. His amendment was overwhelmingly defeated, 3–22. Olin Teague, who as a Hansen Committee member supported the reform recommendations, voted against the amendment—a testimony to the peculiar *esprit de corps* and loyalty of the Hansen Committee. Since each committee caucus retained the right to turn down this proposal, this action didn't violate the letter of the new rules, though it indicates both that individual committees have their own particular internal dynamics[18] and that writing and passing reforms is not tantamount to implementing them.

The staff reform, permitting each subcommittee chairman to hire a professional staffer, had little overall impact. As noted above, the issue was raised, and the reform rejected, by the Science and Astronautics Committee. The Foreign Affairs Committee changed its rules and practices to conform to the Hansen reforms. Other committees which in 1971 permitted subcommittee chairmen to hire their own staffs were Banking and Currency, Education and Labor, Interior, Commerce, Judiciary, Merchant Marine and Fisheries, and Post Office and Civil Service. Many of these committees, however, had instituted this practice prior to the Hansen Committee recommendations.

There were no other formal or blatant rejections of the new regulations immediately, though other violations came to light in late 1971 involving the Armed Services and District of Columbia Committees.[19] On balance, the subcommittee chairmanship limitation had a three-fold effect in the 92d Congress:

1. *The reform itself brought in a minimum of sixteen new subcommittee chairmen.* In the 91st Congress, the House had 110 legislative subcommittees with 93 different chairmen; in the 92d Congress there were 108 legislative subcommittees and 108 different chairmen. Altogether there were 29 new subcommittee chairmen in 1971; sixteen got their positions solely because of the reform.

2. *The reform spread power to younger, less senior members.* The reform-aided new chairman had an average seniority in 1971 of 7.3 years; the men they replaced, 17.8 years. For comparison, the other thirteen new subcommittee chairmen in 1971 averaged 11.9 years in seniority, and the remaining seventy-nine subcommittee chairmen averaged 18.5 years. Table 2 gives a partial committee-by-committee breakdown, to demonstrate the magnitude of these differences in seniority.

TABLE 2

AVERAGE SENIORITY IN YEARS, REFORM-INSTITUTED
SUBCOMMITTEE CHAIRMEN, AND OTHERS,
FOR SELECTED COMMITTEES, 92d CONGRESS

Committee	Average Seniority Reform-Instituted Subcommittee Chairmen*	Average Seniority Other Subcommittee Chairmen*
Agriculture	0 (0)	16.1 (10)
Appropriations	0 (0)	23.2 (13)
Banking and Currency	10.0 (3)	25.0 (4)
District of Columbia	6.5 (2)	7.0 (2)
Foreign Affairs	7.0 (3)	17.6 (7)
Government Operations	12.0 (1)	19.3 (6)
Judiciary	8.0 (1)	26.5 (4)
Merchant Marine and Fisheries	7.0 (2)	17.5 (4)
Post Office and Civil Service	5.0 (1)	9.4 (5)
Public Works	9.0 (1)	16.2 (5)
Veterans' Affairs	3.0 (2)	10.7 (3)

* Number of chairmen in parentheses

3. *The reform improved the lot of non-Southern and liberal Democrats in 1971.* The Caucus subcommittee reforms did not radically alter the face of the House, at least initially. The changes occurred where more senior members had to choose between two subcommittee chairs, and naturally the openings which arose for the new chairmen were not the most prestigious or powerful subcommittees. Overall, 6 of the 16 reform-based chairmen, or 37.5 per cent, were from Southern or border states, compared with 50 per cent of their reform-replaced counterparts, 45 per cent of all other subcommittee chairmen, and 36.5 per cent of all House Democrats. (The fact that Southerners are disproportionally represented among subcommittee chairmen is itself an indication that a reform spreading out these positions would in future aid non-Southerners.)

The immediate improvement for liberals occurred especially with openings on the more powerful committees—Banking and Currency, Judiciary, and Foreign Affairs. These committees accounted for seven of the sixteen reform-aided chairmanships; of the seven, only one chair fell to a conservative, Robert Stephens (Ga.), on Banking and Currency. The other six, including Henry Gonzalez of Texas, all were DSG-type liberals.

The biggest change was in the Foreign Affairs Committee. The Hansen Committee reforms brought in three new subcommittee chairmen: Ben Rosenthal (N.Y.), Europe subcommittee; Lee Hamilton (Ind.), Near East; and John Culver (Iowa), Foreign Economic Policy. They replaced Leonard Farbstein (N.Y.), Robert Nix (Pa.), and L. H. Fountain (N.C.)—and in the process injected much more activism into the three subcommittees, raising issues that had remained dormant in the passive pre-1970 Foreign Affairs Committee.[20] The startling 1971 House vote to cut off military aid to Greece was a direct result of Ben Rosenthal's ascendance to the Europe subcommittee chairmanship.[21]

Moreover, each of these three activist liberals brought in a professional staff member whose outlook and activity correspondingly changed the nature of the Foreign Affairs Committee staff, bringing about more hearings (and publicity) on new issues.

While the qualitative change is most significant, we can also make some use of quantitative data. Table 3 shows the

TABLE 3
TOTAL DAYS OF HEARINGS, HOUSE FOREIGN AFFAIRS SUBCOMMITTEE

Subcommittee	91st Congress Days of Hearings	92d Congress Days of Hearings	Change
Foreign Economic Policy	13	21	+8
Europe	13	38	+25
Near East	6	34	+28
International Organizations	21	37	+16
Africa	17	10	−7
Asian and Pacific Affairs	8	17	+9
Others	79	65	+14
Total	159	222	+65

number of days of hearings for subcommittees of the Foreign Affairs Committee, comparing the 91st and 92d Congresses, taken from Committee calendars. In the 91st Congress, all the subcommittees had a total of 157 days of hearings; this rose to 222 days for the 92d Congress, an increase of 65 days.

As the table makes clear, the three reform-chaired subcommittees increased by 61 days of hearings. Hearings alone don't change policy—especially foreign policy—but this is a clear indicator of increased activism. As a 1971 article in *National Journal* noted:

A young challenging minority on the House Foreign Affairs Committee is demanding, and getting, a more critical appraisal of U.S. foreign policy from the House side than anyone on Capitol Hill can recall.

One reason is that four[22] of the younger members became chairmen of subcommittees this year. They are hiring staff consultants who are even younger and more challenging. And these newcomers are trying to keep a correct distance from some senior staff members whose reputation for orthodoxy is well founded. . . . Much of the new zest stems from . . . House Democrats' . . . reforms.[23]

Determining the exact subcommittees which were opened because of the reforms in 1971 was very difficult; it required in some instances drawing complex flow charts involving several choice points for different legislators. To do the same for the 93d Congress, in 1973, would be impossible. We can only say that there are more new chairmen in 1973 than there would have been without the reforms. However, a look at the twenty-four new subcommittee chairmen in the 93d Congress indicates the trend toward youth, "liberalness," and Northernness in these positions, a trend which was accelerated and accentuated by the Hansen Committee 1971 reforms. The average seniority of the new chairmen was 7.2 years, with eighteen of the twenty-four having less than 10 years in the House upon ascending to their chairmanships. Eighteen of twenty-three had Americans for Democratic Action ratings over 50; fifteen had ADA ratings over 75 and only three were under 25. And only four of twenty-four new chairmen were from the South, compared, as we noted earlier, with nearly 50 per cent of pre-1971 subcommittee chairmen.

Through a conjunction of circumstances—the "Republicanization" of the South, the aging of more senior (especially Southern) members, improved retirement allowances, and the increased pace of activity in Congress—older members are leaving, and Democrats as a whole are becoming less senior and less Southern. Moreover, young Southerners are demonstrably less conservative than their predecessors and their more senior colleagues. Thus, we can expect a reform which spreads the power base to continue to create change in similar directions for the near future.

The "Subcommittee Bill of Rights"

As we noted earlier, the impact of the Hansen Committee reforms varied from committee to committee, with the greatest changes coming on Foreign Affairs. Many committee chairmen were able to retain control over their committees' operations even though they could no longer completely dictate which men would hold positions of power. It remained possible for a committee chairman to defuse a subcommittee by making its jurisdictions vague (thus not assigning it important or controversial legislation), by limiting funds for staff or hearings, by controlling floor debate himself on the subcommittee's legislation. Relying on the incremental approach, liberals in 1973 focused attention on solidifying their gains of 1971 by specifying subcommittee powers.

They were aided in this respect by the 1972 election which, as in 1970, added a significant number of reform-oriented members to the Democratic caucus. The forty-three departing members of the 92d Congress averaged fifteen years in seniority. Though the Democrats as a whole lost thirteen members, electing only thirty new members, the reform-oriented bloc picked up a net of perhaps twelve—which, combined with their gains two years earlier, provide a marked change in the character of the Democratic Caucus in a period of only four years.

The idea for formalization of selection and powers of subcommittee chairmen came from liberals, who approached DSG staff director Dick Conlon with the suggestion that his group take the idea and implement it through the caucus.[24] In addition, Dave Obey (Wis.), a member of the Appropriations Committee, lobbied vigorously with the Hansen Committee to alter the method of subcommittee assignments.

Within the Hansen Committee, the new subcommittee reforms were handled mainly by Burton and Thompson. There was some opposition to them by senior Southern members, but once again the Committee's *esprit de corps* carried the reforms through. As one member said:

> I didn't like the details of that so-called Subcommittee Bill of Rights. I felt it imposed on chairmen; I would prefer some flexibility. But I went along with the majority.

And another member of the Hansen Committee, who also went along, noted somewhat acerbically in March:

> The Subcommittee Bill of Rights is a bunch of bullshit. They [subcommittee chairmen] all pushed to hire their own staff people; you walk into all these offices and you see people sitting on their asses and reading the *Washington Post*. It hasn't changed things a damned bit.

Primarily, liberal members wanted to safeguard against having the prior reforms negated by powerful committee chairman. And, well aware of the character of turnover in the recent past and of their own dominance in the middle and lower levels of seniority, liberals sought to solidify their emerging power. The reforms proposed to the Hansen Committee, considered and approved by it and by the Democratic Caucus in January, 1973, formally institutionalized the party's caucus on each standing committee, which would vote on subcommittee chairmanship vacancies in order of committee or subcommittee seniority. Moreover, subcommittees were granted fixed jurisdictions, guaranteed powers, referral of all appropriate legislation, an adequate budget and staffing. Finally, Obey's subcommittee memberships rule, guaranteeing choice of one subcommittee membership to each Democratic committee member, according to seniority, was carried through the Hansen Committee, and the caucus, with the help of Frank Thompson.

As in 1971, these reforms were secondary issues to most House Democrats; getting automatic votes on committee chairmen, and opening up committee meetings (the "secrecy" issue) were of much greater concern. This of course helped the subcommittee reforms; it made their ratification by the Hansen Committee more important to members of the caucus (especially those not in the DSG) who were preoccupied with the other issues. Liberal criticism of other Hansen Committee recommendations (they failed to give guidelines for voting on each committee chairman) also probably added to their legitimacy on subcommittee reforms.[25]

Two other factors should be mentioned. First, Common Cause, led by David Cohen, director of field operations, was in 1973 present and active in pursuit of a range of reform issues within the Democratic Party, especially seniority and committee secrecy. It dealt with the caucus, however, not the Hansen Committee,[26] and thus played little direct part in subcommittee reforms. But by publicizing and crystallizing the broad "reform" issue, especially among the incoming freshmen, Common Cause at least improved attendance at the series of organizational caucuses in January and February, 1973. Moreover, their grass-roots operation forced many members, especially newcomers, to put themselves on record in favor of reform before the caucuses.

Second, the succession of Thomas P. O'Neill (Mass.) to the post of Majority Leader at the first caucus of 1973 in early January, as a result of Hale Boggs's death, was the first change in Democratic leadership in recent years accomplished without Southern members playing a crucial role.[27] Thus, the leadership was freer to assist in implementing reform objectives; O'Neill, in particular, was quite active.[28]

After Enactment: The Impact of the Reforms

The series of subcommittee reforms informally called the "Sub-committee Bill of Rights" had little immediate effect on most committees; the individual committee caucuses, most of which had cooperated with their committee chairmen in the past, continued to do so. The impact was not as immediate or as measurable as the subcommittee chairmanship limitation initiated two years earlier. Some liberals, frustrated in their committees, attempted, largely unsuccessfully, to use the new reforms to force basic changes. John Moss of California, who in 1971 had fought subcommittee reform in the caucus, went to the leadership and the Hansen Committee in March, 1973, to change the procedures in the Interstate and Foreign Commerce Committee. Moss, unable to garner support for his proposals in his own Commerce and Finance subcommittee, wanted the membership ratio of the subcommittee changed from five Democrats and four Republicans to six to four, on the grounds that the 5 to 4 ratio, 55.56 per cent, was less than the 24 to 19, 55.81 per cent ratio on the full committee. The Hansen Committee referred his complaint back to the Commerce Committee's Democratic caucus, which overwhelmingly rejected his proposal.

On some committees immediate changes did occur, with significant secondary effects as well. One committee chairman commented:

I didn't pay much attention to subcommittee chairmen before—I did it all myself. Now, the subcommittee chairmen handle bills on the floor. They know that when they're answering questions on the floor they had better know what they're talking about. They really study the legislation now; they're much better prepared and more knowledgeable. Now we go to conference and they do the talking—the Senators never open their mouths. Their staffs are the only ones who know anything. So we're more effective with the Senate.

While no exhaustive survey of standing committee practices

was carried out, this type of change does not appear to have occurred in most committees; prior practices prevailed. However, this expansion of expertise is an excellent example of the unintended broader consequences a minor structural reform can produce. In future years, if the Hansen subcommittee reforms take greater hold, this secondary effect could be of great importance to House-Senate interactions and to congressional outputs. An expansion of power and broadening of incentives can give congressmen greater impetus to do legislative work, and can thus expand both expertise and activity.

The Obey amendment was directed at the Appropriations Committee, to guarantee that the younger members of that committee (more liberal than their more senior colleagues) would not be shut out of the most important subcommittees on the Appropriations Committee. Each member would be allowed to "grandfather," or retain two subcommittee memberships, and subsequent vacancies would be open for selection by committee seniority until each member of the committee had two subcommittees, and so forth. Thus, "stockpiling" of three or more subcommittee memberships by senior members would be prevented. This reform effected little immediate change (only one subcommittee assignment changed among the ten most senior members, and that was not caused by the reform), but was clearly enacted with the future in mind.

Conclusion

To this point, we have discussed the causes and short-term consequences of subcommittee reforms in the House. These reforms, we have noted, were not the primary focus or objective of members pushing for change or of the Hansen Committee; indeed, they are only a small part of the large number of reforms which occurred in the House of Representatives in the same time period. It is appropriate now to discuss the broader changes in order to put subcommittee reforms in their proper context.

The Democratic caucus in 1973 enacted several other changes related to committees. Revising a largely unsuccessful 1971 reform, the caucus made each committee meeting open, unless the committee members voted publicly to close the session. A survey done by Common Cause of mark-up sessions from March 7 through June 15, 1973, showed 238 open meetings, and 47 closed. This is a marked change from the past, though most Appropriations and Ways and Means committee meetings have remained closed.[29] A Democratic Steering and Policy Committee, balanced in region and seniority, was set up. The Democratic Committee on Committees was expanded to include the Speaker, Majority Leader, and chairman of the caucus. And, as we have noted, the selection process for committee chairmen was revised to produce a vote on each chairman nominated by the caucus.

Taken as a whole, these measures struck directly at the powers of committee chairmen. They have, at least on paper, reduced the ability of an autocratic committee chairman to dominate his committee and the House, in much the same way that the 1910 House of Representatives reduced the powers of an autocratic Speaker. Each chairman is now theoretically regularly accountable to the full Democratic caucus. Control over subcommittee jurisdictions, chairmen, activities, and powers now rests with subcommittee chairmen (who can be checked by the committee Democratic caucus) instead of committee chairmen, as previously. Informal powers of persuasion are limited by the increasing openness of committee meetings. Power has been spread out to subcommittee chairmen, and concentrated in the hands of the caucus—in both instances at the expense of the standing committee chairmen. The full potential import of these alterations in power has been ameliorated by the continuity of committee memberships (especially among senior members), but the House over the next decade will experience a very significant change in membership, especially at the upper seniority levels. As committees change in their character, we will be able to see whether these reforms have great significance. It must be emphasized that many of the 1910 reforms, which were theoretically tailored to protect the whole House against small concentrations of power, were never widely utilized; the discharge petition is the best example. It is possible that the same fate will befall these 1971 and 1973 reforms.

Moreover, if the liberals who pushed through these reforms take advantage of them in the future to attain power in the House, they may well perceive things very differently than they do now. Long-range goals, more policy-oriented now, might become more personally-oriented when viewed from the top rather than the bottom, as Lord Acton noted, more concisely, some time ago. Over the long run, the fear, mentioned earlier by one liberal, of bringing more members "into the status quo" and thwarting future change, might well prove true.[30]

One of the more significant aspects of these reforms is that they were implemented through the caucus of the majority party, not through the full House membership. While this could greatly limit their future effectiveness (especially if the Republicans were to gain control of the House), they are nevertheless far more important than the changes wrought by the 1970 Legislative Reorganization Act. Working through the caucus meant that a much smaller number of participants was required to achieve success; we can expect the caucus to be a major forum for future reform efforts.

We may also possibly see the Democratic caucus strengthen its position in the House, vis-à-vis the formal leadership and the committees. Unlike the old "King Caucus," this would not be a puppet organization controlled by an omnipotent Speaker. As the caucus grows in power, its inclination to exercise that power and dictate outcomes to other congressional actors would increase; this might well result in widespread Democratic defections which could make all of these other changes academic.

As a final note, we might mention two changes initiated via the Legislative Reorganization Act of 1970—the recorded teller vote and electronic voting.[31] The recorded teller vote reform made public previously unrecorded votes on amendments taken in the Committee of the Whole. In a quantitative sense, turnout on these votes has jumped phenomenally, and some significant outcomes have changed as well.[32] Recording these votes has also made it more difficult for committee chairmen to control events on the floor; their private bargaining must now be weighed by congressmen against perceived public pressure. One member noted simply, "It's more difficult for me to go along now."

Electronic voting has shortened the time of roll call votes from

45 to 15 minutes. This has also had "spillover" effects. The normal practice of cue-taking[33] has been changed somewhat. Examining other members' votes for clues on the "right" way to vote is easier with the large electronic screen and instant reporting featured in the new system; but asking other members for their advice is more difficult because of the time element. This also potentially hurts committee chairmen and senior members, whose expertise made them the predominant sources for information.[34] Thus, these two reforms together, unintentionally perhaps, have diminished the powers of committee chairmen. The extent of their impact remains to be seen.

All of these reforms, passed separately and dealing with different issues, are nevertheless highly interrelated. In interaction, they could well result in a major shift in the power structure of the House in years to come.

NOTES

1. This has been especially true of the work of Price and of Polsby and his colleagues. For additional citations, see the bibliography in this volume.

2. There have been several informal accounts of attempts, led by Joe Waggoner (D-La.), to form a group called the "Boll-Weevils," with staff and structure comparable to the DSG. See the profile of Joe Waggoner by Norman C. Miller, *Wall Street Journal*, April 13, 1973.

3. The twenty-one-day rule, permitting discharge of bills from the Rules Committee, was enacted in the 81st Congress, 1949–50, then resoundingly repealed, by a vote of 247 to 179, at the start of the 82d Congress in 1951. Another twenty-one-day rule was approved in the 89th Congress in 1965, only to be repealed at the 90th Congress.

4. For a good account of the 1961 Rules Committee battle, see Tom Wicker, *J.F.K. and L.B.J.: The Influence of Personality Upon Politics* (New York: Morrow, 1969) chapters 1–5.

5. See Mark Ferber, "The Formation of the Democratic Study Group," in Polsby, ed., *Congressional Behavior* (N.Y.: Random House, 1971) pp. 249–69.

6. The caucus of April, 1969, included the first attack on John McMillan, chairman of the District of Columbia Committee; in the caucus of February, 1970, Speaker McCormack was challenged by Jerome Waldie; the caucus of March, 1970, set up the Hansen Committee; and in the caucus of December, 1970, the Hansen Committee reported back.

7. *Congressional Quarterly Weekly Report*, June 2, 1973, p. 1367.

8. Interview with the author, February, 1973.

9. Interview with the author, March, 1973.

10. *Ibid.*

11. I interviewed Congressmen from all political spectra, including members who rarely agree with each other, and who ranged from strongly pro- to strongly anti-reform. Yet no one criticized the makeup of the Hansen Committee.

12. The committee reporting data was set for January, 1971, which caused some liberals to suspect that the leadership was planning to vote on the new 92d Congress committee chairmen first, thus postponing any seniority reforms for two more years. This was resolved by an agreement to vote on the Hansen Committee recommendations in January, but *prior* to votes on chairmen.

13. Robert L. Peabody, *Leadership in Congress: Stability, Succession and Change*, forthcoming (Boston: Little, Brown, 1974).

14. See Norman J. Ornstein, "Information, Resources, and Legislative Decision-Making: Some Comparative Perspectives on the U.S. Congress," unpublished Ph.D. dissertation, University of Michigan, 1972.

15. In addition, the formation of a group of liberal Democrats that applied pressure from the left on the Hansen Committee thus added to their aura of being in the middle, balanced between extremes. This group was led by Patsy Mink (Hawaii), Brock Adams (Wash.), Tom Rees (Calif.), and Jim Howard (N.J.). See story by Ronald Sarro, *Washington Star*, January 13, 1971.

16. *Washington Post*, March 12, 1971.

17. Three of the subcommittee chairmen elected to keep their Government Operations chairs, forcing them to give up chairmanships they held on other committees. As nearly as I can determine, John Moss (Calif.) and Dante Fascell (Fla.) left their chairs on Government Operations for subcommittees on Commerce and Foreign Affairs, respectively. Bill Moorhead (Pa.) elected to take Moss's chair, leaving one of his own on Banking and Currency to be taken by Fernand St. Germain (R.I.). John Monaghan (Conn.) took Fascell's chair, giving up his option for a Foreign Affairs subcommittee chair to Ben Rosenthal (N.Y.). William Randall (Mo.) took the chairmanship of the remaining Government Operations subcommittee. Jack Brooks of Texas retained his Government Operations chair, thus losing his option for a Judiciary subcommittee to Don Edwards (Calif.). Finally, L. H. Fountain (N.C.) kept his Government Operations subcommittee chairmanship over one on Foreign Affairs, which was taken by Lee Hamilton (Ind.).

18. As is demonstrated superbly by Richard Fenno in *Congressmen in Committees*, Boston: Little, Brown, 1973.

19. Chairmen F. Edward Hebert of Armed Services and John McMillan of the District of Columbia Committee were violating the Hansen restrictions through *ad hoc* subcommittees. Complaints by Committee members caused a letter to be sent to these chairmen from the Hansen Committee in August, 1971; they both changed their practices.

20. See "New Leaders, Staff Changes Stimulate House Foreign Affairs Committee," *National Journal*, June 19, 1971, pp. 1314–22.

21. This move, however, had little more than publicity value; loopholes in the measure were utilized by President Nixon to continue military aid to the Greek dictatorship.

22. A fourth new chairman, Don Fraser, received his subcommittee on International Organizations and Movements without benefit of the reforms; note as well this subcommittee's activity increase in Table 3.

23. "New Leaders, Staff Changes," p. 1314.

24. Peter Barash, an aide to Representative Ben Rosenthal (N.Y.) who handles Government Operations Committee matters, and David Rohde, an APSA Congressional Fellow in Rosenthal's office, formulated the proposals and presented them to Conlon in December, 1972. Representative Richard Hanna (Calif.) independently suggested similar ideas to the DSG.

25. See *Congressional Quarterly Weekly Report,* January 20, 1973, p. 70.

26. My interviews with the Hansen Committee members elicited no responses which recognized a significant role for Common Cause. Talks with congressmen not on the Hansen Committee, especially younger ones, usually resulted in Common Cause being mentioned as an important force in reform.

27. See Peabody, *Leadership in Congress,* for a detailed analysis of these events.

28. See especially, *Congressional Quarterly Weekly Report,* January 20, 1973, pp. 69–72, and January 27, 1973, p. 137.

29. See story by Mary Russell, *Washington Post,* July 5, 1973, p. A-13.

30. See Norman J. Ornstein, "House Reform: Another Year of Seniority," *Washington Post,* Outlook section, December 17, 1972.

31. See *Congressional Quarterly Weekly Report,* September 25, 1971, pp. 1967–70; and U.S. House of Representatives, Democratic Study Group, Special Report, *The First Year of Recorded Teller Voting,* 92d Cong., 2d Sess., January 27, 1972.

32. *Ibid.*

33. See Donald Matthews and James Stimson, "Decision-making by U.S. Representatives: A Preliminary Model," paper presented at a conference on political decision-making, University of Kentucky, April, 1968.

34. See Donald Matthews and James Stimson, "The Decision-Making Approach to the Study of Legislative Behavior," paper presented at the 1969 annual meeting of the American Political Science Association, New York City.

III. Change and Party Leadership

Of what importance are individual members in affecting policy or process in Congress? Could different people filling its positions change the legislature's operations? The impact of personality on congressional politics is most clearcut when we look at party leaders. The formal positions these individuals fill for the most part convey few explicit powers. Thus the personality of the leader becomes crucial; he can shape the leadership position in whichever way he desires.* Nowhere is this clearer than in the contrast between Senate Majority Leader Mike Mansfield and his predecessor, Lyndon B. Johnson. As Rowland Evans and Robert Novak make clear, Johnson was a strong, crafty politician who actively sought to tie together the fragments of formal power available to him—chairmanships of Policy and Steering Committees, the power of recognition on the floor, control of scheduling of legislation—with the informal power of persuasion, so that he could really *run* the Senate.

The Senate is much different under Mike Mansfield, whose personality is the diametric opposite of Johnson's. Mansfield is taciturn and intellectual, apparently without any driving desire for personal power; he sees his leadership role as one of streamlining and expediting the Senate's business. The *National Journal* profile of Mansfield demonstrates how his personality has shaped the operations of the Senate in quite different ways than Johnson's. Leaders can set the tone, dominate decision-making, set priorities for the legislative body. The individuals who make up the leader-

---

* The reference to leaders as "he" is not meant to be sexist; congressional party leaders are reflective of the body memberships: overwhelmingly male.

ship can determine what policies Congress implements or rejects.

How can two such disparate individuals be elected to the same office? One of the most interesting aspects of Congress's internal workings is how leaders are chosen. Situational, strategic and personality factors are all of importance. The first part of the Evans and Novak excerpt shows the fluke circumstances which led to Johnson's initial accession to the Senate Democratic leadership.

How leaders are chosen leads one to ask what *types* of people become leaders in Congress. Garrison Nelson goes back to the earliest Congresses, to evaluate and compare the regional, geographic and social backgrounds of all House party leaders through five distinct historical periods. He finds some interesting changes over time in characteristics of House leaders, as well as great distinctions in background between House leaders and other societal elites—differences which might well have an impact on the kinds of policy implemented by Congress.

LYNDON B. JOHNSON:
THE ASCENT TO LEADERSHIP

ROWLAND EVANS and ROBERT NOVAK

When the Democratic majority of the United States Senate caucused on the morning of January 2, 1951, to choose new leaders for the 82d Congress, there was not the slightest indication that a great political career had reached a critical point. Senator Scott Lucas of Illinois and Senator Francis Myers of Pennsylvania, Majority Leader and Majority Whip in the departing 81st Congress, had both been defeated in the 1950 congressional elections. The world outside the caucus had little interest in the Senate Democrats' tribal ritual. For in the postwar years, the official Senate leadership was an unwanted burden, stripped of power and devoid of honor. . . .

The job of the Senate Majority Leader in that era was a misery without splendor. While Russell and Taft pulled the strings from the cloakroom, the "leader" was out there on the floor trying to keep the Senate's creaky machinery in operation. While Truman hurled his legislative thunderbolts from the White House—and conveniently all but forgot them—Lucas was required to make a nominal effort to catch and then pass them. Tied down in Washington far from his constituents, he became an easy target for

Excerpted from Rowland Evans & Robert Novak, *Lyndon B. Johnson: The Exercise of Power* (New York: New American Library, 1966) by permission of the publisher. Rowland Evans and Robert Novak are syndicated political columnists.

the Republican ex-Congressman, Everett McKinley Dirksen, in the 1950 Illinois Senate election. Years later, Lucas confided that those two years as leader were the most unhappy of his life. No wonder there was so little interest among other Democrats to take his place.

The climb of the talented Class of '48 to formal positions of power in the Senate hierarchy was considerably short of meteoric. Clinton Anderson and Robert Kerr did not become standing committee chairmen until 1961. In that same year, Hubert Humphrey was elected Senate Majority Whip. Russell Long did not succeed Humphrey as whip until 1965.

It is entirely possible that Lyndon Johnson would have advanced with no greater speed to a position of formal power had it not been for a remarkable chain of events in late 1950 and early 1951. And Johnson, unlike Russell and Kerr, predicated his rise in the Senate on his *formal* position. Whether Johnson would have leaped ahead of the rest of the Class of '48 into national prominence without these fortuitous events is questionable.

The first, of course, was the simultaneous defeats in the 1950 election of both Majority Leader Lucas in Illinois and Majority Whip Myers in Pennsylvania—a startling double slaying of the majority party's Senate leaders. Their defeats were symptomatic of Harry Truman's state of affairs in the Senate, which had dropped from poor to bad. Considering Lucas's utter inability to move the Fair Deal program against the Russell-Taft coalition, his loss in itself did no further damage to Truman in the Senate. As Whip, Myers had been little help to Lucas. But the Lucas-Myers defeats were part of the general Democratic losses in 1950. Those losses were in part due to the drop in Truman's popularity following the upsurge after his 1948 election victory. The United States had intervened in Korea in June, 1950, launching an unpopular war that was to grow increasingly more so as casualty lists mounted. Truman and his leadership in Congress looked forward confidently to two years of hell on Capitol Hill.

Clinton Anderson, Harry Truman's old Secretary of Agriculture, was deeply concerned about the approaching 1951–52 Senate session. Quite apart from the now-discarded Fair Deal program, Lucas's successor as Majority Leader would have no easy time passing such "must" legislation as the foreign aid bill, including the Marshall Plan funds for Western Europe. Anderson worried whether *anybody* could carry Harry Truman's banner in the Senate and hope to survive politically, particularly if he were up for re-election in 1952.

Stewing over this problem, Anderson hit upon an audacious answer: persuade Richard Russell to become the new leader. The idea of the arch-conservative from Georgia, who in league with Robert Taft had mangled so much Truman legislation, now becoming Truman's Senate chief made a certain sense, quite beyond its boldness. The parts of the Fair Deal legislative program that Russell most objected to—particularly civil rights—were now quite dead. No one was nearly as well equipped as Russell to guide through the Senate the key appropriations bills and a bare-bones legislative program. And if any Democrat could weather close political identification with Truman, it was Russell. In Georgia he was unassailable.

Anderson secretly presented his idea at the White House and got a favorable response from Truman, who was personally fond of most of the Southern Senators and did not resent their opposition. But why should Russell trade the reality of power as director of the ruling coalition for the powerless drudgery of the Majority Leadership? Here again, the facile mind of Anderson conceived a solution for Truman: Russell could be trapped into taking the job.

He proposed that Truman, accompanied by the regular presidential press entourage, visit Russell down in Winder, Georgia. When Truman arrived, he would announce publicly that he wanted Russell for his Majority Leader. As Anderson reasoned, Russell could not say no to the President. Russell was at that time preparing himself for a serious bid for the 1952 Democratic presidential nomination, cautiously edging a bit closer to the national positions of the Democratic party. His refusal of a public request from the President would crush his admittedly slim presidential hopes.

If the Anderson plan had been carried out—and had worked—Lyndon Johnson would have been barred from the Senate leadership indefinitely, because two Senators from the Old Confederacy would never have been allowed to represent the Democratic party as Senate Leader and Whip.

As it turned out, however, Truman was preoccupied with the war in Korea and showed little personal interest in pursuing Anderson's proposal. Instead of making a public expedition personally to Winder as Anderson suggested, Truman dispatched his closest aide—White House counsel Clark Clifford—to put the request to Russell privately. Under those circumstances, Russell could and did decline. Although Russell had no thought of Johnson's future, his refusal was vital to it.

From that point on, White House interest in who would succeed Lucas and Myers was academic. It was Russell who faced the same chore of two years earlier: to pick a sacrificial lamb to replace Lucas, one who would quite probably suffer Lucas's fate at the next election. Russell's choice was Senator Ernest McFarland of Arizona, considerably more of a doughface and a weaker force in the Senate than Lucas. Noting that McFarland faced a struggle for re-election in 1952 anyway, friends advised that to accept Russell's offer of a thankless job identifying him so closely with the Truman Administration would be as fatal to him as it had been to Lucas. Bumbling, genial Ernie McFarland, perhaps yearning for a few moments in the political sun, brushed aside the good advice and accepted. There was no opposition.

Hopeful for one of their own as whip under McFarland, a few liberals began desultory talk in behalf of Senator John J. Sparkman of Alabama, a Southern liberal whose dependable opposition to civil rights might conceivably make his strong support for other aspects of the Fair Deal palatable to Russell. It did not. Sparkman was well outside the Senate's inner circle. Besides, the increasingly powerful Bob Kerr wanted to expand his influence by installing a close friend as whip, and John Sparkman decidedly did not meet these specifications.*

Kerr first felt out Anderson, but the ailing New Mexico millionaire would have sooner taken a job digging Kerr's oil wells. Kerr

---

* There is no sign Sparkman wanted the meaningless job. His close friend and senior colleague, liberal Senator Lister Hill of Alabama, was whip for three terms but resigned in January, 1949, fearing close identification with the Truman civil rights program.

next turned to Lyndon Johnson. The ambitious Johnson readily agreed, but there remained one possible obstacle: Richard Russell. Russell was skeptical. He had not particularly cottoned to Johnson in 1949–50. Although their relationship was to bloom in 1951–52, Russell said he doubted that an all-Southwest team of McFarland and Johnson had the proper geographical balance. Nevertheless, Kerr doggedly argued for Johnson, and Russell eventually yielded. And so, by an uncertain, unpremeditated course of events, Lyndon Johnson at age forty-two entered the official Senate Democratic leadership—thanks more to Bob Kerr than to Dick Russell, despite the future legend that Russell was the guiding hand who pushed the young Texan along the road to Senate leadership. The team of McFarland and Johnson was elected at the January 2, 1951, caucus of Democratic Senators amid massive inattention from the outside world.

In truth, as the 82d Congress progressed, McFarland and Johnson didn't make much of a "team." Lacking close ties to the powers in the Senate, McFarland struggled manfully but ineffectively through two dismal years—without much assistance from his young whip. Johnson haunted the cloakrooms sharpening his connections with the leaders of the conservative coalition in both parties. In terms of what the role of whip later became when Johnson himself was leader, Johnson's aloofness might have appeared to be deliberate sabotage of McFarland, but considering the history of the job, it certainly was not. When Russell asked Lucas to become Barkley's whip in 1947, he confided with characteristic honesty that the job was purely honorary. Thus Johnson was doing only what was expected of him, neither more nor less than his immediate predecessors as whip. In the tight little world of Capitol Hill, power is measured partly in the currency of office space, but the only visible trapping of power received by Johnson was a small one-room "hideaway" in the Capitol itself, complete with brown leather couch, small refrigerator and liquor cabinet— a luxury generally reserved only for very senior Senators—that reflected the puniness of the job of whip. Johnson's main work was performed in a five-room suite in the Senate Office Building. With the Senator's staff crowded in on each other and the walls lined with autographed pictures of politicians, the suite was much the same as any other Senator's—with one distinctive difference: a growing collection of baby pictures from parents (many of them Johnson staffers) who had already begun the practice of naming their offspring Lyndon or Lynda.

But even without precise leadership duties or a special office, Lyndon Johnson as whip was a more formidable Senate figure than Francis Myers. He was a person of consequence in the Senate, while McFarland was a mediocrity. That made for an uncomfortable relationship. Sensitive about the prerogatives of his newly achieved office, McFarland would have resented efforts by Johnson to share the duties. Consequently, Johnson made not the slightest effort to vitalize the office of whip, and his life in the Senate proceeded much as it had before. He added to his vital store of information about the Senate and its members, and made mental notes how one day he would improve its operation. . . .

LBJ: The Leader

On the cold, rainy day of January 3, 1953, a new era, exciting and turbulent, was opening for the United States Senate. To those in the packed galleries, the most vivid figure on the floor was Lyndon B. Johnson, only four years in the Senate and at forty-four the youngest floor leader of either party. Johnson had taken his front-row center-aisle seat on the left (Democratic) side of the aisle as the just-elected Minority Leader, and assumed a physical stance that was to become a Senate trademark in the next eight years: sprawled almost full length, the tip of his spine balanced on the outside edge of his chair, legs crossed, laughing and joking across the center aisle with his Republican opposite number, the reserved Robert A. Taft of Ohio. An inveterate attention-grabber, Johnson kept sliding his chair over to Taft's side, then back to its place. For the first time, he was flexing his muscles as a new Democratic power.

If Johnson was nervous (which he was) or slightly overwhelmed by his sudden new prominence in the Democratic party (which he also was), the view from the gallery gave no hint of it. There was an incongruity, however, about this long, restless bean pole from the Texas hill country conversing as an equal across the narrow aisle with the distinguished, patrician Taft, even then wasting away from cancer.

Like Johnson, Taft had just been elected floor leader of his party. But—unlike Johnson—from the early 1940's Taft had been the *de facto* Republican power in the Senate (just as Richard Russell had been the *de facto* Democratic power). Thus, Taft was now merely getting *de jure* sanction for what had long existed.* Yet it seemed strange that newcomer Johnson should be the picture of self-satisfaction as he contemplated battle against the formidable "Mr. Republican."

But the galleries did not realize much about Lyndon Johnson in January, 1953, including how hard he had tried to become Democratic floor leader, the powerless job shunned since the late 1930's.

The polls had scarcely closed on the Eisenhower landslide in the 1952 presidential election two months earlier when Johnson, operating from the LBJ Ranch in Texas, began the maneuvers that led him to the job he coveted—Senate Minority Leader, now that Republicans had won control of the Senate. In that 1952 election, a prominent but not unexpected victim was Senator Ernest McFarland, who lost narrowly to a conservative, young Phoenix department-store owner, Barry M. Goldwater. McFarland's 1952 loss proved to be the first act in a drama to be concluded by Goldwater and Johnson on the presidential stage twelve years later. For 1952, however, the significant point was the indispensability of Goldwater's triumph to Lyndon Johnson's next move up the Democratic party ladder. Just as Scott Lucas's defeat in 1950 and Harry Truman's failure to get Russell to succeed Lucas were necessary, so did McFarland's departure leave Johnson room at the top.

It was only natural that Johnson's first telephone call, after McFarland's defeat, was to Richard Russell. Johnson's proposal:

---

* Until 1953, Taft held power as chairman of the Senate Republican Policy Committee, preferring that the routine of floor leadership be borne by somebody else (who, of course, would be responsive to Taft's wishes). With the election of a Republican President in 1952, Taft knew that Eisenhower would be dealing primarily with the Majority Leader; he made himself available for that post and was quickly elected to it.

Russell himself should succeed McFarland as Democratic leader and Johnson would be Russell's aide-de-camp.

"I'll do the work and you'll be the boss," Johnson told Russell.

But Russell still preferred to exert his influence in less official but no less significant ways. Besides his unofficial leadership in the conservative coalition, he was chief of the Southern bloc (at that time twenty-two out of forty-seven Democratic Senators) and a senior member of both the Appropriations and the Armed Services Committees. With glacial disdain for the title of leader, Russell said no to Johnson, and then asked Johnson himself to be the new leader. Johnson, who must have had a strong suspicion that this was precisely what Russell would do, quickly agreed. But he extracted a promise that Russell would move his seat in the Senate to the desk directly behind the leader's desk. Johnson wanted Russell's advice available at all times.

Johnson hungered for the leadership for two basic reasons. First, his ambition propelled him automatically to the next rung on the ladder. Second, he was afraid that if he—the whip and heir apparent—were not picked to fill the vacancy, his own state of Texas would mark him a failure.

And so, after talking to Russell, Johnson began a series of long-distance telephone calls to Democratic Senators around the country, informing his friends that he had decided to run for leader and letting others know obliquely that, with McFarland gone, Johnson was the natural successor.

One new Senator he called was John F. Kennedy, fresh from an upset first-term victory in Massachusetts, unseating Republican Henry Cabot Lodge. Kennedy and his campaign aides could scarcely believe their ears when the Johnson call came through from Texas even before the polls had closed. Johnson's goal with Kennedy was not to tie down his vote on the leadership question, but to let the new Senator know that Johnson was aware of Kennedy's triumph. Johnson was "romancing" Kennedy, and Kennedy was highly impressed.

He "romanced" a score of other Senators, some of whom he asked outright for support, while handling others as he handled Kennedy. Johnson was careful not to tip his hand to Senators who might end up in someone else's camp. Instead of telephoning direct to Mike Mansfield of Montana, a Congressman elected to the Senate for the first time in 1952, Johnson called one of Mansfield's close friends, Montanan James Rowe—the same Rowe who as a White House aide had helped usher Johnson into Franklin Roosevelt's New Guard in the late 1930's. Johnson and Mansfield had never been close when they served in the House together. So Johnson asked Rowe to find out whether Mansfield would support him for leader. The implication was that Rowe might help out if needed. The Johnson call to Rowe turned out to be superfluous. Mansfield already had wired Johnson on his own with a pledge of support.

The next steps in the Johnson campaign were "spontaneous" public statements by three carefully chosen Senators proposing Johnson for leader while Johnson maintained a shy reticence at the LBJ Ranch. The first of the trio was Russell himself, who declared: "He [Johnson] is highly qualified for the job and, in my opinion, he will be chosen for it." Next was Johnson's faithful follower from the Class of '48, Delaware's Allen Frear. The third endorsement was perhaps the most important. It came from Earle C. Clements, a bald, beefy Kentuckian elected to the Senate two years earlier.*

Clements was uniquely valuable to Johnson for his ability to move in two worlds—the inner world of the Senate oligarchy and the outer world of the liberal-oriented, national Democratic party. A former House member well known in Washington, Clements was quickly taken into the Senate's Inner Club through the sponsorship of Virgil Chapman, Kentucky's senior Senator and a minor member of the oligarchy. It was through Chapman that Clements quickly struck up a warm relationship with Johnson. When Virgil Chapman died on March 8, 1951, Johnson pushed Clements—sworn into the Senate little more than two months earlier—to assume Chapman's seat on the Senate Democratic Policy Committee. Two liberals, Herbert Lehman of New York and Paul Douglas of Illinois, applied for the vacancy. Both had

---

* Johnson's public reaction to the triad of encomiums was suitably modest: "I have been honored and am very grateful to the Senators who have expressed confidence in me. It is a matter that the Senate conference [caucus] later will decide."

seniority over Clements, and Lehman wanted the spot badly. The omnipotent Russell, wanting to keep the Policy Committee in friendly hands, disregarded seniority and selected Clements. But unlike Johnson and Russell, Clements had liberal credentials hard to assail. His voting record was solidly liberal, his contacts with organized labor were excellent, and his stance on the emotion-charged oil and gas issue was solidly on the side of the consumer. Visceral liberals like Paul Douglas might distrust Clements but they could scarcely brand him a Dixiecrat. Moreover, while Russell stayed home in Georgia during the 1952 presidential campaign and said not a word for Adlai Stevenson, and Johnson only went through the motions of a few speeches for Stevenson in Texas quite late in the campaign, Clements was a bona fide loyalist. He came out strongly for the Stevenson-Sparkman ticket from beginning to end.

Consequently, Clements's early endorsement of Johnson as leader served a particularly useful purpose. Friendly journalists quickly interpreted it as a sign that all Democrats, liberals as well as conservatives, were closing ranks around Johnson following the 1952 election defeat (even though Clements was certainly not of the Douglas-Lehman school of liberals).

Johnson had an additional use for Clements. He wanted Clements to succeed him as Minority Whip, partly as an ostensible "concession" to liberals, but mainly because he wanted to give the job a new, more powerful dimension. Johnson wanted to take advantage of Clements's proficiency at the back-room political arts. He wanted him to become an assistant *to* the floor leader, rather than just the assistant floor leader. As a visible sign of this enlarged stature, the whip was given a special office and staff for the first time.

But Johnson had in mind far more sweeping reforms in Senate leadership than merely giving the whip something to do. Johnson's instinct for the glittering prospects of new political power served him well during those fast-moving days after the 1952 election. With Dwight Eisenhower preparing to move into the White House as head of the first Republican Administration in twenty years, he realized that Democratic leaders in Congress would assume an overnight importance far transcending the congressional role of the Roosevelt-Truman years.

The entire Democratic power structure was in a state of upheaval and Johnson was quick to perceive his opportunity. Sam Rayburn, of course, was secure in the House as number one Democrat. But in the Senate, the liberals were certain to try to elect one of their own as Minority Leader. Johnson sensed that whoever became the party's floor leader in the Senate would be at the center of action in the defeated, demoralized party, able to exert massive influence over party policy and program. Now the Senate Democratic leader had a singular opportunity to rescue that office from its continuing decline since 1938—and Johnson knew it. The Senate liberals, symbolized by Lehman and Douglas but with no real leader, were also aware of the new potential in Senate leadership. Characteristically, however, they were quite unable to organize an effective countermove against Johnson.

The liberal countermove that December, 1952, was marked by an excess of ineptitude that amazed Johnson himself. When Johnson returned to the Capitol from the LBJ Ranch he had far more than one-half the forty-eight Democratic Senators in his pocket committed to vote him in as leader. But now Johnson was aiming higher. He wanted unanimous election, not only to dramatize his new pre-eminence in the party but also because, with well over a majority already committed to him, he saw no advantage for himself in humiliating a liberal who might be foolish enough to run against him.

Johnson's method was to seek out the Senator with the reputation as the chamber's most militant liberal: Hubert Humphrey of Minnesota. When Humphrey and Johnson entered the Senate together four years earlier, they were worlds apart. To the Senate, Humphrey was not the anti-Communist founder of the Minnesota Democratic-Farmer-Labor party but a radical agitator who in 1948 split his party's national convention in two ("the black knight of civil rights," as Humphrey years later described himself).

By contrast, the skinny young Texan was very much in his element in those early Senate years, very self-assured in Humphrey's somewhat envious eyes. Yet Johnson had spotted in

Humphrey a potential ally of value—even when Humphrey's Senate status hit rock bottom his freshman term. Suffering deep frustration as a liberal outsider in the conservative Senate, Humphrey had exploded on the Senate floor with an attack against an unlikely target: mild-mannered Senator Harry Flood Byrd of Virginia, the aging high priest of economic conservatism. Humphrey had shocked the Senate by indicting Byrd's Joint Committee on Nonessential Expenditures (which consisted largely of Byrd press releases decrying federal spending) as the most nonessential expenditure in Washington. Outraged by the freshman Senator's brash attack on a ranking oligarch, the Senate retorted with a withering repudiation of Humphrey's attack from both sides of the aisle.

Johnson, of course, did not defend Humphrey's indiscretion either publicly or privately. But he refused to join the rest of the Senate in treating Humphrey as an untouchable. Asking Humphrey to visit him in the Senate Office Building, Johnson suggested that he might get along better in the Senate if he studied and came to know the Senate's inner directors—instead of attacking them. Smooth some of the rough edges off your liberal politics, he urged Humphrey. Specifically, he suggested that Humphrey make friends with one of the Senate's most imperious grandees— Walter George of Georgia—because some day he might need George's friendship. Humphrey took the suggestion to heart and slowly recovered from the Byrd affair to make friends with Walter George.

That wasn't the only advice Johnson supplied Humphrey. As the year passed, he gave Humphrey a short course on the Senate and how it really functioned. He explained the importance of knowing the strengths and weaknesses of every Senator, of concentrating on committee work and of mastering a specialty. He explained that Muriel Humphrey ought to become friendly with other Senators' wives. Teasing Humphrey about his pals in the ADA and the CIO, Johnson made it clear that Humphrey was *his* kind of liberal.

How far down the road Johnson was looking on that distant day he did not say, but with his instinct for the ebb and flow of politics, and his eye on the long chance, he may well have had in his mind some faint plan that would link himself and Hubert Humphrey. One was a moderate Southerner with a Populistic heritage, the other a militant Northern liberal who, Johnson well knew, would be bound to move toward the middle of the road. Humphrey would become indispensable to Johnson in his rapid rise to power in the Senate, defending him time and again against suspicious liberals. Indeed, as the years went by, Humphrey's own liberal credentials would become slightly blurred, at first just in the eyes of the few political insiders who knew of his generally shrouded relationship with Johnson but later, after the 1964 election, by many more critical liberals.

Now, in December, 1952, seeking liberal acceptance of him as Majority Leader, Johnson turned to Humphrey. In a post-election talk with Humphrey, he carefully avoided specific mention of the leadership question. Instead, Johnson revealed for the first time his daring plan to modify the Senate's historic seniority rule. He added that the Democrats needed a "good, strong man" on the Foreign Relations Committee, a much sought-after post Humphrey could not demand because of his short Senate tenure, and that Harry Truman, then in his last days as President, had personally recommended Humphrey. For Humphrey, that was heady stuff. He told Johnson he indeed wanted the Foreign Relations Committee slot.

Silent on the leadership question, Johnson's only purpose was to make Humphrey aware of the fact that Johnson regarded him as a rather special fellow. That, thought Johnson, would be enough to cool off Humphrey's participation in the leadership question. But Humphrey already had decided that the liberals must make a bid for the leadership that would display their strength, even though bound to lose. The liberal Democrat whom Humphrey picked (Humphrey himself was far too controversial) was aging, millionaire Montana cattleman James Murray. Never more than a pedestrian politician, Senator Murray by now was in his twilight years, a benign Western liberal who specialized in introducing federal aid to education bills that passed the Senate and died in the House.

Humphrey, Murray, and other liberal Democrats began recruiting and on the eve of the first Senate Democratic caucus of the 83d Congress, at which the new leader would be elected, they thought they had a respectable seventeen or eighteen votes for Murray and against Johnson, out of the total forty-eight. Then Johnson summoned Humphrey to his office for their second chat. Johnson came quickly to the point. He wanted Humphrey to back him for leader. He outlined his plans for running the Democratic party in the Senate. He spoke of broadening the Steering and Policy Committees (the leader is automatically chairman of both), so as to give the liberals a larger voice. Humphrey, he said, was a key element in Johnson's grandiose plans for reshaping the Democratic party in the Senate and making it a more vital instrument of party policy and action. When Humphrey explained that he was irrevocably committed to Murray—that he was pledged, locked in, and couldn't change—he got a hard lesson in the Johnson method of doing political business. Johnson pulled from his pocket the printed list of Democratic Senators of the 83d Congress. Humphrey, he said bluntly, was foolish to have allowed himself to be sucked in to support Murray. Humphrey hadn't done his homework, Johnson added, because if he had, he wouldn't be talking about seventeen or eighteen votes for Murray. Johnson started down the list, alphabetically.

He got to Rhode Island's octogenarian Theodore Francis Green, who generally was counted in the liberal camp, and asked Humphrey where Green stood. With Murray, Humphrey replied. You see? said Johnson, that's what I mean. You don't know the facts. You don't even know that Green is going to nominate me. And so it went, down the list of forty-eight Democrats, until only a handful was left and Murray's total dwindled. Johnson bore down. Humphrey and the liberals, he said, would look foolish when the vote was taken. Murray would be humiliated. Why make a fight under these conditions? But Humphrey, although thoroughly chastened, could not break his commitment. He changed the subject, and asked Johnson about liberal representation on the Steering and Policy Committees.

Almost curtly, Johnson said: No, I don't want to talk about that now. You put up your man [Murray] and we'll put up our man [Johnson] and we'll see what happens. If you want to talk to me later, I'll discuss these other matters with you.

And so, on that rainy January 3, just before the convening of the new Senate, when the Democrats met to elect their new leaders, the result was precisely as Johnson predicted. Murray's total was so small it was not even announced, to spare Murray his humiliation. (No record was kept and the exact number—Humphrey remembers just three votes—is now lost forever.) Humphrey himself moved to make Johnson's selection unanimous.

After the Senate adjourned that day with Johnson now established as Democratic leader, he visited Humphrey's office and offered to talk *now* about the Steering and Policy Committees. Despite his lopsided victory, it rankled Johnson that the liberals hadn't supported him. He told Humphrey: I'll talk to you, but I'm not going to deal with any of those other blankety-blank liberals. I'm not going to talk to those so-and-so's. You tell me what liberals you want on Policy and Steering, and I'll put them on but I won't talk to them. . . .

True to his tip to Humphrey, Johnson added to the Policy Committee two bona fide liberals to join the only holdover liberal, Green of Rhode Island, in those first days of 1953: Thomas Hennings of Missouri, and Johnson's challenger for the leadership, old Jim Murray. He also added Ed Johnson of Colorado, who had been Russell's campaign manager for the presidential nomination the previous year, and Earle Clements. With the four carry-overs, this meant that the liberals now had three out of nine Policy Committee seats, far from a majority but a fair number in proportion to their ratio in the Senate then.*

As for the fifteen-man Steering Committee, Johnson gave Humphrey a seat along with three other liberals, raising the left-of-center ratio to its highest peak, but short of a majority. The Steering Committee had only one function—to assign Senators to standing committees, a seemingly innocuous role. In fact, since the committees were the heart of the Senate, the assignment role could make or break individual Senators.

* Of the four carry-overs, three were to the right of center: Russell of Georgia, Hayden of Arizona, and Kerr of Oklahoma. The fourth, Lister Hill of Alabama, voted the straight Southern line on all issues touching race but took a strong liberal position on many social welfare issues, particularly in the field of health.

Nevertheless, despite the new change in the Steering Committee, the inner directorate headed by Russell held the real power over committee assignments, and Russell wasn't even on the Steering Committee.

It was vital, therefore, for Johnson to win Russell's consent before he could carry out his historic reform of the seniority system. With Russell behind him, the Steering Committee presented no problem. Without Russell, the Johnson reform couldn't succeed.

Before Lyndon Johnson's leadership, the criterion for getting assigned to a committee was length of service in the Senate. For example, if two Senators sworn into office the same day were competing for a single committee vacancy, and one of them had served previously in the House, he automatically got preference. Similarly, a former governor had priority over a Senator with equal seniority who had never been a governor. This rigidity made it impossible to place a new Senator where his talents best suited him if a Senator with one day more seniority happened to want that committee.

A concrete case confronted Johnson in January, 1953. Newly elected Senator Stuart Symington of Missouri, who had grown close to Johnson in fighting alongside him for a seventy-group Air Force as Secretary of the Air Force under Truman, would have been barred by the seniority system from the Senate Armed Services Committee. Johnson had watched the seniority system deprive qualified younger members of committee seats during his fifteen years in the House and Senate. He personally had been immune to it, simply because of patronage by President Roosevelt in the House in 1937 and by Russell and the other Southerners in the Senate in 1949. Now, as the new Senate leader, he decided to risk a major party row by proposing to break the seniority system.

Johnson's first step, naturally enough, was to minimize that risk by talking to Russell. In those days Johnson never made a tactical move without getting—and generally taking—the advice of the dour-faced Georgian whose grasp of Senate politics and innate common sense gave him towering prestige among his colleagues. Russell was Johnson's touchstone on every conceivable problem.

When Johnson broached his revolutionary idea, Russell surprised him by replying that he, too, had always favored giving new Senators one good committee instead of making them cool their heels for years on the Post Office and Civil Service Committee. The cautious Russell characteristically added, however, that Johnson would be playing with dynamite in tampering with the hallowed seniority system. As a result of Russell's benign neutrality, the Steering Committee tamely followed Johnson's proposals. Symington was immediately assigned to Armed Services; Humphrey (as Johnson had hinted) to Foreign Relations, along with the just-elected Mike Mansfield; Herbert Lehman of New York to Banking and Currency; and John F. Kennedy to Labor and Public Welfare. With Russell not objecting, this fracturing of the seniority system went by without visible anger from any of the old Senate grandees. Instead, Johnson was praised in the press—and, far more important, collected political IOU's from the freshman Democrats whom he helped. In one blow he had accomplished a multiple increase in the power of his office. . . .

The Johnson System

The new Senate force *implicit* in Johnson's two years as Minority Leader (culminating in [Sen. Joseph] McCarthy's censure) became *explicit* when Johnson took over as Majority Leader, with narrow Democratic control of the Senate, after the 1954 elections. George A. Smathers, the debonair young Senator from Florida (who was only dimly aware of Johnson's presence when they served together in the House), years later described Johnson's presence in the Senate as "a great, overpowering thunderstorm that consumed you as it closed in around you." Bryce Harlow, who twice had turned down job offers from Johnson and by now was President Eisenhower's chief congressional lobbyist, perceived in Majority Leader Johnson "a new hauteur" that made him scarcely recognizable to Harlow and other old friends in the House a decade before. Charles Watkins, the sage parliamentarian of the Senate, watched a new force at work in the Senate. Not long after Johnson became Majority Leader, Watkins remarked: "Lyndon's passed bills in a few days that I thought would take weeks. He does more buttonholing and going around than anyone I've ever seen."

Smathers, Harlow, and Watkins each was describing in his own way the Johnson System by which the young Senator from Texas stretched the limits of the Majority Leader's inherently meager power to unimagined boundaries.

The informal directorate of the Senate, headed by Richard B. Russell, insensibly yielded operational control and power to Johnson. It was a remarkable surrender considering that the power ratio of the Senate—evenly divided between Republicans and Democrats, ideologically weighted in favor of the conservatives—was unchanged from the earlier postwar years and was not to be altered until the 1958 elections. When Smathers, Harlow, and Watkins—and many others as well—described the momentous changes of the Senate in terms of Lyndon Johnson's personality, they reported the surprising truth. For the Johnson System was a highly personalized, intensive system of Senate rule adaptable to no successor. Because it involved so little institutional change, the Johnson System vanished overnight once Lyndon B. Johnson himself left the Senate. It was as though it had never existed.

Through most if its history, the Senate had been a cockpit of debaters—Websters and Calhouns, La Follettes and Tafts. Only twice before Johnson's rule had a Majority Leader achieved real power and control. The first occasion was a two-year reign by the imperious Republican aristocrat, Nelson W. Aldrich of Rhode Island, in 1908 and 1909. Under Aldrich, the majority leadership reached its peak of institutional authority. Aldrich had sole power to name all members of standing committees—a power destined for short life in a feudal-like institution whose members possessed baronial equality. Not until the long tenure of Democrat Joseph Robinson of Arkansas—Minority Leader from 1923 to 1928 and Majority Leader from 1928 to 1937—was the Senate again brought under tight control. Robinson utilized his personal authority, born of fourteen years as party floor leader, to compensate for his lack of institutionalized power.

Lacking both Aldrich's institutional power and Robinson's long tenure, Johnson had to concoct his own System. Highly personalized and instinctive as it was, the Johnson System stemmed from no grand master-plan or tightly organized chart. Simply stated, the System can be broken down into two interlocking components: the Johnson Network and the Johnson Procedure. The Network was the source of Johnson's power, the tool essential to put into effect the Procedure that enabled one man to tame the Senate and bring it under control for the first time in eighteen years. . . .

Indispensable to the Johnson System were generous rewards for consistent good conduct. While distinguished economist Paul Douglas spent years angrily and anxiously waiting for a seat on the tax-writing Finance Committee, Frear went on it quickly (as well as onto the Banking and Currency Committee). Moreover, Johnson did all in his power for Frear's pet bill: a tax-relief measure for Delaware's dominating industry, E. I. Du Pont de Nemours & Company. Du Pont's request was opposed even by the conservative Treasury Department of the Eisenhower Administration.* . . .

At the core of the Johnson Network were his peers—Senate grandees to whom he turned more for advice than for votes. Richard Russell, of course; Clinton Anderson; Styles Bridges, the Senate's senior Republican; and—one to whom he turned far more often than most realized—his old seat-mate from the Class of '48, Robert S. Kerr. Sometimes unsure of himself on the fine points of complex bills, Johnson often picked Kerr's retentive brain. Once when White House officials traveled secretly to Capitol Hill to give Johnson a confidential advance peek at a new Eisenhower farm bill, they were taken aback to find Kerr waiting for them with Johnson.

Essential to the Johnson Network was the informal, uncoordinated system of lieutenants that he established soon after becoming Majority Leader. Senator Earle Clements of Kentucky—now the Majority Whip—was general handyman and assistant to Johnson and was still able to move moderately well among all

---

* The fact that a combination of liberal Democrats and Eisenhower Administration officials prevented passage of the Du Pont bill contributed to Frear's defeat in 1960. Ironically, the bill passed in 1961, with support from the Kennedy Administration.

factions of Senate Democrats (though he had become increasingly distrusted by the liberals). Taking up that slack with the liberals was Senator Hubert Humphrey of Minnesota. By 1955, though the general public and even much of the Senate failed to realize it, the one-time stereotype of ADA-style liberalism had become a full-fledged lieutenant of Lyndon Johnson. They still disagreed about many matters, just as Russell and Johnson often disagreed. But as much as Russell, though less openly, Humphrey was a Johnson man.

The most important of Johnson's lieutenants in 1955 was no Senator at all. Bobby G. Baker, now twenty-six, had been promoted to Secretary of the Senate Majority when the Democrats regained control in 1955, approved routinely by the Senate Democratic caucus on the Majority Leader's recommendation. Baker promptly remade that job to fit his own specifications, just as Johnson was remaking the majority leadership to fit his. Thus, a routine housekeeping sinecure became in Baker's hands—and with Johnson's blessing—a position of great authority. Mistakenly shrugged off for years by many Senators as a cloakroom chatterbox, Baker now began to eclipse Senator Clements himself as Johnson's top assistant. When Johnson was running the Senate from the Bethesda hospital bed after his heart attack, he relayed his instructions through Bobby Baker. The bouncy, ingratiating—and immensely able—young man from Pickens, South Carolina, came to be called "the ninety-seventh Senator" and "Lyndon, Jr." . . .

To build his Network, Johnson stretched the meager power resources of the Majority Leader to the outer limit. The mightiest of these was his influence over committee assignments. Still, it was not comparable to the absolute power enjoyed by Nelson Aldrich a half century before. As chairman of the Democratic Steering Committee, Johnson steadily widened the breach in rigid seniority rules, working delicately with a surgical scalpel, not a stick of dynamite. . . .

Johnson's use of power to influence committee assignments cut both ways. "Good" liberals, such as Humphrey, could be prematurely boosted into the Foreign Relations Committee, and a "bad" liberal, such as Kefauver, could be made to cool his heels for years. A "bad" liberal such as Paul Douglas could be barred from the Finance Committee for eight long years, while five fellow members of the Class of '48 (Kerr, Long, Frear, Anderson, and Johnson himself) and one from the Class of '50 (Smathers) were finding places there.* Senators who dared to function too far outside the Johnson Network waited long to get inside the prestige committees. . . .

The Johnson Procedure

At the opening of the 1951 Senate session, when Richard Russell named Lyndon Johnson as floor manager of the universal military training bill (his first major floor assignment), the Senate could justly claim itself to be "the world's greatest deliberative body." The Korean War was raging, and President Truman badly needed passage of the bill to bring the armed forces to full strength. But the Senate took its time, as it had since its earliest days. Debate on the bill—stretching from February 27 to March 9—had the urgency of a chess game at an exclusive men's club. There was an unhurried discursive tone as the learned Senators—Richard Russell, Wayne Morse, Robert Taft, Henry Cabot Lodge, Herbert Lehman—probed every corner of the bill. The sessions seldom ran beyond six o'clock in the evening, and the chamber was closed over the weekends. Senator Ernest McFarland, the Majority Leader, tried to hurry the Senate along, but he wasn't overly concerned by the languorous pace or the frequency and uncertainty of roll calls on amendments. As floor manager of the bill, Johnson naturally joined in debate, delivering long, rambling speeches. But Johnson did not enter the game with the zest of a Taft or Russell. He seemed impatient with this kind of Senate.

* This extraordinary treatment of Douglas also reflected Johnson's desire to keep the Finance Committee free of Northern liberals opposing special tax advantages for the oil and gas industry. But if Douglas had been a "good" liberal in the Humphrey mold, Johnson could have shaved a point, since the Finance Committee was already so stacked in favor of the oil and gas industry.

The Senate had always been that way, even in the days of Nelson Aldrich and Joe Robinson. In 1883 the young Woodrow Wilson wrote of the Senate in *Congressional Government:*

It must be regarded as no inconsiderable addition to the usefulness of the Senate that it enjoys a much greater freedom of discussion than the House can allow itself. It permits itself a good deal of talk in public about what it is doing, and it commonly talks a great deal of sense.

But it would not be hurried, and, without a rule of germaneness, it could not stick to the point, as Senator Lester Hunt of Wyoming perceived in 1952, on the eve of the Johnson System. Hunt complained: "Any state legislature in the United States would make the Senate of the United States look very bad in connection with procedure." Indeed, the "procedure" of the Senate was geared to slow talk, not vital action.

Johnson was quite aware that he could never establish an efficient procedure by modernizing the encrusted Senate rules. His only recourse, then, as the new Majority Leader, was by trial and error, to evolve slowly the Johnson Procedure—along with the Network, the second major component of the Johnson System.

The principal ingredient of the Procedure was flexibility. On any major piece of legislation, never make a commitment as to what will pass; determine in advance what is *possible* under the best of circumstances for the Senate to accept; after making this near-mathematical determination, don't reveal it; keep the leader's intentions carefully masked; then, exploiting the Johnson Network, start rounding up all detachable votes; when all is in readiness, strike quickly and pass the bill with a minimum of debate.

Essential to making the Johnson Procedure work in this fashion was divided government: a Democratic Majority Leader and a Republican President. Freed of obligation to shepherd a White House program through a Democratic Senate (because the White House was in Republican hands), Johnson could hold his own cards and play his own game. Although divided government had come to Washington before, as recently as the Republican 80th Congress of 1947–48 under President Truman, no previous leader in a divided government had had Johnson's political wit. Besides,

Johnson genuinely wanted to *pass* bills, not just block everything sent up by the Republican President.

Johnson had another advantage: the Johnson Intelligence System. Unlike his predecessors, Johnson was constantly probing beneath the Senate's bland exterior to discover what the Senate was really thinking. The Intelligence System was a marvel of efficiency. It was also rather frightening. One evening in the late 1950's, Senator Thruston Morton of Kentucky (the Republican who defeated Earle Clements in 1956) dined with seven political reporters at the Metropolitan Club. The meeting was off-the-record. The reporters had been working as a team for several years. All were sworn to secrecy, and there had never been a leak. Morton laid bare some fascinating behind-the-scenes divisions in the Republican party. A few days later, one of the reporters called on Johnson in his Capitol office. Johnson bitterly chided him and the Washington press corps for writing column after column about the divisions in the Democratic party while ignoring internal tensions in the Republican party. To prove his point, Johnson dipped into one of the deep wire baskets on his desk and fished out a memorandum on the "confidential" Morton session—complete in every detail.

The thoroughness of Johnson's Intelligence System worried his fellow Senators, some of whom began to half doubt the security of their own telephone conversations. But Johnson needed no help from electronic eavesdropping. His intelligence had a dazzling multiplicity of sources tucked away in surprising places all over Washington. Bobby Baker and his team of cloakroom attendants were in constant touch and conversation with Senators. Johnson's staff was alert to report what they heard on the floor from other Senators and their staffs. The Johnson Network of friendly Senators kept him informed. Johnson himself was constantly probing and questioning other Senators in the cloakrooms, over late-afternoon drinks, during hamburger lunches, in his office. Occasionally aides of other Senators were invited to lunch with the Majority Leader. Immensely flattered, they eagerly volunteered what they— and more important, what their bosses—were thinking.

Speaker Rayburn and the Texas congressional delegation kept Johnson fully informed about what was going on inside the House.

Beyond this, moreover, Johnson had loyal friends scattered throughout the government agencies who regularly tipped him on developments.

Johnson took special precautions to maintain a flow of intelligence about the activities of liberal Democrats, his greatest source of trouble in the Senate. Gerry Siegel and later Harry McPherson, his two most liberal staff members, kept lines open to staff members of liberal Senators and sometimes liberal Senators themselves. Robert Oliver, the United Auto Workers staff member from Texas who had maneuvered the CIO behind Johnson in his 1948 campaign and who was now Walter Reuther's chief lobbyist in Washington, was in constant touch with both Johnson and the liberals. But the most important conduit to the liberals was Hubert Humphrey. Johnson had such intimate knowledge of liberal battle plans to reform Rule XXII (the filibuster rule) in January, 1957, that liberals suspected a leak in their own camp. Specifically, they suspected that Humphrey, Bob Oliver, or possibly both, were passing word of their secret meetings to the Majority Leader.

The distillation of intelligence was the head count—the report on how each Senator would vote on a given issue. This delicate judgment of each Senator's intentions was entrusted to Bobby Baker, who compiled the famous head counts in their final form. Baker's head counts were an invaluable asset for Johnson not available to labor, to business, to the Republicans, or even to the White House. Baker's invariably precise count not only gave Johnson the odds on a bill, but what votes he had to switch. This enabled Johnson to energize the Network and get a sufficient number of Senators to change their votes, or at least arrange for Network Senators who opposed the Johnson position to linger in the cloakroom while the roll was called. Johnson controlled the speed of the actual roll call by signaling the reading clerk—slowing it down until the Senator with the deciding vote (on Johnson's side, of course) entered the chamber, then speeding it up (by a quick rotary movement of his forefinger) when the votes he needed were in hand.

Very infrequently the Johnson-Baker count would be off by a single tally. Perhaps an anti-Johnson Senator would return unexpectedly from out of town to vote. If that happened, Johnson would flash an S.O.S. to the cloakroom and a Network Senator would emerge, then signal the reading clerk that he wanted to cast his vote and tip the balance to Johnson.

That was the dramatic culmination of the Johnson Procedure. Never had a Majority Leader maintained so precise a check on the preferences and the possibilities of every colleague. But inherent in the Johnson Procedure were basic changes in the daily operation of the Senate, changes emanating from the personality of the Majority Leader and evolving so slowly that they were ignored by the public and scarcely recognized in the Senate itself. Yet they were insensibly transforming the Senate. No longer was it the deliberative body described by Woodrow Wilson in 1883 and found relatively intact when Lyndon Johnson arrived in 1949. . . .

Just as Thomas Jefferson was a strong President who weakened the presidency as an institution, so did Lyndon Johnson tame the Senate and make it work for him but leave it a weaker institution than he found it.

MIKE MANSFIELD, MAJORITY LEADER

ANDREW J. GLASS

In January, 1966, Senate Majority Leader Mike Mansfield, (D-Mont.) was summoned to the White House for one of the bipartisan advice-seeking sessions favored by former President Lyndon B. Johnson on the eve of major policy decisions. When it came Mansfield's turn to speak, he unfolded a three-page typewritten statement drafted in the dry style of a college professor—which he once was. He argued in the statement that air raids over North Vietnam, which had been suspended for a month-long "peace offensive," should not be resumed. Some days after the White House meeting, Mansfield watched on television in his Capitol office, S-210, as Mr. Johnson announced that the bombing halt was over. "I feel so sorry for him," Mansfield said. "I can imagine what he's going through."

The remark reflected a compassionate side of Mansfield's complex character. Sen. Hubert H. Humphrey (D-Minn.) once alluded to this quality when he observed that "there is no meanness in him." "Keep in mind," Humphrey added in an interview, "the things he says, no matter how critical, do not spring from personal ambition, but rather as a reflection of his own mind and conscience."

Mansfield now says of the Johnson period: "It's not easy to say

Excerpted from *National Journal*, March 6, 1971, pp. 499–512 by permission of the publisher. Andrew Glass is a staff writer for *National Journal*.

'no' to the President in that oval office, where he is surrounded by all of his advisers and chiefs of staff. I guess I had to do that half a dozen times." Mansfield's forgiving approach to politics remains one of the chief reasons why a Senate in which personal ambition is no stranger manages to function with a minimum of rancor.

While the Mansfield and Johnson political styles are poles apart, Mansfield shares with Johnson, who was his predecessor as Majority Leader, a somewhat mystical sense of the Senate's dignity and integrity. In spite of his forgiving nature, Mansfield cannot abide behavior that tends to throw the Senate into disrepute.

Senate Minority Leader Hugh Scott (R-Pa.) describes Mansfield as "the most decent man I've ever met in public life. He's fair. And his word rates in fineness above the gold at Fort Knox."

There is a certain bleakness to the Mansfield landscape: his smile, while warm, is not quick in coming. Mansfield's public life is increasingly governed by the credo once espoused by the seventeenth-century English poet John Dryden when he wrote:

> For all the happiness
> Man can gain
> Is not in pleasure,
> But in rest from pain.

At 67, Mansfield is six feet tall and weighs 170 pounds. He speaks in short declarative sentences in a flat style that has been compared to that of a sheriff of the Old West. The Majority Leader has long been one of the most casual dressers in the Senate. Lately, the contrast with his colleagues has sharpened; he often appears in the Senate wearing a sport jacket and yellow socks.

Career

Michael J. Mansfield was born March 16, 1903, in Manhattan's Greenwich Village. He was reared in Great Falls, Montana, the first son of Irish immigrant parents, who ran a grocery store below their apartment. As a youth, Mansfield ran away from home three times, ending up twice in the Great Falls city jail, the second time overnight, before his third and successful attempt.

He entered the Navy on February 23, 1918, at age 14, for the duration of World War I. In 1919, he enlisted in the Army for one year, and then enlisted in the Marine Corps for two years, serving mainly in China.

In 1922, he returned to Montana to work in the Butte copper mines, 3,000 feet below the surface, for the next eight years. While working as a miner, he met Maureen Hayes, a Butte schoolteacher. Miss Hayes encouraged him to resume his studies (he had never finished grade school) while Mansfield encouraged her to marry him, which she did.

He attended the University of Montana at Missoula from 1930 to 1934, where he received his bachelor's and master's degrees. Mansfield then embarked upon a new career as an associate professor of Latin American and Far Eastern history at the university, where he taught for ten years. He still retains permanent tenure there as a professor of history.

Mansfield ran for Congress in 1942 and served five terms in the House (1943–53). He was elected to the Senate in 1952 and re-elected in 1958, 1964, and 1970. Johnson engineered his election as Majority Whip in 1957. When Johnson became Vice-President in 1961, John F. Kennedy persuaded a reluctant Mansfield to serve as Majority Leader. He has held that position longer than any other Senator.

Mansfield wields the full power inherent in his position only to protect the interests of his 682,000 Montana constituents. [He] has been known to keep Cabinet officers waiting in his outer office while he chatted amiably with a touring Montana family. Over the years, copper mining legislation and other measures of direct interest to his state have been safely guided through the Senate. Should Mansfield come to feel that Montana has been short-changed in its slice of federal funds, he is apt to summon the agency chief to his office for a head-to-head talk. This is a fearsome and parochial side of Mansfield which outsiders rarely see. In nonelection years, he returns to Montana only a few times a year, mainly to speak on college campuses.

Mansfield's campaign style is to come into a hotel lobby an hour or so before the scheduled start of a political dinner and to stand quietly in a corner with his wife, smoking a pipe. As soon as he is recognized, a reception line forms and everyone comes up to shake his hand.

Last year, in an October 28 Great Falls campaign speech, Mansfield said: "Every candidate who runs for public office has the duty and obligation to lay his whole life before the people he seeks to represent."

In 1970, Mansfield ran against Harold E. (Bud) Wallace, a Missoula sporting-goods salesman. Wallace accused Mansfield during the campaign of "being soft on communism." The issue failed to take root when President Nixon sent an Air Force plane to Glasgow Air Force Base in Glasgow, Montana, to fly Mansfield to New York, where he accompanied the President on an October 23 visit to the United Nations.

Mansfield ignored his opponent, never mentioned him in the campaign, and won 150,060 to 97,809.

While in Washington, Mansfield usually arrives at the Capitol before 7 A.M. in a car chauffeured by Lorenzo M. Lee. He has breakfast with his closest friend in the Senate, George D. Aiken (R-Vt.) and Aiken's wife, Lola, who is her husband's administrative assistant. By 8:15, he is in his Capitol office, dictating letters, drafting speeches, and conferring with his senior staff. Mansfield leaves the office ten minutes before the start of a Senate session for his daily press conference behind the Majority Leader's desk on the Senate floor. Normally, he skips lunch; when he does eat, it is alone in his office.

Depending on the nature of the business before the Senate, Mansfield will remain on the floor or ask his deputy, Sen. Robert C. Byrd (D-W.Va.) to monitor the debate. He will see visitors throughout the afternoon, coming off the Senate floor or from the cloakroom retreat to meet with them in his office. In late afternoon, Mansfield usually returns to his "Montana office," a six-room suite in the old Senate Office Building, where he dictates and signs mail until he leaves for home.

The Mansfields' social schedule is comparatively light. He prefers to be home by 10 P.M. The Mansfields' only child, Anne, is an economics writer in London.

Humphrey once observed that Mansfield "is a political leader who refuses to be pressured. He resents outside contacts. He calls that 'lobbying.'"

Mansfield also abhors the idea of acquiring or exercising power for his own account. When he became majority leader, he halted the practice of conducting the kind of painstaking pre-ballot senatorial head counts that Robert G. (Bobby) Baker once handled for Lyndon Johnson in their years together. The White House filled the void until 1969; since then, the policy committee staff has quietly resumed head counts—without the vote-by-vote fine tuning that marked the Johnson years.

Mansfield is unwilling to say whether the Johnson high-pressure power-broker system or his own far more gentle approach ("Senators will have to live up to their responsibilities; all Senators are equal") works best in the long run. "We're different personalities, and we have faced different problems," Mansfield said in an interview. "It's just not a fair comparison. But Johnson was the greatest Majority Leader the Senate ever had."

In 1970, most rank-and-file Senators quite predictably favor the Mansfield technique. As former Sen. John J. Williams (R-Del., 1947–71) once observed: "When Lyndon was the leader, he liked to play tricks on you. The game was always trying to outfox Lyndon. But I would never try to pull anything like that on Mike. Why, he'd just turn around and say, 'The Senator, of course, is perfectly within his rights.'"

Senate Leadership: A Twentieth-Century Innovation

In 1885, Woodrow Wilson wrote in his book *Congressional Government* that "No one is *the* Senator. No one may speak for his party as well as for himself." Well into the twentieth century, the Democrats and Republicans elected a chairman for their respective conferences, but no Senator was elected to serve as the Majority or Minority Leader, as those offices are known today. The party conference is in theory the supreme organ of the legislative party, as the national convention is of the national party. But, until Senate Majority Leader Mansfield, D-Mont., recently revived the conference machinery, its principal function was to elect party leaders at the start of each session.

In the view of Lyndon B. Johnson, once a Senate Majority Leader (1955–61), not much can be accomplished in a conference. Johnson maintained that the issues that divide a party cannot be settled in a plenary forum, even when it is held in secret.

On January 15, 1920, a Democratic conference was called for the first time for the purpose "of selecting a leader for the Democrats of the Senate." They elected Senator Oscar W. Underwood (Ala., 1915–27) as "Minority Leader." (The Republicans elected a leader of their own in 1925.) But down into the 1930's, it was common practice for committee chairmen to take up a bill on the Senate floor without consulting the party leader.

The office of Majority Leader is not mentioned in any Senate rule. But the leader is recognized by law in that special funds are appropriated each year for the office. (Mansfield currently earns $49,500, a $7,000 premium over the annual salary of other Senators. In addition, he is entitled to several special staffs and such additional perquisites of office as the use of a telephone-equipped Cadillac.) Since 1927 and 1937, the Democratic leader and the Republican leader, respectively, have continuously occupied the front row seat on their party's side of the center aisle.

In 1946, the Joint Committee on the Organization of the Congress, then in GOP hands, reported that "strong recommendations" had been made to it concerning the need for a body to express formally the main policy lines of the majority and minority parties. The Senate had provided for the creation of Republican and Democratic policy committees for each chamber in the Legislative Reorganization Act of 1946 (60 Stat 812), but the House deleted the provision from the bill. The Senate established the committees by attaching them as a rider to the fiscal 1947 legislative money bill (60 Stat 911). The law fixed membership at seven Senators each, with the party leader to serve as chairman.

The original policy committee concept called for a membership chosen to provide both ideological and geographic balance, a concept that has been followed ever since. Committee chairmen were to be omitted from the roster. While this precept was also followed, committee members in time gained in seniority and influence. Many of them eventually became committee chairmen, but retained their policy committee seats.

Sen. Alben W. Barkley (D-Ky., 1927–49) was Minority Leader when the policy committee was born. Barkley's Senate leadership, which began in 1937 and lasted until he resigned to become Vice-President, was personal, intuitive, and highly informal. While he set out to hold weekly meetings of the policy committee, he seldom did.

Barkley's successor, Sen. Scott W. Lucas (D-Ill., 1939–51) utilized the policy committee to formulate the legislative schedule and help map floor strategy. But no votes were ever taken, and no decisions were ever held as binding. Barkley came to the meetings and added his weight as Vice-President. Lucas established the principle that the leader cannot be forced to take a man on the committee that he doesn't want. He left a seat vacant for two years rather than name the only logical geographical replacement, a Senator with whom he didn't get along.

Senator Ernest W. McFarland (D-Ariz., 1941–53), who served one term as Majority Leader, viewed the policy committee as a kind of legislative cabinet. He said: "These are the men that the leader would have to deal with anyway, even if there were no policy committee, if he wanted to do his job, although he would not have to deal with them as a group."

The committee declined in influence after Johnson became Minority Leader in 1953. Few votes were taken and few decisions made. The minutes were brief and confidential. Public announcements of committee actions were a rarity. The committee's decline reflected Johnson's personal ascendance. "Lyndon ran his own show," Senator Stuart Symington (D-Mo.), a veteran policy committee member, told National Journal.

One Johnson innovation, dating from 1959, was the addition of three freshman Senators to the policy committee. This group, which was geographically balanced and subsequently expanded to four Senators, is known as the Legislative Review Committee. Originally, its main function was to keep track of minor bills which fellow Democrats objected to and to block their passage on the Senate floor. Sen. Philip A. Hart (D-Mich.), one of the original trio named by Johnson, recently told National Journal: "I remember the days when we ate with the policy committee and participated in the discussion. But it was a gray area whether we were allowed to vote. Johnson kept the issue from ever coming to a head."

The Johnson method of running the Senate eventually incurred the wrath of former Senator Albert Gore (D-Tenn., 1953–71). At a Democratic Conference which Johnson convened January 12, 1960, Gore moved to remake the policy committee into "an organization for evolving coherent party policy on legislation." He sought to have its membership increased to fifteen and selected by the entire conference. The Gore motion lost, 51 to 12.

Ralph K. Huitt, a political scientist who once worked for Johnson when he was Majority Leader, has observed that "leadership in the Senate is highly personal and exceedingly complex. People who know a great deal about it are the ones most reluctant to talk about it." In discussing the subject with *National Journal*, [Mansfield], the [current] Majority Leader, said: "I'm not a king and I have no princes. I have less power than any other Senator. . . . This is a job which is not in the Constitution. It (the power available) is whatever the Senate gives us in the way of cooperation. Basically, we have less power than all the other Senators. But the power of the Senate is tremendous. Yet my power is neither defined nor understood.

"Senators realize that they are treated as I'd like to be treated— as mature men. Their independence is not infringed upon. They know that everything is on the table. They know all about our moves ahead of time. There are no surprises. Lyndon Johnson once said—and he was quite right about this—that 'the only power available to a leader is the power of persuasion. There is no patronage, no power to discipline, no authority to fire Senators like the President can fire members of his Cabinet.' Johnson was an effective Majority Leader. But I look toward the long range. I'm not interested in immediate victories. We're trying to keep the party together despite all the pressures that might divide us."

One divisive pressure, Mansfield acknowledged, would be any contest to succeed him as Majority Leader. Mansfield, however, said he would never seek to designate a successor as had former

Speaker McCormack in choosing to support Representative Carl Albert (D-Okla.) for the Speakership. "Senators are grown men and can make up their own minds," Mansfield said.

A Senator who took his seat in 1953, as did Mansfield, agreed to comment on Mansfield's remarks if he would not be quoted by name. He said: "I'm not at all surprised, although of course it isn't true that he has less power than any other Senator. He doesn't believe that for a moment. But what he was trying to say —and what he *does* believe very strongly—is that other Senators are able to twist and to turn this way and that to suit their political needs—exploiting the rules or even abusing them—whereas Mike to remain effective must play fair. His attitude is sometimes interpreted as one of weakness, but that isn't it at all."

Another Senator who knows Mansfield well and who similarly declined to be quoted, by name said: "The only time I've seen Mike get uptight is when someone crowds his authority as leader. But he has no ego-trip hang-ups and so the others like to work with him. He is also scrupulously fair. I've heard him say, as I'm sure you have, that there is no difference between the oldest and the newest Member. While, strictly speaking, that isn't true, it is Mansfield's approach."

A Southern Democrat told *National Journal* privately: "Mansfield has an acute awareness that Senators must play different and conflicting roles and that the task of his leadership is to structure a situation so that a Senator can select a role that will allow him to stand by his party."

Asked to comment on the statement, Mansfield reflectively chewed on his pipe for several moments and then said: "I guess that's fair."

In his book *The Congresssional Party: A Case Study*, David Truman wrote: "The Majority Leader builds his influence upon a combination of fragments of power." Mansfield is, at one and the same time:

• majority floor leader of the Senate
• chairman of the Democratic Policy Committee
• chairman of the Democratic Conference
• chairman of the Democratic Steering Committee.

Each title adds to his influence and to the size of the professional staff that he controls, although Mansfield is anything but an empire builder.

Republicans divide these tasks among four senators. Currently, Scott serves as minority floor leader; Allott (Colorado) as chairman of the policy committee, Margaret Chase Smith (Maine) as chairman of the Republican Conference, and Wallace F. Bennett (Utah) as chairman of the GOP Committee on Committees, which is the equivalent body to the Democratic Steering Committee.*

Mansfield also possesses what Lyndon B. Johnson once termed "the power of recognition." This is essentially the time-honored duty of the Vice-President, or whomever is presiding over the Senate in his stead, to recognize the Majority Leader above the claims of all others whenever he wants the floor. (Once a Senator is recognized, he may speak or control the debate, until he agrees to yield the floor.) The "power of recognition" has evolved by tradition and is not stated in any Senate rule. The first presiding officer who announced that he would abide by the policy was Vice-President (1933–41) John N. Garner.

This year, the Senate for the first time adopted a unanimous consent agreement, requested by Mansfield and Scott, that the two party leaders be automatically recognized before any other Senators are permitted to speak at the start of each Senate day. The agreement, which will remain in effect for the duration of the Senate session, ensures that the leadership will retain day-to-day control.

Several political scientists have observed that the powers of the Majority Leader are limited by:

• the direct relationship between Senators and their own constituencies, which the leader cannot usually penetrate

• the national constituencies of some Senators, including those who are running or weighing a race for the Presidency

• the system of standing Senate committees with virtually pre-emptive jurisdiction over wide areas of legislation.

---

* Editor's note: In the 1972 election, Gordon Allott and Margaret Chase Smith were defeated. In the 93d Congress, John Tower (R-Tex.) became chairman of the Policy Committee; Norris Cotton (R-N.H.), chairman of the Conference; and Jacob Javits (R-N.Y.) became chairman of the Committee on Committees for Senate Republicans.

A member of the policy committee, who is also a committee chairman, said privately: "Around here, committee chairmen are tribal chiefs to be bargained with, not lieutenants to be commanded. The persons who are least enthusiastic about a strong policy committee composed of committee chairmen, as has been suggested in some quarters, are the chairmen themselves, who have no desire to trade their sovereignty for a vote in council."

Mansfield is sensitive to the power of committee chairmen to bottle up legislation. In order to keep his lines open, he makes it a practice to confer with the chairmen of the Senate's seventeen standing committees on a regular basis, usually over lunch in his office.

Pressure, when applied, is of the gentlest sort. For example, in early February, Mansfield informed Senate Finance Committee Chairman Russell B. Long (D-La.) that the policy committee had approved a resolution urging that social security, welfare reform, and trade matters be considered separately and not as part of a package, as had occurred in the waning days of the 91st Congress.

Mansfield himself has little time for committee work. (He is a member of the two most prestigious Senate committees—Appropriations and Foreign Relations.) Mansfield ranks behind Fulbright and Sen. John Sparkman (D-Ala.) on the Foreign Relations Committee. But Sparkman is already chairman of the Banking and Currency Committee, so if Fulbright should die, resign, or retire, Mansfield would be in line to succeed him. But Mansfield told *National Journal* that "under no circumstances" would he serve in the Senate as a committee chairman.

Although Mansfield said he is willing at all times to confer in private with any of his fellow senators, he sees his colleagues only rarely on that basis. One Mansfield staff aide explained: "The older guys know better than to bother him, and the younger guys are in awe of him." Another Mansfield aide who also requested anonymity said: "Mansfield is an arms-length guy. He'll play a straight and honest game with Senators and with Nixon. He won't have it any other way. The type of politician he can't stand is the guy who will go whisper in the corner. With him, it's all on the table, head-to-head."

Mansfield devotes particular attention to "bringing along" relatively junior Democrats from Southern states by using his influence to ensure that they receive responsible committee posts early in their Senate careers. In this vein, he has named South Carolina's Hollings to the policy committee, and Virginia's Spong and newly elected Senator Lawton Chiles (Fla.) to the steering committee. In addition, with Mansfield's help, Hollings this year won a seat on the Appropriations Committee while Spong, again with a push from Mansfield, was named to the Foreign Relations Committee.

"We've got to look to our younger Members," Mansfield said. "They are a new generation, and they look at the problems of the South in a new way. It should be clearly recognized within their constituencies that the Senate in general and the Democratic Party in particular welcome them and will provide for them. I have told all the new senators—North and South—that I expect them to be seen and heard if they have something to say."

In commenting on Mansfield's "Southern Strategy," Minnesota's Mondale said: "Spong and Chiles represent a shift toward moderation. That probably explains the election of (Sen. Gaylord) Nelson (D-Wis.) to the Finance Committee and of (Sen. Daniel K.) Inouye (D-Hawaii) to the Appropriations Committee. It is not a revolution, but it's a change, in my opinion in the right direction. I think it's almost unprecedented to reach behind a whole army of senators and pick a brand new freshman and put him on the steering committee—which is what he did with Chiles."

Mansfield blocks off a wide swath of potential pressure by refusing to see any Washington or out-of-town lobbyist, in or out of his office, no matter what his background or his cause. Thus, when such major issues as tax reform, civil rights, or the effort to repeal Section 14(b) of the Taft-Hartley Act (61 Stat 136) have reached the Senate floor, Mansfield has remained aloof from the large and diverse group of lobbyists who have sought to affect the course of the legislation on Capitol Hill.

But Mansfield will readily see any constituent from Montana who comes to Washington or will talk with any long-distance caller from the state with a legitimate reason for telephoning him. He does not regard any of his fellow Montanans as lobbyists, and he personally dictates replies to all his mail from the state. . . .

In contrast with lobbyists, congressional reporters enjoy easy access to the Majority Leader. While Mansfield is held to be an extremely poor "leak" on Senate matters that have not been publicly announced, he is most willing to discuss his own views on issues with a candor that is rarely seen on Capitol Hill. All of Mansfield's conversations with reporters and editors are "on the record," in contrast to other Washington politicians who often talk with correspondents on a "not-for-attribution" or "not-for-publication" basis.

Mansfield does not have a press secretary. He is usually available to reporters for about ten minutes before the start of a Senate session. On Saturday mornings, he often meets with the "regulars" within the press corps over coffee in his Capitol office.

Because he refuses to discuss personal relationships and often glosses over Senate disputes in his remarks to reporters, Mansfield has acquired a reputation among some reporters for being politically naive. But one Senate colleague, who is well versed in this aspect of Mansfield's personality, said, "You can be sure that he knows what's going on, including all the bad blood between senators. But he doesn't want to let on that he does know what's going on because he doesn't want to say anything that would tend to bring the Senate into disrepute. . . ."

A high-ranking official of the Democratic National Committee privately told *National Journal*:

". . . Mansfield lives in the institution of the Senate and not in the institution of the Democratic Party. In short, he's a Senate man, not a political man, and in many ways an inscrutable figure."

CHANGE AND CONTINUITY IN THE RECRUITMENT OF U.S. HOUSE LEADERS, 1789–1975

GARRISON NELSON

Whatever their fondest illusions, legislators are no special breed of the human animal fitted by nature to make laws. Legislators are human beings, filled with the same strengths and weaknesses of other members of society. What makes them different is the span of institutional control over our lives. Consequently, one must be aware of the forces that press upon a legislature, for they are far greater than the sum of forces which affect the individual members of it. They are far greater for they span the lifetimes of mere individuals and invest these institutions with the momentum of the accumulated past. Regardless of a legislator's level of awareness or his propensity to act, there can be no question that whatever decisions he makes will have far greater ramifications than decisions made by individual citizens. He can affect more people with greater impact and for a longer duration. He is able to do this through the institutional framework which his society creates for the making of laws, irrespective of the strength and persuasiveness of his own being.

The legislative institution which is to be examined in this study is the U.S. House of Representatives, and if there is one observa-

Garrison Nelson is Assistant Professor of Political Science at the University of Vermont.

tion in which both its critics and its defenders are united, it is the "humanness" of its membership. Fisher Ames, one of Massachusetts' first representatives in Congress, felt secure in the knowledge that the House "is composed of sober, solid, old-charter folks."[1] Alexis de Tocqueville however was less impressed in 1831 when he wrote:

> On entering the House of Representatives at Washington, one is struck by the vulgar demeanor of that great assembly. Often there is not a distinguished man in the whole number. Its members are almost all obscure individuals, whose names bring no associations to mind. They are mostly village lawyers, men in trade, or even persons belonging to the lower classes of society.[2]

Contemporary observers share the same sentiments as both Ames and de Tocqueville. "One absorbs the feeling that this is quite the ordinary America," California's late Representative Clem Miller discovered, "with its narrowness, its humanity, and its immediacy."[3] To William S. White, who, like de Tocqueville, found the Senate more congenial to his tastes, the House is "an agglomeration . . . of middle-class, middle-aged, middle-abilitied Americans who together form an almost perfect microcosm of nonurban America."[4]

Whatever one's attitudes toward typicality may be, it should be clear that representatives are not a breed apart from other members of American society. However, rather than attempting to study each of the thousands of men (and some women) who have been members of the House, we shall limit our attention to those members who have become first among equals by achieving some "positional" or "formal leadership" status in that body. We shall expect to find that our society has left its identifying marks upon those who govern its institutions just as it has upon those who are governed by them. In addition to comparing the social characteristics of House leaders to those of the nation as a whole, we shall examine how these leaders are like, or unlike, the men at the top of the other two branches of the federal government.

The occupants of eight formal leadership positions will be considered the leaders of the House. Apart from the Speakership, no leadership position can be consistently defined over the entire course of House history, for different positions during different eras fulfilled the functions of floor leadership. For this reason, the positions and the relevant years which will be used here to denote the House leadership population are (1) Speaker of the House, 1789 to 1975; (2) the appointed Chairman of the Ways and Means Committee from its inception in the 4th Congress to its separation from floor functions in the 62d Congress, 1795 to 1911; (3) the appointed Chairman of the Appropriations Committee from its inception in the 39th Congress through the 55th Congress, when only the Ways and Means chairman was designated as Majority Leader, 1865 to 1899; (4) the caucus-elected Majority Leaders from the 62d Congress to the present, 1911 to 1975; (5) the minority's nominee for the Speakership, 1863 to 1911; (6) the caucus-elected Minority Leaders, 1911 to 1975; (7) the Republican Party Whips, 1897 to 1975; and (8) the Democratic Party Whips, 1899 to 1909, 1913 to 1915, and 1921 to 1975.[5] These eight positions have been occupied 169 times by 124 different individuals throughout the history of the House. Because many of the House leaders have held more than one of these positions during their leadership careers, the positions themselves will not be separated for analysis.

The Boundaries of Time: Five Party Control Periods

The House, like all institutions that have endured through time, has changed. Very often these changes have been so dramatic and their effects have been so lasting that they make it possible to identify various eras within the two centuries of House history. Because the House is a political institution and its formal power structure is based on partisan considerations, the variables used to differentiate House eras are ones dealing with political party control (e.g., number of parties, sizes of party majorities, frequency and duration of control, alternation rates, and degrees of inter-institutional competition). Using these variables it is possible to detect five distinct and separable periods of political party activity in the House. The eras which appear most evident are:

Period I, 1st through 18th Congresses (1789–1825)
Period II, 19th through 36th Congresses (1825–61)
Period III, 37th through 53d Congresses (1861–95)
Period IV, 54th through 71st Congresses (1895–1931)
Period V, 72d through 93d Congresses (1931–75)

The first period is marked by the growing dominance of the House by the Jeffersonian Democratic-Republicans and the disappearance of the Federalists. This period ends with the election of 1824 and the collapse of the congressional caucus. Period II was beset by extraordinary interparty and intraparty conflict, reflecting the national political disarray which preceded the Civil War. From the Civil War through 1895, Period III, the House had more evenly balanced two-party competition than at any point in its entire history. However, the financial disasters of the 1890's and the gold vs. silver debate within the Democratic party gave the Republicans their greatest opportunity to control the House, which they did in fourteen of the next eighteen Congresses. The Republican hegemony of Period IV was replaced by the Democratic one of Period V when the combined effect of the Depression and Franklin D. Roosevelt created the large and heterogeneous Democratic majority that has organized the House in all but two of the last twenty-two Congresses.

These five period groupings will be used to analyze House leadership changes over time and, where possible, reference will be made to comparable findings concerning other social and political elites and the general public itself.

THE GEOGRAPHY OF LEADERSHIP RECRUITMENT

Any nation which spans and populates a continent in less than two centuries is bound to be fascinated by its spatial dimensions. Geographic and demographic factors, such as location, dispersion, and size, are all likely to affect the beliefs of those individuals who conceived the nation itself and those who have been responsible for its growth and maintenance through time. Thus, it is not surprising that geography has been an essential ingredient of both the formal governmental requirements and the informal political practices of the nation.

The nativity requirement for all presidential candidates, the residency stipulations for all congressional officeholders, and the constitutional provision that presidential electors cannot cast their votes for a President and Vice-President from the same state are manifestations of this belief in geographical determinism. Implicit in these requirements is the belief that one's places of origin and of residence shape one's attitudes and values. We will look briefly at two types of geographical variables in the backgrounds of the leaders: region (both of birth and district represented) and size of place as it relates both to birthplaces and district residences.

Region and Recruitment

The regional origins of the House leaders as reflected in their birthplaces have been slightly similar, but certainly not identical to the westward-moving patterns of the American population.[6] Prior to the Civil War, forty-two (95 per cent) of the forty-four native-born leaders were born in the states of the South and the Northeast; only two leaders began life in the Midwest. In the century since then, twenty-one Midwestern natives and one California-born Republican whip have been able to reduce the older regions' dominance of leaders' birthplaces to 71 per cent. This is not a staggering drop in light of American folklore about the sons of the pioneers.

A closer examination of regional birthplaces indicates that the two older regions have shown differing rates of decline. The ten Northeastern states of New England and the Mid-Atlantic area have declined as a region of leaders' births from 45 per cent in the first three periods to only 29 per cent in the two twentieth-century periods. The South, however, has survived. The percentage of native-born leaders from the South was 52 per cent in the two antebellum periods and 45 per cent in the two most recent ones. In fact, the proportion of Southern-born House leaders in Period V (46 per cent) is almost as high as it was in the heyday of the Jeffersonians in Period I (47 per cent).

The overrepresentation of the South through time is due primarily to the control which its leaders have enjoyed over the Democratic Party in the House. Of the sixty-eight native-born Democratic leaders, forty-three were born in either the border states or those of the Confederacy. If one eliminates the eight non-Southern Democrats who first gained their leadership posts during the Civil War and Reconstruction (1861–77), the proportion of Southern-born leaders among the Democrats rises to 72 per cent. Only the Period I Federalists who lived in a much more geographically compact America show a similar degree of regional homogeneity in leadership recruitment (71 per cent).

Perhaps a more meaningful measuring point would be to examine the regions of the districts that the leaders represented during their careers in the House. As in the case of birthplaces, the South has had more districts represented by leaders than any other major region, from 55 per cent in period I to 46 per cent in Period V. Only in the Reconstruction era, Period III, does the South's representation fall to 20 percent of House leaders. In the middle eras, from 1861–1931, the Midwest is more heavily represented with 43 per cent of House leaders in Period III (1861–95) and 37 per cent in Period IV (1895–1931). In the contemporary era, the South again is dominant. If we compare the regional proportions of leaders to the distributions of the population at large, the South is considerably overrepresented in four of the five time periods. The expectation that the "newer" regions of the nation would be more equitably represented in places of residence was not fulfilled. Certainly, this represents a far more important trend than any revealed in the birthplaces, since where one was born may or may not have left a specific imprint upon a life, but the places represented in a legislative assembly have a continuing impact upon one's behavior within it. This is particularly true of American legislatures which are wholly committed to the representation of geographical units. The American public expects its legislators to be "district-oriented" and members of the House generally share that expectation.[7] Remaining in the House is the first prerequisite of leadership and to ignore this sentiment of the public would end a legislative career long before leadership opportunities appeared.

The logic of geographical determinism would suggest that if the leadership of a legislative body is overrepresentative of a particular region, then there is a great likelihood that the legislature itself will be more responsive to the aspirations and anxieties of that region's residents than it will be to feelings expressed elsewhere in the nation. This was the sentiment which led to the requirement in the Constitution that House seats be reapportioned among the states after every dicennial census. The principle of numerical representation that the drafters of the Constitution wished to encourage has been distorted by the recruitment patterns of House leaders.

A legislative body as large as the House of Representatives needs effective management. Such a need enhances the procedural power of the floor leadership. Therefore, if a region is consistently overrepresented in the leadership, the values of that region, particularly if they are as unique as the South's,[8] will soon become a major part of the value structure of the entire body. The long-standing complaints that the House is estranged from many areas of national concern may be attributed in part to the historic overrepresentation of the South in its leadership and the underrepresentation of the South in the leadership of other power centers.[9]

City and Countryside

American politics is a "politics of places" and the sizes of those places are presumed to affect the behavior of those who were born in them or who reside in them.[10] A recent example of a study based on this assumption is Rieselbach's analysis of the conservative voting propensities of House members from rural and small town America.[11]

Regarding size-related voting patterns in the House, Rieselbach discovered that birthplaces were more predictive of ideological propensities than sizes of residence,[12] but it is the residence which serves as the launching pad for a political career. The following table summarizes the population distribution of residence sizes for all leaders at the time of their first election to the House.

Table 1 shows a movement away from rural areas to the small

TABLE 1
SIZE DISTRIBUTION OF LEADERS' RESIDENCES BY PERIOD

Size of Place	1789–1825	1825–1861	1861–1895	1895–1931	1931–1975	Total*
Rural/Plantation	50%	52%	30%	27%	17%	34.7%
2500–9999	20%	26%	27%	33%	29%	25.8%
10,000–24,999	30%	4%	23%	17%	21%	19.5%
25,000–99,999	0	7%	7%	17%	4%	7.2%
100,000–249,999	0	11%	0	0	21%	6.4%
250,000 + over	0	0	13%	7%	8%	6.4%
Totals %	100	100	100	101	100	100.0
N of Cases	(20)	(27)	(30)	(30)	(24)	(124)*

* Adjusted for period overlapping

towns and cities. Comparing these figures to those of the general public, one can see some evidence of the urbanization which has characterized population growth in the United States. However, even the most recent period shows only one-third of the House leaders residing in cities with more than 25,000 people. An even more striking fact is that half of the eight leaders who represented major cities (250,000 + over) in the House served *prior* to 1895. In proportional terms, 13 per cent of Period III's leaders represented major cities while only 8 per cent of the leaders in Periods IV and V did so. This relative *decline* (38 per cent) of major city representation in the House leadership stands in sharp contrast to national population trends which showed a relative *increase of* 162 per cent as the proportion of the public residing in cities of this size rose from 8.8 per cent in 1880 to 23.1 per cent in 1950, the midpoint of this most recent era.

If we combine these data with information on leaders' birthplaces, we find a consistent underrepresentation of rural and plantation areas as leaders' residences. Leaving the family farm in quest of wealth and prominence in urban America is a continuing theme of leadership success stories, but the leaders of the House who have moved from these areas have not gone very far in terms of size. Eighty leaders were born in rural and plantation areas and forty-eight of them (60 per cent) moved away from these places by the time of their first elections to the House.

However, forty-two landed in towns and cities of less than 100,000 people, leaving only six "country boys" courageously braving the perils of the large cities. Two arrived in Nashville from rural Tennessee. Thus, only four of the House's 124 party leaders made the fabled move from the backcountry to the major metropolitan areas of the nation. The last one to do so was Hale Boggs of Long Beach, Mississippi, whose career was launched in New Orleans. But once again, a curious anomaly appears. Three House leaders reversed the pattern. They were born in major cities yet came to the House as residents of small towns and villages. The most recent instance is that of the present Democratic Whip, John McFall of Manteca, California, who began life in Buffalo, New York.

The decline in large-city representation in the more recent eras may be due in part to the impact of the Seventeenth Amendment and other reforms early in the century. With the Senate open to elected politicians, it is quite likely that urban representatives may have found the move tempting. Rather than relying upon the good will of rural-dominated state legislatures to propel them into office,[13] the urban representatives now had access to the big-city media and to sizeable blocs of urban votes which made senatorial candidacies far more attractive and easy to win.

The question of atypicality of the House leaders arises in the urban-rural data much as it did in the regional comparisons. Comparisons of leadership hierarchies in various fields indicate that political leaders generally are more likely to be rural-born than are others. Roy Hinman Holmes ranked political leaders in tenth place of twelve leadership groups based upon the proportion with urban origins.[14] Only the educational and agricultural leaders ranked lower. Suzanne Keller's review of the literature indicated that political leaders are more rural-born than the journalistic, diplomatic, and business elites of the United States; only military leaders were more likely to be rural-born than politicians.[15] Comparing the 1959 Senate to presidents of major corporations, Andrew Hacker found that 64 per cent of the senators came from rural or small-town America while only 29 per cent of the corporation presidents did.[16]

Knowing that political leaders are more likely to come from

rural and small town America and that the leaders of the House share that similarity, the next question must focus on the typicality of the House leaders vis-à-vis other national officeholders. Once again, the uniqueness of the House leaders emerges. The predominance of rural and plantation origins among the House leaders (71 per cent) is not matched by any other segment of America's political hierarchy. The most comparable study in terms of time span and number of cases is John Schmidhauser's composite portrait of the Justices of the U.S. Supreme Court. Schmidhauser found that only 24 per cent of the Justices were rural-born.[17]

Even the leaders of the most recent party control period (1931–75) in the House are likely to be rural-born: 54 per cent. This is slightly higher than that found for members of the U.S. Senate (52 per cent) by Donald Matthews in the years from 1947 through 1957.[18] Casting the net further to include births in small towns and cities under 25,000, the 75 per cent registered for the House leaders of Period V is 11 per cent higher than Hacker's study of the 1959 Senate.[19]

Places of residence show the same patterns of atypicality for the House leaders, even among other members of the political hierarchy. Urban America dominates every other leadership structure. Eighty-nine per cent of the top federal political executives who served in the five administrations from Franklin Roosevelt to Lyndon Johnson came from urban places with populations larger than 25,000.[20] Forty-nine per cent of the senators studied by Matthews came from places of this size, but only one-third of the Period V House leaders did. The inferred communication gap which Hacker, Rosenau, and Huntington see between elected political leaders and their counterparts in appointed political posts and in nongovernmental positions[21] is greatest in the case of the House leadership. If similarity of background facilitates interpersonal exchange, then the House leaders would appear to have the most difficulty relating to other elites for the simple reason that their rural birthplaces and their small-town and small-city residences are quite uncommon. Obviously, a most crucial factor operating in the case of the House leaders is the geographical dispersion insisted upon by the Constitutional Convention of 1787. Unlike the other hierarchies, the House leadership is drawn from a pool of eligibles which attempts to be geographically representative of the entire nation. Add to this the apportionment act of 1842 which imposed single-member districts throughout the country[22] and there are statutory factors forcing the dispersion principle into the states themselves, thereby limiting urban concentrations of power.

These two elements operate in such a way as to include sizable numbers of rural and small-town members within the pool of eligibles for House leadership. The informal requirement that they be residents of the districts which elect them reinforces these factors because most of the congressional districts throughout House history have been nonurban ones (due in part to the "natural" dispersion of the population and in part also to the creation of these districts by rural-dominated state legislatures). No other leadership group has its parameters defined in such narrow geographical terms, not even the U.S. Senate. And perhaps most important of all, House leaders not only come from nonurban areas, they represent them in Congress and their leadership careers are dependent upon the continuing good will of their constituents.

Apart from their disproportionate share of Southern and nonurban backgrounds, House leaders are not all that geographically dissimilar from the American public. It is their dissimilarity with other political elites and the "Metroamericans" whose goals and values shape much of contemporary life that has made their provincialism seem more pronounced.[23] Obliged to function in Washington, D.C., a metropolis quite unlike the cities at home, the leaders still have to be attentive to the demands of their own constituents and those of their fellow partisans in the membership. Consequently, their nonurban backgrounds may facilitate their intraparty relationships, but they may also make more difficult their dealings with the other political elites whose origins and interests are more urban and cosmopolitan.

SOCIAL STATUS FACTORS AND RECRUITMENT

One of the early victims of "realism" in the biographies of political decision-makers was the "log cabin myth." The myth states that every young man, regardless of his social origins, can rise to the top of the political ladder by dint of hard work, native intelligence, and unassailable integrity. It has been debunked so often by biographers that one wonders if the belief still exists. Apparently it does, because most of the discourses on the subject continue to open with the demythologizing paragraphs.[24] If the need for refutation remains, then the myth must be receiving periodic refueling. Presidents Truman, Eisenhower, Johnson, and Nixon were all born in social circumstances not very different from the rags-to-riches heroes of nineteenth-century American literature. The "log cabin myth" survives because it has a continuing empirical reality and that reality extends to the leadership of the House.

Family Status and Father's Occupation

"The most important single criterion of ranking in the United States seems to be occupation," asserted Donald Matthews in his social background analysis of the U.S. Senate.[25] Building upon this assumption, Matthews hypothesized that "information on the occupations of the senators' fathers should provide a remarkably accurate portrait of senators' class origins."

There are a number of ways to deal with this particular piece of information. Table 2 presents the occupations of the leaders' fathers in a modified version of the Census Bureau's eleven-category breakdown by party and period.[26] The largest modification is in the category of "other occupations" wherein appear clerical, sales, skilled, semi-skilled, unskilled, and service workers. The percentages in the table are based on the known occupations of 113 leaders' fathers. All but eleven of these occupations could be found.

The top two occupational categories, professionals and proprietors, comprise slightly less than half of the known occupations (49 per cent) of leaders' fathers. There is a 5 per cent difference between the Democrats and their opponents over time, which would seem to indicate some degree of interparty similarity in this aspect of the recruitment process.

Comparable studies have been done by John Schmidhauser on the Supreme Court[27] and by H. Dewey Anderson on Presidents,

TABLE 2

PERCENTAGES OF HOUSE LEADERS' FATHERS' OCCUPATIONS IN
ADJUSTED CENSUS CLASSIFICATION BY PARTY AND PERIOD

Period and Party	Professional and Technical	Proprietor, Manager and Office-worker	Agricultural	Other	N
Period I, 1789–1825	45%	20%	30%	5%	(20)
Democratic-Republicans	46%	8%	38%	8%	(13)
Federalists	43%	43%	14%	0	(7)
Period II, 1825–61	35%	12%	50%	4%	(26)
Democrats	33%	6%	60%	0	(15)
Non-Democrats	36%	18%	36%	9%	(11)
Period III, 1861–95	29%	21%	33%	17%	(24)
Democrats	45%	27%	27%	0	(11)
Republicans	15%	15%	38%	31%	(13)
Period IV, 1895–1931	41%	15%	37%	7%	(27)
Democrats	54%	9%	36%	0	(11)
Republicans	31%	19%	38%	12%	(16)
Period V, 1931–75	9%	22%	52%	17%	(23)
Democrats	0%	19%	69%	12%	(16)
Republicans	29%	29%	14%	29%	(7)
Totals, 1789–1975*	30%	19%	42%	10%	(113)*
Democrats	32%	14%	48%	5%	(62)
Non-Democrats	27%	24%	33%	16%	(51)

* Adjusted for overlapping

Vice-Presidents, and Cabinet members.[28] Fathers of Justices and of the executive branch officers showed clear majorities of 65 per cent and 58 per cent respectively in the combined totals for these two occupational divisions.

It makes sense to move the agricultural aristocracy, the planters, from a lesser status agricultural designation to an upper status: the estates of "Horseshoe," "Blenheim," "Macon Manor," and "Mount Pleasant" which housed the fathers of four House leaders in the antebellum South were separated as much in status as in time from the dreary hardscrabble farms where Sam Rayburn, John Garner, and Carl Albert were raised. Adding planter fathers increases the occupational levels of all three leadership groups. The adjusted percentages of fathers in the upper occupational categories become:

Supreme Court Justices (1789–1957)   90%
Executive branch officers (1789–1934)   72%
U.S. House leaders (1789–1975)   58%

On the basis of this categorization, the evidence indicates that House leaders are more likely to have been recruited from lesser social origins than other members of the federal hierarchy. Another consequence of moving the planters is a reversal and increase in the status gap between the political parties. Adding the plantation owners to the upper levels increases the proportion of Democratic leaders with fathers in this combined category to 65 per cent, while the fathers of their various political adversaries remain stable in their total percentage (51 per cent).

At no time in the history of the House has there been a majority of sons of professionals in the leadership. The highest proportions occurred in Period I, 1789–1825, a full 150 years ago. The democratization of American politics in the wake of Andrew Jackson resulted in a general lowering of social status among the leaders over time which has continued through the present era. Only the fathers of Period V Republican leaders Charles Halleck and Harry Englebright were professional men. The relative disappearance of sons of professionals is most dramatically displayed in the case of the Democrats. Ten of twenty-one Democratic fathers were professionals from the Civil War until the Depression. Since then, no Democratic fathers have been professionals. Even Senator John H. Bankhead, the father of Speaker William B. Bankhead (1937–40), spent most of his pre-political life as a planter. Comparing the Period V figures to studies done on other governmental decision-makers during the era indicates that the House leaders are more likely to come from farm backgrounds and less likely to come from professional ones than U.S. Senators, upper level bureaucrats, and, even more remarkably, the general membership of the House itself. Their backgrounds are typical of one another, but not of any other leadership group in the government.

TABLE 3

OCCUPATIONS OF THE FATHERS OF HOUSE
LEADERS COMPARED TO THOSE OF OTHER DECISION-MAKERS

Decision-Makers	Professional and Technical	Proprietor, Manager, and Office-worker	Agricultural	Other	Total
U.S. House leaders 1931–1975	9%	22%	52%	17%	100%
U.S. Senators 1947–1957	24%	35%	32%	9%	100
U.S. House members 1941–1943	31%	31%	29%	9%	100
High-level Civil Servant, 1940	28%	30%	29%	13%	100

SOURCES: Donald R. Matthews, *The Social Background of Political Decision-Makers* (New York: Random House, 1954), p. 19; and Donald R. Matthews, "United States Senators: A Collective Portrait," *International Social Science Journal* 13 (1961): 623.

Another important factor appears when the fathers' occupations are compared to those of the population during the census years closest to the birth dates of the leaders. For example, only 8.7 per cent of Period V's leaders were the sons of professionals. Comparing this figure to the proportion of professionals in the census of 1890, one discovers that House leaders are not very unrepresentative of the population as a whole. Professionals accounted for 3.9 per cent of the working population that year,[29] thus making the index of professional overrepresentation a relatively low 2.231. This is quite a decline from Period I when the sons of professionals had their largest proportion of House leaders (42.1 per cent). When this figure is compared to the estimated 1 per cent of the population which was professional in the years from 1750 to 1775,[30] the index of overrepresentation becomes astronomically high (42.100). In this occupational category, the leaders of the "people's house" are becoming more representative of the public.

Comparing the agricultural population of 1890 to the proportion of House leaders in Period V from agricultural backgrounds, a rather remarkable development appears. The social backgrounds of House leaders are *more* agricultural than the American population of 1890 ($\frac{52.2}{42.1} = 1.240$). This is the only time in the history of the House leadership that this occurs. The preceding four periods all show an underrepresentation of agricultural backgrounds in the leadership vis-à-vis the population: Period I, .343; Period II, .625; Period III, .472; and Period IV, .627.[31] Agricultural overrepresentation in the fathers' backgrounds of Period V's leaders is the social analogue of their nonurban geographical origins. The House leadership appears to be reversing the demographic trends of the population. The social lag which contemporary critics see in the House may be increasing as its leadership becomes more small-town and agricultural in its origins.

In summarizing the ascribed social status factor of one's father's occupation, it appears as if the "log cabin myth" still has relevance for the House leadership. In fact, Sam Rayburn, Period V's best-known House leader, was born in a log cabin in Roane County, Tennessee, a few years before his father, a subsistence farmer, brought the family to north Texas in search of more fertile fields. His successor in the Speaker's chair, John McCormack, was born in the urban equivalent of the log cabin, the tenement flat in an ethnic ghetto. McCormack's father was a bricklayer who died when John, his oldest child, was only thirteen. Poverty stalked McCormack as it did Carl Albert, who served as whip under Rayburn and as floor leader under McCormack, and who is now Speaker. He came from a family of poor farmers and coal miners from southern Oklahoma, not far from the north Texas country of Sam Rayburn. On the Republican side, Joe Martin, the only member of that party to preside over the House during Period V, was born in North Attleboro, Massachusetts, the son of a blacksmith. Martin's family was not poverty-stricken, but they were too poor to fulfill their son's dream of a college education.

Horatio Alger's Jed, the poorhouse boy, may not have become a House leader, but his slightly more affluent cousins in the lower-middle and working classes would appear to have had that opportunity.

Leaders and Their Major Pre-Political Occupations

The other half of the "log cabin myth" is the poor boy's ascent through the social structure once the shackles of his lesser origins have been removed. Generally, ascent has been measured by comparing the occupations of the fathers with the occupations of the sons. Like the other occupation-based measures, it has its limitations and unexamined assumptions, but it has acquired a degree of validity through widespread usage.

Although the leaders had varying experiences throughout their occupational life histories, 102 (82 per cent) were comfortably situated as professional men by the time of their first forays into politics. Another thirteen (10.5 per cent) were either proprietors or managers. Six entered politics from the agricultural sector— three as planters and three as farmers. Only Thomas Bell of Georgia (Democratic whip, 1913–15) came from another occupational category: Prior to his political career, he was a traveling salesman. Two of Period I's leaders, Jonathan Trumbull and John Randolph, entered political life so early that no reliable pre-political occupation for either of them could be ascertained.

The most distinctive occupational characteristic is the very high incidence of lawyers among the leaders. Ninety (73 per cent) were practicing attorneys. In addition, there were eleven others who received legal training, six of whom practiced law on a part-time basis. With 81 per cent of all leaders having received legal training, it would appear as if this factor was an essential element in their recruitment for party leadership positions in the House. Among the five periods, the proportions of leaders with legal training are: Period I (80 per cent); Period II (89 per cent); Period III (87 per cent); Period IV (83 per cent); and Period V (71 per cent).

There has been a steady, but not very steep, decline over the years of legally trained leaders since the peak period, 1825–61. In this regard, the leaders are similar but not identical to the membership. Davidson's ten-Congress analysis indicates the highest proportions of lawyers in the membership occurred during the two Congresses of Period II; then there was a leveling off throughout the nineteenth century, followed by a decline during the more recent Congresses.[32] However, the membership proportion of practicing lawyers runs ten to twenty points below that of the leaders who were similarly trained and employed.

The high incidence of lawyers in the House leadership, and among other political leadership groups in America is neither new nor unique. Alexis de Tocqueville noted in the 1830's that lawyers pervaded the entire upper structure of American life, financial as well as political. In his assessment:

> The government of democracy is favorable to the political power of lawyers; for when the wealthy, the noble, and the prince are excluded from the government, the lawyers take possession of it, in their own right, as it were, since they are the only men of information and sagacity, beyond the sphere of the people, who can be the object of the popular choice.[33]

Why there are so many lawyers in politics is not difficult to understand. Matthews pointed out that the lawyer's career, more than that of any other professional man, can be adapted to public life, for "the lawyer, in his everyday occupational role develops not only ability in interpersonal mediation and conciliation but also skill in verbal manipulation."[34] A similar theme of transferability appears in Heinz Eulau and John D. Sprague's book, *Lawyers in Politics*.[35] In that book, the authors contend that movement between law and politics is readily possible because the two occupations exhibit professional convergence in sharing similar values and expectations.

It was this knowledge which led to Woodrow Wilson's remark, "The profession I chose was politics; the profession I entered was the law. I entered the one because I thought it would lead to the other."[36] However, the most intriguing observation on lawyers and politics belongs to Tocqueville. Even if one discards his vision of lawyers and judges as America's real aristocracy, there is a great deal of truth in his observation that "lawyers belong to the people by birth and interest; and to the aristocracy by habit and taste; they may be looked upon as the connecting link between the two great classes of society."[37] This link makes it possible for them both to be elected and to govern.

It is this observation which is the most germane one for this portion of the study. The way out of lower social origins was the legal career. Reading law at home, at work, in libraries, or in lawyers' offices served as the functional equivalent of the law school in the nineteenth century.[38] The bar examinations were not difficult. The biographer of Speaker Nathaniel Banks (1855–57) recounts, "After scanning a few books in Rantoul's office, Banks won admission to the Suffolk County (Boston) bar."[39] Although he did not formally practice law, Banks, "the Bobbin Boy of Waltham," was one of many House leaders who used his legal training to escape the limitations of his background. Of the 101 House leaders trained in law, sixty-nine received no formal schooling in the law. This was particularly true of the leaders in the first three periods. Fifty-seven of the sixty-four leaders trained in law who served prior to 1895 read law. In Period V, only John McCormack received legal training outside of the classroom. The sixty-nine informally trained leaders read law under a wide variety of practitioners, from Daniel Webster and John C. Calhoun to a number of unknown village lawyers. In thirty-six cases, all that is known is that the leader "studied law."

The other occupations fall into four groups: editors, businessmen, non-lawyer professionals, and planters and farmers. The editorial career appears most frequently among Republicans. Five of the thirty-seven Republican leaders in Periods III-V entered politics from this profession. Only two Democrats did. In status terms, editors were once considered to be lesser professionals because they were not far removed from the printer's trade.[40] Only six leaders were farmers and planters and all were Democrats. It was better to be off the farm and plantation at the time of the launching of a political career. The man behind the plow or in the fields is not as visible to local slate-makers as the in-town lawyer. While many leaders were the sons of farmers and planters, they had generally abandoned the soil for lives in trade and in the law by the time of their entry into politics.

Of the thirteen businessmen who became leaders of the House, six were Democrats and seven were Republicans. None of the Federalist or Whig leaders came from the ranks of business. The absence of businessmen among Federalist House leaders contrasts with the merchants and traders who were appointed to 17.7 per cent of the executive positions by President John Adams.[41] Businessmen constituted only 8.6 per cent of the Democratic leaders while they represented 18.9 per cent of the thirty-seven Republican leaders who have served since the Civil War. Their firms were not very large, but they were successful enough to permit their owners and managers sufficient time to make a substantial contribution to policy-making in the House of Representatives.

The other professionals were randomly scattered between parties and periods. Little can be learned from their pattern.

Social Mobility

Social mobility as a concept has both macropolitical and micropolitical uses. The macropolitical analysts, such as Weber and Durkheim, have focused upon the effect of new occupational groupings entering the political realm and the changes they have wrought in the functioning of various political systems.[42]

Micropolitical analysis of social mobility has not captured the attention of many social scientists interested in leadership. Two studies that used intergenerational occupational differences to measure the impact of social mobility on the political ideology of state legislators produced contradictory results; thus, the evidence about mobility's impact upon political beliefs of legislators remains in doubt.[43]

In this study, the socioeconomic index devised by Otis Dudley Duncan will be used to measure social mobility.[44] Based on a combination of the National Opinion Research Council's studies of occupational prestige and median income of occupations reported in the 1950 Census, the Duncan scores have a wider range of values and a more standardized mean than the NORC ratings.[45] These scores have been used infrequently in political analysis, but this will be no bar to their utilization in this study. Because averages can be misleading, however, the social mobility data has been reanalyzed using the socioeconomic index in a different way. The leaders were placed in three categories: upwardly mobile (at least 26 points above father's occupation); stable (an occupational differential from 25 points above to 25 points below father's occupational score); and downwardly mobile (at least 26 points below father's occupation).[46] Leaders for whom no occupational information could be found on either their fathers' or their own major occupation were eliminated.

More than seventy House leaders (63.4 per cent) moved at least twenty-six points beyond their father's occupations. This is an enormous degree of social mobility. The Anderson study found that only 25.7 per cent of the executive branch officers could be classified as "climbers." Although the two measures of mobility are not strictly comparable, there is little reason to believe that a gap of this magnitude would be completely eliminated by a redefinition of variables.

Since Anderson periodized his data, it is possible to compare the two sets of national elites. The periodization utilized in each study is not identical, but the results are so consistent that it is doubtful whether changing seminal and terminal points in time would affect the conclusions.

Leaders of the House are more socially mobile than their counterparts in the various administrations. Had we stopped our analysis in the 1930's it would have appeared that the proportion of socially mobile House leaders had reached a plateau which

TABLE 4

SOCIAL MOBILITY OF EXECUTIVE BRANCH
OFFICERS AND HOUSE LEADERS

Executive Officers		House Leaders	
Periods and Years	Percentage of "Climbers"	Periods and Years	Percentage of Upward Mobiles
Colonial		Period I	
1789–1824	13.9%	1789–1825	38.9%
Commoner		Periods II & III	
1825–77	30.6%	1825–95	60.9%
Modern		Period IV	
1877–1934	24.4%	1895–1931	60.0%
Total		Total	
1789–1934	25.7%	1789–1931	57.8%

SOURCE: H. Dewey Anderson, "The Educational and Occupational Attainments of Our National Rulers," *The Scientific Monthly*, 40 (June 1935): 517.

it maintained for more than a century (1825–1931), but the Period V figures reveal an even more interesting finding. The proportion of Period V leaders who were socially mobile is the highest for any House period (82.6 per cent). Only two Democrats and three Republicans who served in leadership positions since the Depression came from socially stable backgrounds.

The various measures of social status have indicated that the level of social origins of House leaders has undergone a steady decline. The sons of farmers and workingmen have replaced the sons of planters and professionals in the leadership of the House. Yet, there has been relatively little change over time in the status of occupations held by the House leaders prior to their entry into politics. The proportion of lawyers in the leadership has shown a slight decline in more recent periods, but it still remains the largest single occupational group. The dual trends of status decline in social origins and status stability in major pre-political occupations have produced a degree of social mobility uncommon among political elites. In order to achieve the occupational status which seems to have been a stable feature of leadership recruitment, leaders in recent periods have had to go farther and work harder than their predecessors.

Overcoming a status gap of this enormity may take its toll. Rapidly gained social status takes its psychic toll by heightening insecurity.[47] Presuming that the House leaders are similar to the general population of socially mobile people, it is possible to see some of the behavioral manifestations of this likely insecurity. Among these manifestations would be deference to the executive branch and its prerogatives, the high concern for institutional loyalty, the policy of "going along" to avoid internal conflict, and the general defensiveness exhibited by House leaders in the presence of senators, federal bureaucrats, and the mass media. This is not the sole reason for these particular behavioral patterns, but it may explain much of the generally acknowledged lack of assertiveness in the House.

Continuity coexists with change. Political institutions often survive because of the internal changes which they make to cope with external social and political ones. In many ways, the U.S. House of Representatives has changed less than any legislative body of similar duration. Its basic form of representation has remained the same for almost two centuries and new standards of electoral eligibility have not altered significantly the social composition of its membership. It still remains a white male bastion. The two-party system which exists within it today is very similar to the one that it spawned early in its existence.

However, change has occurred. Thirty-seven states have been added to the Union and the House has increased from 65 seats to 435. The average district contained 30,000 residents at the time of the 1st Congress and now contains 490,000. Committees have been created and abandoned; leadership roles have been defined and redefined; and relations both within the Congress and between it and other institutions have undergone alteration over the years.

Keeping institutions functioning through time is a task assigned to the individuals who hold leadership positions. Leaders and the institutions which they guide have a symbiotic relationship; each shapes the other. Consequently, understanding the leaders and their backgrounds may help to explain the motivations which affect the character of the institution and the society of which it is an integral part. This is particularly true of a legislative institution which is dependent upon popular authority. The people are presumed to rule themselves through their elected assemblies, so it is these bodies that should be the most reflective of their origins and most responsive to their demands.

It was this assumption that guided this study of the leadership of the U.S. House of Representatives. Two basic questions were posed: In what ways are the leaders of the House similar to the public which endows them with law-making power, and in what ways are they similar to the other political decision-makers with whom they must share policy-making for the nation?

Regionally, the House leadership has been consistently more Southern in its places of origin and residence than the rest of the nation. But its greatest contrast on this characteristic is with the other elites and it is this factor which makes its Southern over-representation more pronounced. The values of the South differ from those of other regions of the United States, and a legislative leadership overrepresentative of that region is likely to become isolated and inbred.

With regard to urban-rural differences, the House leadership is becoming more urban, but at a slower rate than the public. Their rural origins and their small-town residences do not separate them as much from the people as they do from the members of other social and political leadership groups. Also, unlike the other elites, they are obliged to represent their local interests in the course of their leadership activities. Maintaining one's seat in the House is the first responsibility of the leadership. Thus, the impact of their nonurban backgrounds on their attitudes and behavior is intensified.

Perhaps the most important finding in this study is that the House leadership is becoming more similar to the general population in terms of its social origins. It has become very "representative" of the population, but concomitantly very atypical of the other elite groups. Only in the area of their major pre-political occupations do the leaders of the House seem to converge with other leadership groupings, but herein lies an irony. In order to attain their exalted occupational status as professionals, House leaders have had to move great social distances. They have become "marginal men," arising from one status level and operating on another. It is their social mobility that separates them from both the American mass and the American elite. The full dimensions of this uniqueness remain to be explored, but it may go a long way towards explaining the clubby, self-absorbed, and seemingly encapsulated U.S. House of Representatives.

Biographical Sources

The major source for the geographical and occupational information on the leaders used in this study was the U.S. Congress, *Biographical Directory of the American Congress, 1774–1971*, comp., Lawrence F. Kennedy, (Washington, D.C.: U.S. Government Printing Office, 1971). Information on leaders' fathers' social status came primarily from three major biographical compendia: Allen Johnson and Dumas Malone, eds., *Dictionary of*

American Biography, Vols. I-XX (New York: Charles Scribners Sons for the American Council of Learned Societies, 1928-1936), with two supplemental volumes, Volume XXI (1944) edited by Harris E. Starr and Volume XXII (1958) edited by Robert L. Schuyler and Edward T. James; the *National Cyclopedia of American Biography*, 65 volumes (New York: James T. White Co., 1891-date); and *Current Biographies* (New York: H. W. Wilson Co., 1940-present).

In addition to these sources, a number of biographies, autobiographies, diaries, memoirs, and memorial addresses were consulted. And lastly, the Biographical Directory files in the U.S. Capitol Building at Washington were examined for leaders' obituaries. All told, it was possible to complete social status information on 113 of the 124 House leaders (91 per cent).

NOTES

1. Fisher Ames, letter to George Richards Minot, April 4, 1789, in *Works*, ed. Seth Ames (Boston: Little, Brown, 1854), I, p. 33.

2. Alexis de Tocqueville, *Democracy in America*, Phillips Bradley, ed. (New York: Vintage Books, 1956), I:211.

3. Clem Miller, *Member of the House: Letters of a Congressman*, ed. John W. Baker (New York: Charles Scribner's Sons, 1962), p. 79.

4. William S. White, *Home Place: The Story of the U.S. House of Representatives* (Boston: Houghton Mifflin, 1965), p. 5.

5. The sources for the leaders' names were the following lists: Speakers, 1789-1961, in George B. Galloway, *History of the House of Representatives* (New York: Thomas Y. Crowell, 1961) pp. 287-89; Chairmen of the House Ways and Means Committee, 1795-1911, and Chairmen of the House Appropriations Committee, 1865-1899, in DeAlva Stanwood Alexander, *History and Procedure of the House of Representatives* (Boston: Houghton Mifflin, 1916), pp. 399-402; elected Majority Leaders, 1911-67, designated Minority Leaders, 1911-67, and designated whips of both parties, 1897-1967, in Randall B. Ripley, *Party Leaders of the House of Representatives* (Washington: The Brookings Institution, 1967, pp. 26, 30-31, and 34-35; Minority nominees for the Speakership, 1863-1911, in various volumes of the *House Journal*. In addition to these sources, official congressional publications such as the *House Journal* and the *Congressional Directory* were used for corroboration and updating.

6. The four regions used in this study are (1) the Northeastern region—the six New England states, the three Middle Atlantic ones, and Delaware; (2) the Southern region—the eleven states of the Confederacy, the "border"

states of Maryland, Kentucky, Oklahoma, and West Virginia, and Washington, D.C.; (3) the Midwest region—the Census Bureau's East North Central and West North Central states; and (4) the Western region—the Mountain and Pacific states, Alaska, and Hawaii.

7. On the "district-oriented" expectations of the public, see Carl D. McMurray and Malcolm B. Parsons, "Public Attitudes Toward the Representational Roles of Legislators and Judges," *Midwest Journal of Political Science* 9 (May 1965): 167–85. The "district" orientations of House members are examined in Roger H. Davidson, *The Role of the Congressman* (New York: Pegasus, 1969), pp. 121–26.

8. Among some of the studies which indicate the uniqueness of Southern congressional voting patterns are: Robert Boynton, "Southern Conservatism: Constituency Opinion and Congressional Voting," *Public Opinion Quarterly* 29 (1965): 259–69; George L. Grassmuck, *Sectional Biases in Congress on Foreign Policy* (Baltimore: The Johns Hopkins University Press, 1951), pp. 152–54; Charles O. Lerche, Jr., "Southern Congressmen and the New Isolationism," *Political Science Quarterly* 75 (September 1960): 321–37; Malcolm E. Jewell, "Evaluating the Decline of Southern Internationalism Through Senatorial Roll Calls," *Journal of Politics* 21 (November 1959): 624–46; LeRoy N. Rieselbach, *The Roots of Isolationism*, (Indianapolis: Bobbs-Merrill Co., 1966), pp. 113–14.

9. On the underrepresentation of the South in the "national [political] structure," see Joseph A. Schlesinger, *Ambition and Politics* (Chicago: Rand McNally, 1966), p. 24; James N. Rosenau, *National Leadership and Foreign Policy* (Princeton: Princeton University Press, 1963), pp. 99–101; and Alex B. Lacy, Jr., "The White House Staff Bureaucracy," *Trans-Action* VI (January, 1969), p. 51. The underrepresentation of the South in leadership circles is documented in two works of Ellsworth Huntington, "Where Our Leaders Come From," *American Magazine* 141 (June 1946): 38–39 and 157–59; and *Mainsprings of Civilization* (New York: John Wiley and Sons, 1945), pp. 80–89.

10. The phrase is from James David Barber's *Citizen Politics: An Introduction to Political Behavior* (Chicago: Markham, 1969), pp. 7–8. The "size of place" hypothesis holds that smaller communities will be more resistant to "progressive" attitudes than larger ones; see Leon D. Epstein, *Politics in Wisconsin* (Madison: University of Wisconsin Press, 1958), Chapter 4.

11. Leroy N. Rieselbach, "Congressmen as 'Small Town Boys': A Research Note," *Midwest Journal of Political Science* 14 (May 1970): 321–30.

12. Rieselbach, "Congressmen as 'Small Town Boys,' " p. 326.

13. See David J. Rothman's discussion of state politics in his *Politics and Power: The United States Senate, 1869–1901* (Cambridge, Mass.: Harvard University Press, 1966), Chapter 6.

14. Roy Hinman Holmes, "Origins of Distinguished Living Americans," *American Journal of Sociology* 34 (January 1929): 683–84.

15. Suzanne Keller, *Beyond the Ruling Class: Strategic Elites in Modern Society* (New York: Random House, 1963), p. 310. The military leadership is

quite unique; see Morris Janowitz, *The Professional Soldier* (New York: The Free Press, 1960), Chapter 5.

16. Andrew Hacker, "The Elected and the Anointed: Two American Elites," *American Political Science Review* 55 (September 1961): 541.

17. John R. Schmidhauser, "The Justices of the Supreme Court: A Collective Portrait," *Midwest Journal of Political Science* 3 (February 1959): 17.

18. Donald R. Matthews, "United States Senators: A Collective Portrait," *International Social Science Journal* 13 (1961): 621. See also his *U.S. Senators and Their World* (New York: Vintage Books, 1960), pp. 14–18.

19. Hacker, "The Elected and the Anointed," p. 541.

20. David T. Stanley, Dean E. Mann, and Jameson W. Doig, *Men Who Govern: A Biographical Profile of Federal Political Executives* (Washington, D.C.: The Brookings Institution, 1967), p. 115. See also Dean E. Mann, "The Selection of Federal Political Executives," *American Political Science Review* 58 (March 1964): 81–99. Nonpolitical federal officials are examined in W. Lloyd Warner, Paul P. Van Riper, Norman H. Martin, and Orvis F. Collins, *The American Federal Executive* (New Haven: Yale University Press, 1963). Urban-rural information appears on pp. 56–67.

21. Hacker, "The Elected and the Anointed," pp. 547–49; Rosenau, *National Leadership* pp. 30–31 and 347–50; and Samuel P. Huntington, "Congressional Responses to the Twentieth Century," in David B. Truman, ed., *The Congress and America's Future* (Englewood Cliffs, N.J.: Prentice-Hall, 1965), pp. 5–31, esp. 12–16.

22. George B. Galloway, *History of the House of Representatives* (New York: Thomas Y. Crowell Co., 1961), p. 27.

23. The phrase is from Eric F. Goldman, *The Tragedy of Lyndon Johnson* (New York: Alfred A. Knopf, 1969), pp. 16–17.

24. A classic and typical debunking of the myth may be found in Richard B. Morris, "Where Success Begins: Rags to Riches—Myth and Reality," *The Saturday Review* 36 (November 21, 1953): 15–16, 65–71. A more recent version appears in Kenneth Prewitt, *The Recruitment of Political Leaders: A Study of Citizen-Politicians* (Indianapolis: Bobbs-Merrill, 1970), p. 23.

25. Donald R. Matthews, *U.S. Senators and Their World*, p. 19.

26. U.S. Bureau of the Census, *1960 Census of Population: Alphabetic Index of Occupations and Industries*, rev. ed. (Washington, D.C.: U.S. Government Printing Office, 1960), pp. xix–xxiv. A six-category version was devised by Alba M. Edwards, *Comparative Occupation Statistics for the United States* (Washington, D.C.: U.S. Government Printing Office, 1934), pp. 164–69.

27. Schmidhauser, "The Justices of the Supreme Court," p. 7.

28. H. Dewey Anderson, "The Educational and Occupational Attainments of Our National Rulers," *The Scientific Monthly* 40 (June 1935): 511–18, esp. 516. A nonquantitative study which comes up with similar conclusions is C. Wright Mills, "The American Political Elite: A Collective Portrait," in Irving Louis Horowitz, ed., *Power, Politics and People: The Collected Essays of C. Wright Mills,* (New York: Ballantine Books, 1963), pp. 196–207.

29. This figure comes from H. Dewey Anderson and Percy E. Davidson, *Occupational Trends in the United States* (Stanford: Stanford University Press, 1940), pp. 16–17.

30. This percentage may be found in Sidney H. Aronson, *Status and Kinship in the Higher Civil Service* (Cambridge, Mass.: Harvard University Press, 1964), p. 46.

31. Proportions of the agricultural population may be found in Aronson, *Status and Kinship*, p. 46; and U.S. Bureau of the Census, *Historical Statistics of the United States*, (Washington, D.C., U.S. Government Printing Office, 1960) p. 74. The base years used for each period are Period I, 1770; Period II, 1800; Period III, 1830; Period IV, 1860; and Period V, 1890.

32. Davidson, *Role of the Congressman*, pp. 41–45.

33. Alexis de Tocqueville, *Democracy in America*, ed., Phillips Bradley, I: 285–86.

34. Donald R. Matthews, *U.S. Senators and Their World*, p. 33.

35. Heinz Eulau and John D. Sprague, *Lawyers in Politics: A Study in Professional Convergence* (Indianapolis: Bobbs-Merrill, 1964), esp. pp. 132–44.

36. This remark appeared in a letter of Wilson's to his future wife, Ellen Axson, October 30, 1883. It may be found in Alexander L. George and Juliette Y. George, *Woodrow Wilson and Colonel House: A Personality Study* (New York: Dover Publications, 1964), p. 14.

37. Tocqueville, *Democracy*, p. 286.

38. On this point, see James Willard Hurst, *The Growth of American Law: The Law Makers* (Boston: Little, Brown, 1950) Chapter 12, esp. pp. 252–55.

39. Fred Harvey Harrington, *Fighting Politician: Major General N. P. Banks* (Philadelphia: University of Pennsylvania Press, 1948), p. 14.

40. Aronson, *Status and Kinship*, p. 88.

41. *Ibid.*, p. 89.

42. See Ioan Davies's interpretation of their writings in *Social Mobility and Political Change* (New York: Praeger Publishers, 1970), pp. 18–23.

43. Heinz Eulau and David Koff, "Occupational Mobility and Political Career," *Western Political Quarterly* 15 (September 1962): 507–21; and Samuel C. Patterson, "Intergenerational Occupational Mobility and Legislative Voting Behavior," *Social Forces* 43 (October 1964): 90–93. Eulau and Koff found that social "mobiles" were more liberal than "status-stables" in the Ohio, Tennessee, New Jersey, and California legislatures. Patterson found contradictory results in Wisconsin's State Assembly.

44. Duncan's socioeconomic index appears in Albert J. Reiss, Jr., with Otis Dudley Duncan, Paul K. Hatt, and Cecil C. North, *Occupations and Social Status* (New York: The Free Press, 1961), pp. 263–75.

45. The original NORC ratings appeared in Paul K. Hatt and C. C. North, "Jobs and Occupations: A Popular Evaluation," *Opinion News* 9 (September 1947): 3–13. A full assessment of this scale and others may be found in Robert W. Hodge, Paul M. Siegel, and Peter H. Rossi, "Occupational

Prestige in the United States, 1925–63," *American Journal of Sociology* 70 (November 1964): 286–302.

46. These cutting points are the same as those used by Blau and Duncan with the exception that their intermediate categories (+6 to +25 and −6 to −25) have been subsumed by the stable category in this study. See Peter M. Blau and Otis Dudley Duncan, *The American Occupational Structure* (New York: John Wiley & Sons, 1967), p. 509.

47. On this point, see Robert A. Ellis and W. Clayton Lane, "Social Mobility and Social Isolation: A Test of Sorokin's Dissociative Hypothesis," *American Sociological Review* 32 (April 1967): 237–53.

IV. Formal and Informal Change: Rules, Norms, and Roles

Although Congress is part of the U.S. governmental system and of American society, it can also be regarded apart from these larger groups as a highly structured social institution, with the characteristics possessed by all social institutions. It has formalized laws, or rules, of procedure and behavior; it has less formal but equally rigorous norms of proper conduct; and it has clearly defined roles and role expectations.

Rules of parliamentary procedure, like the rules of basketball or football, are theoretically neutral. Unlike rules of sport, congressional rules in practice often turn out to work to the advantage of one particular group of legislators; sometimes the advantage shifts to another group over time. Such was the case with the filibuster in the Senate, which was used primarily by Southern conservatives in the early 1960's to delay action on civil-rights legislation. Now, it is used just as frequently by Northern liberals concerned about antibusing legislation or defense expenditures.

In this section articles on the 1970 Legislative Reorganization Act and on the House electronic voting system are concerned with formal rules changes which have significantly altered congressional behavior. The recorded teller voting provision of the 1970 act has greatly increased voting attendance, has been credited by knowledgeable observers with killing the SST, and in general has probably produced advantages for congressional liberals. The electronic voting system has affected all members by altering the pace of congressional life, changing the normal methods of obtaining voting information, and changing leadership influence on the House floor.

Each house of Congress, as a social institution, has informal leaders and followers, who set norms and role expectations for members of each institution. Expected and actual behavior by congressmen is conditioned by the times, expectations in the society itself, and the characteristics of the members. In the last century, as Neil MacNeil has noted, "It was not unusual to see representatives intoxicated on the House floor;"[1] and fist fights or personal vilification were not uncommon. As the House membership stabilized and the country became more urban and less frontier, behavior in Congress changed. Through the 1950's, the norms or "folkways" of conduct were much more circumscribed. Interpersonal courtesy (in Matthews's term) was an important norm of congressional floor behavior; John McCormack, former Speaker of the House, used to claim proudly that the worst insult he had ever unleashed against a colleague on the House floor was to note that he held the gentleman "in minimum high regard." In recent times, the use of epithets like "potato-head" and outcries such as "This chamber reeks of blood" have become more frequent. The Vietnam war, and the increasing focus on the Senate as a Presidential arena, are in part responsible for the change in norms.

Nelson Polsby's "Goodbye to the Inner Club" and Herb Asher's "The Changing Status of the Freshman Representative" speculate on other reasons for the changes that the 1970's have wrought upon norms and role expectations in the House and Senate. The "Inner Club"—senators like Johnson, Richard Russell (D-Ga), Bob Kerr (D-Okla.), and Bob Taft (D-Ohio); and congressmen like Carl Vinson (D-Ga.), "Judge" Smith (D-Va.), or Mendel Rivers (D-S.C.)—could use the carrot and the stick (committee assignments, office space, floor amendments) to reward followers and punish transgressors. Former Speaker Sam Rayburn, for years head of the House Establishment, always told freshmen congressmen, "If you want to get along, go along." These admonitions no longer work. Recognizing these "changes in the climate of the House," House Majority Leader "Tip" O'Neill (D-Mass.) has commented, "If you got out of line in the old days you were a pariah. These new members are brighter, better educated, more talented. There's doctorates in Congress now. Sam Rayburn used to be able to glare people down. You just don't glare these people down. . . . The times are different now. The ethics are different."[2] The Inner Club, as Polsby points out, is gone, and younger members, as Asher notes, have achieved a new role of influence in Congress.

Most of these changes are largely evolutionary. Stiff resistance to abrupt transformations that might upset the comfortable old ways of operation still remain. This helps us to understand the congressional reaction to the onset and growth of television, and its impact (or lack thereof) on legislative role expectations and behavior.

NOTES

1. Neil MacNeil, *Forge of Democracy*, (N.Y.: McKay, 1963) p. 10.
2. Quoted in the *Washington Post*, Sunday, March 31, 1974, p. E 5.

1970 LEGISLATIVE REORGANIZATION ACT: FIRST YEAR'S RECORD

The House of Representatives, according to conventional wisdom, is run by a score of powerful committee chairmen who long ago wrote the rules and now wield them to their own advantage. The Senate, the same wisdom decrees, is a gentlemen's club where insiders wheel and deal behind the guise of unanimous consent.

How close to the truth the conventional wisdom comes is a matter of conjecture, but a 1970 law revising the rules by which Congress works has been in effect a year and has brought a few demonstrable changes in the way the tradition-bound body operates.

The law was the Legislative Reorganization Act, and most of its provisions changing floor and committee procedures in the House and Senate went into effect at the beginning of the 92d Congress in January 1971. At least one provision—providing for recorded teller votes in the House—has already produced dramatic effects. Another change limiting the number of committees on which senators can serve will probably bring changes when it takes full effect—though this might take up to ten years. At least one new procedure set by the act—the issue of germaneness in House-Senate conference committees—has proved to be a major source of contention between the two bodies.

Other changes in Title I of the act, the section dealing with congressional rules and procedures, have a record ranging from compliance to defiance.

Excerpted From *Congressional Quarterly Weekly Report*, March 4, 1972, pp. 485–91, by permission of the publisher.

Requirements of Law

The act required committees in both chambers to:

• Provide that all record votes be made public, and that roll-call votes on final approval of a bill be printed in the written report
• Encourage open hearings and business meetings
• Provide for advance notice of hearings and allow a majority of committee members to call meetings when the chairman fails to do so
• Prohibit the use of general proxies; specific written proxies are allowed through procedures determined by each committee
• Require prompt filing of committee reports once a committee has acted and allow committee members to file minority or additional views in a reasonable time
• Seek annual funding in a single request covering the committee and its subcommittees
• Allow the minority party committee members to call their own witnesses at hearings
• Permit broadcasting of hearings—a practice already in effect in the Senate but not in the House
• Require committees to issue biennial reports reviewing their activities regarding legislation within their jurisdictions

In addition, Senate committees were required to publish their rules in the *Congressional Record* by March 1 of each year. No equivalent provision in the Legislative Reorganization Act applied to House committees, but the bill did state that House rules would apply to committees and subcommittees. In a separate resolution the House stipulated that committees must adopt rules although it did not specify they must be published.

Provisions affecting floor procedures in the Senate:

• Prohibited consideration of any bills for which the written reports had not been available for at least three days in which the

Senate was in session, unless waived by the Senate majority and minority leaders

• Allowed committees to meet while the Senate was in session, with the approval of the leadership

Provisions affecting House floor procedures:

• Required a three-day layover between the time the report on a bill was made available and the time the measure was taken up on the floor; the procedure contained no specific waiver procedure

• Allowed committees to meet while the House was in session, except when it was in the process of amending bills

• Set a procedure for a committee member to call up a bill when it had been cleared for floor action but the committee chairman failed to bring it to the floor

• Guaranteed that copies of proposed amendments would be made available and that debate time would be provided for amendments printed in advance in the *Congressional Record*

• Permitted recorded teller votes during the amending process, which traditionally took place under a procedure which banned roll-call votes

• Authorized electronic voting and recording machinery

• Allowed quorum calls to be completed when a majority of members have announced their presence, thus dispensing with the need to complete such calls, which take about 30–35 minutes each

• Allowed debate on motions to recommit a bill back to committee with instructions on how to rewrite it. In effect this was another way to amend a bill

• Permitted dispensing with the reading of the Journal each day and provided that doors of the House would be closed to keep members in or out of the chamber only when ordered by the Speaker

Conference procedures were altered to:

• Require conference reports to be filed in both chambers and include a single explanatory statement

• Divide debate time in both chambers on conference reports between the two parties

• Prohibit House consideration of conference reports until three days after they have been printed in the *Congressional Record*, unless a waiver of this rule has been requested by the Speaker. This provision is not in effect during the last six days of a session

• Specify that House conferees cannot include in the final version of the bill matter not committed by either chamber or modifications beyond the scope of the issues committed to the conference (This would mean, for example, the conferees on an appropriations bill could settle on a funding level anywhere between the levels voted by the House or the Senate but not above both or below both.)

• Allow separate votes by the House on nongermane amendments added to House-passed bills by the Senate, with 40 minutes of debate divided between supporters and opponents of the amendment . . .

Other titles of the Legislative Reorganization Act, not covered by the scope of this review, provided Congress with additional fiscal and budgetary information, analytical support and new procedures; expanded committee staff resources and increased aid in research and analysis from the Congressional Research Service in the Library of Congress; established a Joint Committee on Congressional Operations and an Office of Placement and Office Management; and revised the statute governing the House Office of the Legislative Counsel.

Background

The Legislative Reorganization Act of 1970 (PL 91-510) was the first congressional reform measure since 1946. The drive for enactment of a new law began in the early 1960's, and several of the key supporters were no longer in Congress by the time the 1970 law was enacted.

In 1965 Congress set up a Joint Committee on the Organization of Congress. The following year the committee issued a report calling for reforms, including tightening committee procedures to curtail the powers of chairmen, limiting committee assignments, increasing committee staff resources, strengthening fiscal controls, improving the Legislative Reference Service (the forerunner of the Congressional Research Service), and strengthening lobbying rules. In 1967 the Senate passed a bill embodying many of these proposals, but it died in the House. In 1969 the Senate Government Operations Committee reported a similar bill but did not bring it to the floor until after the House acted on companion legislation. The House Rules Committee set up a special subcommittee to consider reform.

In 1970 the Rules Committee reported a bill which did not contain provisions dealing with seniority, electronic voting, reform of the *Congressional Record*, lobby reform, or campaign spending provisions.

The House debated the measure off and on for 11 days, eventually accepting 36 amendments—including recorded teller votes and electronic voting—and defeating 29. The Senate later added on provisions similar to those in the bill passed in 1967 to deal with Senate reforms, and the bill cleared Congress late in the 1970 session.

In the House, task forces in both the Democratic and Republican caucuses devised new procedures modestly modifying the rigid seniority system by which committee chairmen and ranking minority members were selected. The Democratic Committee on Committees (the Democratic members of the Ways and Means Committee) would nominate members for committee chairmanships which would not necessarily follow seniority. In fact all chairmen were named according to seniority, and a challenge to John L. McMillan (D-S.C.), chairman of the District of Columbia Committee, failed by a 258–32 vote by the full House following a 126–96 vote by the Democratic caucus early in 1971.

The Republican conference adopted a system whereby GOP members would vote by secret ballot on each nomination for ranking minority member. All these posts were filled by senior members as well.

Recorded Teller Vote

Easily the most dramatic change brought about by the Legislative Reorganization Act involved the recorded teller vote in the House. During 1971, 108 such votes were taken, most of them on amendments to bills which under the previous system would have been decided by a small number of anonymous members.

Most major bills in the House are considered in the Committee of the Whole—a system devised by the British Parliament to act without arousing the ire of a tyrannical king. Although the British abandoned the system of non-record voting in the early nineteenth century, the U.S. House of Representatives carried it on until 1971. One hundred members comprise a quorum of the Committee of the Whole, and often amendments were voted on with only a handful of members present. Votes were taken in three ways—voice, standing, and tellers. Under the latter system members would walk up the aisle to be counted by tellers who would record numbers but not names of members voting each way. Amendments approved by the Committee of the Whole could be recorded by roll-call votes just before final passage, but amendments rejected in that fashion could not be voted on by the full House in a record vote.

The 1970 act for the first time allowed record votes by the House on amendments to bills considered in the Committee of the Whole. One fifth of the committee (20 members) could demand "tellers with clerks." Members would still file up the aisle, but would hand the tellers colored pieces of paper bearing their names and positions. Recorded teller votes were sometimes used in the full House when demanded by one-fifth of the full membership (44 members) because it took only 12 minutes rather than the 30–35 minutes allowed for a regular roll-call vote.

A survey by *Congressional Quarterly* based on the 108 recorded teller votes found that voting participation increased by more than 90 per cent compared to non-record votes on amendments the previous year. The study showed that only 23 of the 108 recorded teller votes were decided by a margin of 150 votes or more.

Early in the year the potential importance of the recorded teller vote was realized when the House defeated funds for the controversial supersonic transport plane by a 217–204 vote on March 18. It was the first time House members had voted on SST funding by recorded vote. Another significant recorded teller vote on March 31 defeated an amendment cutting the President's authority to draft men into the armed services to one year from his requested two years; the amendment failed by a 198–200 vote. Another amendment extending the draft for 18 months failed by a 30-vote margin.

Pressures were exerted to modify the recorded teller vote procedure by some disgruntled members who claimed that the procedure was being abused by small numbers of representatives seeking votes on minor issues. Although some members backed a move to modify the rule—perhaps by increasing the number of people who could request a recorded teller vote—support for the present system voiced by Speaker Carl Albert (D-Okla.) early in 1972 effectively squelched the attack.

On February 23 the Democratic Caucus voted to change the recorded teller vote rule to permit such votes to last 15 minutes rather than the existing 12 minutes. In addition, it voted to change the rules to allow quorum calls to be taken by a 15-minute teller vote procedure rather than by calling the roll. Both changes were adopted by voice vote. No attempt was made during the caucus session to modify the procedure for having recorded teller votes. The proposed rule changes had to be adopted by the full House before they would go into effect.

Richard P. Conlon, staff director of the Democratic Study Group, comprised of about 160 House Democrats, most of them liberals, said that the recorded teller vote was "working beyond any expectations" of its original backers. He said that the House leaders "underestimated its potency" before the SST vote, but the popularity of that vote made it "untouchable."

Representative Barber B. Conable, Jr. (R-N.Y.), the Republican leader of a bipartisan group sponsoring a series of strengthening amendments during House passage of the 1970 bill, said the recorded teller vote ensured majority participation in the amending process. Before its adoption, 100 members could usually amend a bill any way they sought—"a serious gap in the legislative process," Conable said.

Conlon said the new system had produced a few liberal cracks in the committee chairmen's control of the Committee of the Whole. That body was generally dominated by conservatives, and a committee chairman could usually guarantee success for his bill by getting his supporters on the floor during votes on amendments.

Instead of worrying about only the Committee of the Whole, today chairmen must "assess the entire membership of the House —the SST burned into their consciousness," Conlon said. He said [that] during 1971, liberals prevailed on about 25 votes under the recorded teller system that they would probably have lost before under the non-record system.

Senate Committee Memberships

Another provision whose effects have not yet been fully felt but which is expected to make a major impact is the Senate limitation on committee memberships. In both chambers, most of the work in drafting and amending legislation is accomplished in committees rather than on the floor. The Legislative Reorganization Act reduced in size most Senate committees and limited members entering the Senate beginning in 1971 to two major and one minor committee assignments. In the future, no senator may hold the chairmanship of more than one committee or of more than one subcommittee of a major committee.

The bill contained "grandfather" clauses to protect the committee assignments held by senators when the act was voted on in 1970. This meant that numerous senior senators could hold more than the three committee posts allowed.

In addition, the law prohibited membership on more than one of the following committees: Appropriations, Armed Services, Finance, and Foreign Relations. These four committees are generally the most powerful and most sought after of all Senate committees, and the law would spread membership on them among more members.

At the beginning of the 92d Congress at least eight senators with membership on two of the four committees were protected by grandfather clauses in the act. They included Senate Majority Leader Mike Mansfield (D-Mont.), who sat on both Appropriations and Foreign Relations, and two committee chairmen. John C. Stennis (D-Miss.) was chairman of the Armed Services Committee and also sat on Appropriations; he was third-ranking Democrat on the Defense subcommittee of the Appropriations Committee, which gave him a major role in writing both defense authorizations and appropriations. J. W. Fulbright (D-Ark.), chairman of the Foreign Relations Committee, also served on the Finance Committee. . . .

Despite the numerous waivers for senior senators, incoming members in both parties were assigned to committees in strict accordance with the requirements of the law. The Senate did vote in 1970 to waive the act for senior members making transfers in class and for memberships on certain joint committees, but the waivers affected only the 92d Congress and expire after 1972. Aside from these waivers, senior senators seeking new committee appointments have also complied with the law.

Walter Kravitz, senior specialist in American national government for the Library of Congress's Congressional Research Service, said that both parties have tried "conscientiously" to conform to the law. Kravitz, who is directing a study of compliance with the law, predicted that because of the grandfather clauses, the full effect of this provision will not be felt for another 8 to 10 years.

Germaneness Issues

The provisions of the bill dealing with germaneness have caused more problems between the House and Senate than any other section of the bill. The germaneness matters were contained in the House provisions of the bill, which were not amended by the Senate when it considered the measure.

As enacted, the bill required that House conferees could not include any language in a conference version of a bill which concerned a topic which neither chamber sent to conference or beyond the scope of the differing versions of a similar provision voted by both chambers. It also authorized separate votes with 40 minutes of debate on any non-germane amendments added by the Senate to a House-passed bill and prohibited House conferees from agreeing to a non-germane Senate amendment unless authorized to do so by a vote on that amendment.

Several House-Senate disputes arose because of the House provisions and subsequent interpretations of the law by the House leadership and parliamentarian. . . .

In several . . . instances House and Senate conferees went beyond the scope of language in either version of the bill. For instance, the House had approved a pay raise whose benefits cost more than $2.7 billion and the Senate pay raise would cost nearly $2.8 billion. The final version, enacted into law, cost less than $2.4 billion, considerably lower than the amount voted by either chamber.

Snarls also arose over the different versions of the Mansfield amendment, passed by the Senate three times and each time either killed or watered down by the House. The amendment attempted to set a specific date for withdrawal of troops from Vietnam and was introduced by the Senate Majority Leader.

One Mansfield amendment was added by the Senate to the House-passed defense procurement authorization bill. The House leadership, which opposed the Mansfield amendment, refused to allow a separate vote on the proposal as a non-germane amendment. Instead there were two separate roll calls on procedural motions dealing with instructing House conferees. Lucien N. Nedzi (D-Mich.), a supporter of the Mansfield amendment, called the move "a very transparent effort to avoid a clear-cut vote on the most serious issue in the United States today." He said the issue of germaneness was not raised before the House until "after very high-level strategy meetings."

Later, when the procurement bill had been through the conference and had emerged with three non-germane amendments attached, the Rules Committee cleared the measure for the floor with a special rule waiving points of order on all parts of the conference reports except those amendments. One of the three amendments was an amended Mansfield proposal; a second repealed the ban on imports of chromium ore from Rhodesia.

In connection with the bill, Speaker Albert ruled that the entire conference report would fall if any part of it were rejected. No vote was asked on the Mansfield amendment, but the chromium provision was challenged by Donald M. Fraser (D-Minn.). It was supported by the House on a 251–100 roll-call vote; this was the only record vote on a non-germane amendment to take place in the House in 1971.

Another germaneness problem arose in connection with a ruling by the House parliamentarian that conferees could not amend sections of a bill added by the House onto a Senate-passed bill. This problem arose once during the year, in connection with the regional development bill. The Senate passed the bill originally; it contained provisions on Appalachian regional development and other economic development projects. The House added a new Title I which had no counterpart in the Senate bill; the House Title I contained funds for accelerated public works for areas of high unemployment.

In conference, the Senate delegation tried to offer a modified accelerated public works proposal, but House conferees refused to consider it. The House conferees cited a ruling by the parliamentarian that a substantially different Title I would be beyond the scope of the bill sent to conference by the House and would violate that chamber's germaneness rule. The House version of the title remained in the bill, but three Republican senators refused to sign the conference report. They were John Sherman Cooper (Ky.), Howard H. Baker Jr. (Tenn.) and Robert Dole (Kan.).

Cooper explained his position on the floor: "The Senate became subject, in a conference, to a prior ruling of the parliamentarian of the House. I do not think that is right. . . . It denies to the Senate the authority to act upon measures added by the House. . . . It denies to the body . . . a voice upon the substance of amendments placed by the House in any bill which originates in the Senate." Cooper warned that continued incidents could wreck the conference system of resolving differences in House and Senate versions of a bill.

In spite of his protests, the conference report was adopted by the Senate. The bill was subsequently vetoed by the President.

Several Senate staff members expressed concern that the Senate's hands were tied by the germaneness rules. One pointed out that the Senate often uses non-germane riders to get around the opposition of House committee chairmen. One such example was the 18-year-old vote in federal elections, added to the 1970 voting rights bill by the Senate. House Judiciary Committee Chairman Emanuel Celler (D-N.Y.) opposed the 18-year-old vote for years but would not hold up the civil rights measure because of it.

Mansfield has written to Albert concerning the effects of the germaneness rules, but the Democratic leadership of both chambers had not yet agreed to meet and work out their differences.

Other Provisions

Some provisions of the act have never been invoked, and many others are observed in most or all instances. The new procedure for House quorum calls—ending the roll call after a quorum is reached—has never been used. Neither has the procedure allowing House debate on recommitting a bill to committee with instructions for rewriting it. The latter provision was designed to allow votes on amendments defeated in the Committee of the Whole and was rendered superfluous by the recorded teller vote system.

No sources could recall instances in which House committee members called meetings when the chairman refused to do so or in which bills were brought up on the floor for a vote when the chairman refused to act. Apparently no member was denied the chance to submit an amendment for advance printing in the *Congressional Record* with 10 minutes of guaranteed debate. Debate time divided by the parties is regularly observed in the House.

Most committees published rules in 1971—and in some cases adopted them for the first time. By October 27, when the Joint Committee on Congressional Operations compiled all committees' rules in a single document, only the House Administration and the Senate Judiciary and Armed Services Committees had not made their rules public. The rules themselves vary greatly among committees. Several committees have very detailed rules, while others sum theirs up in three or four paragraphs.

Proxy voting is another area in which committee voting varies widely. A few committees allow only very specific proxies—detailing in writing the bill and specific positions on proposed amendments. Others allow less stringent proxies. Some committees will not allow proxy votes to reverse decisions made by members actually present and voting.

One well-publicized proxy vote came when Mundt, who had been absent for two years following a stroke, gave Minority Leader Hugh Scott (R-Pa.) a blanket proxy during Senate Foreign Relations Committee consideration of the foreign aid bill. Mundt's proxy read: "This is to authorize you to cast my vote by proxy in the Foreign Relations Committee in any way you see fit on the amendments to, and the reporting of, HR 9910, the Foreign Aid Authorization bill, when that matter is taken up by the committee on October 19 and 20."

Written proxies are required and generally are kept on file by the committees, in contrast to previous practices when committee chairmen had broad blanket proxies on any matter to arise.

Televised or recorded hearings, long popular in the Senate, occurred on more than 30 occasions in the House during 1971. Twelve different committees held between one and five broadcast hearings on subjects such as prisoners of war, water pollution, the SST and the Lockheed loan guarantee. Although many members were initially afraid of disruption by cameras, microphones and lights, response among members was generally favorable. "Now some of them may comb their hair before they go into the hearing room," said one House committee aide.

Congressional Quarterly's annual study of committee secrecy showed that 36 per cent of all committee meetings in both the House and Senate were held in secret. Most of the open meetings were hearings; in general, congressional committees still voted to close their business or bill-drafting sessions. The House Appropriations Committee, which traditionally held even its hearings in secret session, in 1971 opened 36 hearings—8 per cent of all its meetings.

One House privilege included in the act but reversed early in 1971 would allow one-third of committee investigative funds to be used by minority staff members. The House Democratic Caucus voided this rule, and this decision was made binding on all Democratic members during the 1971 vote adopting House rules. Other provisions of the 1970 law guaranteed at least some minority staffing. The Senate provisions allowed the minority committee members to select two of the six professional staff members plus clerical support. In the House, minority committee members could nominate two professional and one clerical staff member.

Other provisions affecting minority rights—such as the right in the House for minority members to call witnesses during committee hearings—are apparently being observed. . . .

Assessing the Act

The Legislative Reorganization Act had three major goals, according to Representative Conable: streamlining the legislative processes, opening up the operations of Congress to more public scrutiny, and democratizing the system to protect minority rights.

"I think it's been a plus generally," Conable said. Many of the reforms, especially the recorded teller vote, "have been a constructive force in the life of this body. . . . It is always reassuring (to the public) to see reform accomplished. There is so much cynicism about hardening of the arteries in public institutions. Just the accomplishment of reform has been a refreshing thing."

Conable echoed a view expressed by numerous members who felt the bill had accomplished at least some of its reforming goals —that just the existence of the bill acts as a sort of curb on the leadership in both parties and in both chambers. The act "makes those in power realize they can't exercise their power capriciously," he stated.

All observers agreed that the act did not preclude wheeling and dealing by powerful committee chairmen and high-ranking party members in their accustomed fashion. But especially in the House, leaders must be more conscious than before of gaining majority acceptance for their actions.

"In a way the bill was a symbol," said Representative Thomas M. Rees (D-Calif.). "It was a symbol to the leadership they just couldn't run over us like they used to." Rees was a Democratic member of the bipartisan group which fought successfully in 1970 to add liberalizing amendments to the act.

In the Senate, some members and staff aides are chafing to get the germaneness dispute ironed out between the House and Senate leadership. "That has had more impact than anything else. It has thwarted the ability of the Senate to get things in ways which we were always able to do," said one Senate Republican staff member.

Some House members and staff aides like it for just that reason. They argue it prevents the Senate from adding numerous extraneous amendments to House bills in the famous "Christmas-tree" fashion. Some members say accommodation is needed on the issue. "Our germane rule is ridiculously narrow and they (the Senate) don't even have one. We should both have one but somewhere in the middle," Rees said.

Another potential problem relating to the germaneness issue was pointed out by Representative William A. Steiger (R-Wis.). He objected to the ruling by the Speaker in connection with the Rhodesian chromium amendment, which held that if a non-germane amendment failed, the entire conference report was rejected. Such a vote should be bound up only on the amendment and not on the whole conference measure, he said.

Conlon said that efforts to get the entire appropriations process opened up for more public scrutiny was "a bust." The DSG director said that the House committee generally complied with the three-day layover provision, but before it reported the bill it held months of hearings and days of mark-up sessions in private. "The bills are not visible for more than a week. . . . A couple of days isn't enough to digest what the committee has done over several months in secret."

He added, "The major things still get decided at the last minute or just as everybody is leaving town."

Further Reform Proposals

Backers of reform said they are still concerned with further changes in procedures but will probably wait until the 1970 provisions have had a longer shake-down period.

B. F. Sisk (D-Calif.), chairman of the House Rules subcommittee which originally drafted House provisions of the act, said his subcommittee was reactivated last fall and has begun evaluating some changes. The subcommittee may look into further amendments to the law.

"We may conclude the act itself needs to be reopened," Sisk said.

Frequently mentioned proposals for further reform include:

• Changes in the rules governing the *Congressional Record* to assure it chronicles what actually happened on the floor of both chambers. At present, members may add, delete, or change material from official records of floor proceedings

• More open committee meetings—especially hearings but perhaps executive sessions as well

• Changes in House voting procedures as a result of electronic voting

• Improving staffing procedures and restoring minority rights regarding investigative funds in the House

• Modifications of the seniority system—avoided by both the House and Senate when they originally passed the bill

Nobody expected dramatic changes as a result of the reform provisions of the act. Several observers expressed surprise that the recorded teller vote provision succeeded as well as it did. Congress is an institution bound by traditions, and internal changes are generally measured by small increments.

"The House is still the House. We didn't change it much but we did change it," Rees said of the reformers' efforts. "They know that we're looking. If someone gets way off base we can bring it up in the caucus or even on the floor."

WHAT MAKES CONGRESS RUN?

Norman J. Ornstein

Senator William Proxmire is not the only one jogging on Capitol Hill these days. On sunny afternoons tourists are apt to see half the House of Representatives chugging across Independence Avenue toward the House floor for a roll-call vote. Meanwhile, their colleagues are plugging along labyrinthine underground passages toward the subway that links the Rayburn House Office Building with the Capitol. All this haste is decidedly uncongressional and most closely resembles a class change on a busy college campus.

It wasn't always this way. Until 1973 voting in the House of Representatives was one of the more leisurely activities in the entire federal government, an institution never known for its frenetic pace. Generally, it took the House clerks 35 minutes to read through the roster of 435 members and then record the absentees. And if this wasn't long enough for procrastinating members, understanding clerks could always stretch the process out another five minutes to accommodate latecomers.

These good old days are now fondly remembered. As one veteran Democrat recalls, "I used to have the old system down pat. They would ring the bells, call the roll once, then the bells rang again, and they called the names of the non-responding members. I had about 12 minutes after that point, and if I left my office five

Originally published in the *Washington Monthly*, December 1973, pp. 47–49.

minutes after the second bells, I made it to the floor easily." Now congressmen must bolt their bean soup in the House dining room and head for the Capitol as soon as the bells ring for a vote.

The big change in the pace of congressional life occurred last February, when an electronic voting system was installed in the House of Representatives. No longer do the clerks drone through an alphabetical list of 435 names. Instead, congressmen now have just 15 minutes to register their votes on computer consoles triggered by the insertion of individualized plastic cards. Instantly, their vote is flashed on a tote board which is mounted over the Speaker's head and which resembles nothing so much as the latest advance in basketball scoreboards.

Reforming the way Congress votes is far from a new idea. In fact, tradition has it that Thomas Edison's first patent was for a device to automatically record congressional roll-call votes. Although nineteenth-century legislators refused to consider Edison's gadget, several state legislatures have adopted computerized voting within the past decade. The issue was raised repeatedly in the House during the 1960's but was thwarted by a mixture of congressional inertia and the reluctance of many members to alter their hallowed traditions.

That's why it was rather surprising when electronic voting was finally adopted in July, 1970, as an amendment to the Congressional Reorganization Act. Unlike other reforms, such as the modification of the seniority system and the adoption of the recorded teller vote, computerized voting was not debated along ideological lines. In fact, the key advocate of reform was Wayne Hays, then ranking Democrat on the House Administration Committee and now its chairman. Hays, one of the most conservative of Northern Democrats, has a sadistic disposition which has won him a reputation as the most genuinely unpleasant man in Congress. He has become one of the powers of the House, not only from other members' terror that his attention will light on them, but also through his control of routine housekeeping tasks and his supervision of all House employees. The new voting system provides him with more than 40 additional employees to supervise and puts him in control of the House's only computer.

Joining Hays in support of computerization were such technology-oriented Republicans as Robert McClory, who had long been advocating that Congress be run more like a business, with efficient, modern equipment. In addition, the project had the support of Democrat B. F. Sisk, chairman of the Rules subcommittee that had jurisdiction over the project. Most House liberals supported electronic voting, but they did not consider it a priority issue and spent little time gathering support for it. The major objection Hays and his cohorts faced was the predictable complaint about the cost to the taxpayers.

All of this would be of interest solely to Capitol Hill tour guides if electronic voting did not have some significant—and rather unexpected—side effects. For example, the instantaneous flashing of votes on the tote board has greatly increased the congressional leaders' ability to pinpoint party defectors on close and important votes. Take the vote earlier this year in which the House rejected by one vote, 197 to 196, an effort to increase minority staffing for House committees. Electronic voting allowed Carl Albert and Tip O'Neill to quickly locate a couple of errant Democrats and strong-arm them into changing their votes before the 15-minute roll-call was up.

But the real impact of computerized voting stems from the rigid time limit. Fifteen minutes is just not very much time to get from a congressional office to the House floor and cast your vote, especially, as is the case with many members, if you have no idea what's being voted on. Originally, proponents of electronic voting wanted the time limit to be 12 minutes, but when confronted with a chorus of objections they settled for a quarter of an hour. Despite the inconvenience, it would be politically difficult for the House to relax the time limit any further. Allowing 20 or 25 minutes for a roll-call would awaken members' fears of the inevitable AP feature story beginning, "Congress has spent $1.1 million of the taxpayers' money for a new voting system that saves six minutes on each vote." Also, most liberals favor rapid voting, because it allows them to cram in more votes on floor amendments during the House's tightly scheduled legislative debates. And as if all this were not enough to keep Congress from returning to its leisurely old ways, the lurking shadow of Wayne Hays may make members prefer shortness of breath to the whiplash of his tongue.

So life on Capitol Hill has become significantly less pleasant for many senior congressmen. The frequent sprints across Independence Avenue increase the risk of being felled by a coronary in the line of duty. Voting has become particularly irksome for the less issue-oriented legislators who have to commute from the House gym to make roll-call votes. A few members like Harold Donohue, the last of John McCormack's Massachusetts cronies still in Congress, solve the entire problem by merely spending their days dozing on the House floor. But for veteran members who have not reached such a happy accommodation with technology, the allure of the $42,500 salary and the prestige of being in Congress have paled significantly.

Meanwhile, increasing citizen concern with good government has effectively removed for most members the obvious solution—simply ignoring roll-call votes. There are few reliable ways for most voters to measure the performance of their congressmen. It is difficult to analyze their voting records, especially when they indulge in such legislative tricks as voting one way on an amendment and the opposite way on final passage of the bill. But even the most apathetic voter senses something awry if his representative has missed 40 per cent of the roll-calls. Almost nothing in the checkered political career of Adam Clayton Powell inspired more comment than his habit of spending his time on the beach in Bimini instead of on the House floor. In the same way, Margaret Chase Smith was far better known for never missing a Senate roll-call than for any position she ever took on a specific issue.

While congressional reform has become one of Washington's favorite topics during the last five years, reformers have been almost totally oblivious to such mundane matters as voting attendance. Yet in the long run, such non-ideological reforms as increased pensions and electronic voting may have an enormous political impact. The pressure of the new voting system may give older members one more reason not to prolong their congressional careers into their seventies and eighties. Retirement and death have become almost the only way that congressional seats change hands—95 per cent of the incumbents who ran for re-election in 1972 won. Passage of measures like electronic voting may owe more to serendipity than design, but reforms like these may play a significant role in making the House a more responsive institution.

Perhaps reformers should shift their focus to other nuts-and-bolts issues such as closing the congressional gyms or removing the elevators from congressional office buildings and assigning space on the basis of seniority—with freshmen on the ground floor. These are not replacements for more direct ways to keep Congress from being a life-tenure institution—reform of the franking privilege, for example, or public financing of campaigns —but they may be useful weapons against those who should be spending their sunset years elsewhere.

GOODBYE TO THE SENATE'S INNER CLUB

NELSON W. POLSBY

At the opening of the 91st Congress in January, Senator Edward M. Kennedy (D-Mass.) challenged Senator Russell Long (D-La.) for the position of Senate Democratic Whip. Long, chairman of the powerful Finance Committee and a senator for twenty years, had held the Whip post nearly as long as Kennedy had been in the Senate.

The position is elective, by secret ballot in the caucus of Democratic senators at the opening of each Congress, and, as readers of the newspapers could hardly avoid noticing, Kennedy won handily.

A few days later, Senator Robert P. Griffin (R-Mich.) left the Committee on Labor and Public Welfare for an opening on the relatively low-ranked Committee on Government Operations, and Senator Eugene F. McCarthy (D-Minn.) voluntarily left the prestigious Foreign Relations Committee to take up a place on the same committee. His public explanation of the move consisted of a Delphic quote from Marshall McLuhan: "Operations is policy." When Senator Lee Metcalf (D-Mont.) removed himself from the Finance Committee that same week, in order to stay on

Originally published in the *Washington Monthly*, (August 1969), pp. 30–34. Reprinted by permission of the author. Nelson W. Polsby is Managing Editor of *The American Political Science Review*, and Professor of Political Science at the University of California, Berkeley.

Government Operations, he explained that the Finance Committee had become "just a rubber stamp for the House Ways and Means Committee. No matter what the Finance Committee or the Senate does," he said, "when we come back from conferences with the House we have given in to Wilbur Mills. He runs both committees." In part, Metcalf was protesting a decision of the Democratic Steering Committee, which had forced him to reduce his committee responsibilities from three to two while permitting more senior senators to hold three assignments. The Steering Committee also reduced the size of the Appropriations and Foreign Relations Committees in a move widely interpreted as an attempt to staunch the flow of power from senior to junior senators who might otherwise have been able to go a long way toward out-voting the chairmen of these two committees.

To a generation of followers of the U.S. Senate, these were peculiar goings-on. Whoever heard of senators leaving important committees to go on unimportant ones—voluntarily? Or committee chairmen worried about uprisings of the peasants? Or an agreeable young man of negligible accomplishments, one eye cocked on the Presidency, knocking off a senior Southern chairman running for a job tending the inner gears of the institution?

If this sort of thing can happen in broad daylight these days on Capitol Hill, there must be something seriously the matter with the ideas that have dominated conversation about the Senate for the last 15 years. For at least since the publication of William S. White's *Citadel: The Story of the U.S. Senate* (1956), the common assumption has been that the Senate has been run by an "inner club" of "Senate types." "The Senate type," White wrote, "is, speaking broadly, a man for whom the Institution is a career in itself, a life in itself, and an end in itself." Although others might belong to the inner club,

at the core of the Inner Club stand the Southerners, who with rare exceptions automatically assume membership almost with the taking of the oath of office. . . . The Senate type makes the Institution his home in an almost literal sense, and certainly in a deeply emotional sense. His head swims with its history, its lore. . . . To him, precedent has an almost mystical meaning. . . . His concern for the preservation of Senate tradition is so great that he distrusts anything out of the ordinary. . . .

As the Southern members of the Inner Club make the ultimate decisions as to what is proper in point of manner—these decisions then infallibly pervading the Outer Club—so the whole generality of the Inner Club makes the decisions as to what *in general* is proper in the Institution and what *in general* its conclusions should be on high issues.

White conceded, of course, that the Senate had its "public men," who made their way by inflaming or instructing public opinion. But he argued that it was not these grasshoppers but rather the ants of the Inner Club who got their way in the decision-making of the Senate.

Since the publication of *Citadel*, commentators on Senate affairs have routinely alluded to the Inner Club as though to something as palpable as an office building. No senatorial biography—or obituary—is now complete without solemn consideration of whether the subject was in or out. Discussions of senatorial business can hardly compete with dissections of the Inner Club's informal rules, tapping ceremonies, secret handshakes, and other signs and stigmata by which members are recognized. One writer, Clayton Fritchey in *Harper's*, took the further step—in 1967—of actually naming names.

By far the most zealous promoter of the whole idea was someone whose opinion on the matter must be given some weight. This is the way Joseph S. Clark described a lunch that Majority Leader Lyndon B. Johnson gave for Clark's "class" of incoming freshman Democrats in 1957:

> As we sat down to our steaks at the long table in the office of Felton M. ("Skeeter") Johnston, Secretary of the Senate, . . . we found at our places copies of *Citadel: The Story of the U.S. Senate*, autographed "with all good wishes" not only by its author William S. White . . . but by the Majority Leader as well. During the course of the lunch, which was attended by the other recently re-elected leaders, Senator Johnson encouraged us to consider Mr. White's book as a sort of *McGuffey's Reader* from which we could learn much about the "greatest deliberative body in the world" and how to mold ourselves into its way of life.

These days, somehow, the mold seems to have broken. Ten years after the Johnson lunch, Clayton Fritchey's *Harper's* article named Russell Long as a "full-fledged member" of the Inner Club. Of Edward M. Kennedy, Fritchey said:

> On his own, the amiable Teddy might some day have become at best a fringe member of the Club, but he is associated with Robert F., who like John F., is the archetype of the national kind of politician that the Club regards with suspicion. It believes (correctly) that the Kennedy family has always looked on the Senate as a means to an end, but not an end in itself.

And yet, only two years later, Kennedy unseated Long.

Power in the Senate

Some time ago, in *Congress and the Presidency,* I argued that the notion of an inner club misrepresented the distribution of power in the Senate in several ways. First, it vastly underplayed the extent to which *formal* position—committee chairmanships, great seniority, and official party leadership—conferred power and status on individual senators almost regardless of their clubability. Second, it understated the extent to which power was spread by specialization and the need for cooperative effort. Fritchey's list bears this out; of the 92 nonfreshman senators in 1967, he listed 53 as members or provisional members of the Inner Club. This suggests a third point: the existence of an inner club was no doubt in part incorrectly inferred from the existence of its opposite—a small number of mavericks and outsiders. The Senate has always had its share of these, going back at least as far as that superbly cranky diarist, Senator William Plumer of New Hampshire, who served from 1803 to 1807. But the undeniable existence of cranks and mavericks—uncooperative men with whom in a legislative body it is necessary (but impossible) to do business—does not an Inner Club make, except, of course, by simple subtraction.

To dispute that there is an all-powerful Inner Club is not, of course, to claim that no norms govern the behavior of senators toward one another, or that this body of adults has no status system. Any group whose members interact frequently, and expect to continue to do so on into the indefinite future, usually develops norms. All groups having boundaries, a corporate history, a division of labor, and work to do may be expected to have folkways and an informal social organization. What was opened to question was whether, in the case of the U.S. Senate, the informal social organization was as restrictive or as unlike the formal organization as proponents of the Inner Club Theory believed.

To these observations I would now add a number of others, the most important of which would be to suggest that the role of the Senate in the political system has changed over the last 20 years in such a way as to decrease the impact of norms internal to the Senate on the behavior and the status of senators.

One possible interpretation of what went on at the opening of the current Congress is that the Senate today is far less of a citadel than when William S. White first wrote. It is a less insular body, and the fortunes of senators are less and less tied to the smiles and frowns of their elders within the institution.

What is the great attraction, for example, of the Committee on Government Operations? It reports little legislation, has oversight over no specific part of the executive branch. Rather, it takes the operations of government in general as its bailiwick, splits into nearly autonomous subcommittees, and holds investigations. In short, it has the power to publicize—both issues and senators. It takes less of a senator's time away from the increasingly absorbing enterprise of cultivating national constituencies on substantive issues.

The claim that lack of ambition for the Presidency distinguishes members of the Inner Club could not have been correct even 20 years ago, considering the Presidential hankerings of such quintessentially old-style Senate types as Robert A. Taft of Ohio, Richard B. Russell of Georgia, and Robert Kerr of Oklahoma. Today, Presidential ambition seems to lurk everywhere in the Senate chamber.

Over the course of these last 20 years, the Senate has obviously improved as a base from which to launch a Presidential bid, while other bases—such as the governorships—have gone into decline. There has certainly, since World War II, been a general movement of political resources and of public attention toward Washington and away from local and regional arenas. The growth of national news media—especially television—has augmented this trend. The impact upon the Presidency of this nationalization of public awareness has been frequently noted. To a lesser extent, this public awareness has spread to all national political institutions. But of these, only the Senate has taken full advantage of its increased visibility. In the House, Sam Rayburn refused to allow televised coverage of any official House function, and Speaker John W. McCormack has continued this rule. The executive branch speaks through the President, or an occasional Cabinet member, and the Supreme Court remains aloof. Thus, only Senators have had little constraint placed on their availability for national publicity. Senate committee hearings are frequently televised. Senators turn up often on the televised Washington quiz shows on Sunday afternoons. House members, even the powerful committee chairmen, rarely do. National exposure does not seem to be as important a political resource for them.

As senatorial names—Kefauver, McCarthy, Kennedy, Goldwater—became household words, governors slipped into relative obscurity. Where once the governor's control of his state party organization was the single overwhelming resource in deciding who was Presidential timber at a national party convention, television and the nationalization of resources began to erode gubernatorial power. Early Presidential primaries, with their massive national press coverage, made it harder and harder for the leaders of state parties to wait until the national party conventions to bargain and make commitments in Presidential contests. Proliferating federal programs, financed by the lucrative federal income tax, were distributed to the states, in part as senatorial patronage. Governors were not always ignored in this process, but their influence was on the whole much reduced. Meanwhile, at the state level, services lagged and taxes were often inequitable and unproductive. Responsible governors of both parties have often tried to do something about this problem, but it has led to donnybrooks with state legislatures, great unpopularity, and, on some occasions, electoral defeat.

This decline of governors and the shift of public attention to national politics and national politicians goes some distance in explaining how the Senate, in its role as an incubator of Presidential hopefuls, seems to have made it increasingly hard for a Senate inner club to monopolize power. As the stakes of the senatorial game have changed, so has the importance of informal norms and folkways internal to the Senate, in the life space of senators.

In my view, two historical accidents also played a part. The first was the majority leadership of Lyndon B. Johnson. Ambitious for the Presidency, immensely skilled, Johnson sedulously perpetuated the myth of the Inner Club while destroying its substance.

If the idea of the Inner Club was collegiality among the fellowship of the elect, the essence of Johnson's Senate operation was the progressive centralization of power in the hands of the Majority Leader. By the time Johnson left the Senate, after eight years as Majority Leader, the "Inner Club" could command little of the power attributed to it. It had too long been merely a facade for Johnson's own activity—a polite and palatable explanation for the exercise of his own discretion in committee appointments, legislative priorities, and tactics. Under the loose rein of Majority Leader Mike Mansfield, the Senate has again become a much more collegial body whose corporate work has been pretty much determined by Presidential programs and priorities. But it has not recaptured the sense of cohesion, community, and separateness that is supposed to have existed "in the old days." Younger men have come in, and in the last few years liberal majorities on legislation mobilized by the executive departments were by no means uncommon.

The second historical accident that shaped the contemporary Senate was the style of service hit upon by several postwar senators, but most notably pioneered by the late Arthur Vandenberg of Michigan, and, in the 1950's and 1960's, brought to full flower by Hubert Humphrey. This new style combined the concerns over national issues—formerly attributed mainly to Senate outsiders—with patience and a mastery of internal procedure and strategy. Like Johnson, Humphrey entered the Senate in 1949. Unlike Johnson, Humphrey had a large and varied stock of interests in, and commitments to, public policy. These attuned him to demands from outside the Senate. Through his phenomenally retentive mind, insatiable curiosity, and unquenchable optimism, Humphrey could learn enough to hold his own on any issue. Invariably his name went on the bills that reached out for new national constituencies.

Much earlier than most members of his generation, Humphrey sensed the possibilities in the Senate for long-range political education. He spent the Eisenhower era incubating ideas that, in a better climate, could hatch into programs. In the early 1950's a flood of Humphrey bills (many of them co-sponsored by other liberal senators) on civil rights, Medicare, housing, aid to farm workers, food stamps, Job Corps, area redevelopment, disarmament, and so on died in the Senate. A little over a decade later, most of them were law, and Humphrey had in the meantime become a political leader of national consequence.

By reconciling acceptance within the Senate with large public accomplishments, Humphrey set a new style—and it is a style that has grown in popularity among younger senators as the role of the Senate as an appropriate place in the political system for the incubation of new policy and the building of national constituencies emerges more sharply.

THE CHANGING STATUS OF THE FRESHMAN REPRESENTATIVE

HERBERT B. ASHER*

From Woodrow Wilson, who described the freshman representative as "without weight or title to consideration in the House," to Irwin Gertzog, who concluded that "few elected officials are as 'underprivileged' as first-term Congressmen," the situation of the House newcomer has almost uniformly been depicted as an unpleasant one.[1] The freshman is commonly portrayed as a second class representative who is admonished not to speak on the floor or in committee, is assigned to the least desirable committees, and is generally treated with disdain.

The accuracy of the foregoing image of the freshman is in some doubt. In recent years, the very early participation in floor debate by some freshmen, the successful rejection of committee and subcommittee assignments by others, and the sponsorship and organization of serious investigations of major problems all belie the passive image of the newcomer. Charles Clapp observes that many of the truisms that were thought to guide freshman behavior are now outmoded:

The old admonition that new members should observe but not

* I am grateful to John Kingdon, Charles Bullock, Aage Clausen, John Kessel, Norman Ornstein, Randall Ripley, and Herb Weisberg for their helpful comments and suggestions.

Herbert B. Asher is Associate Professor of Political Science at Ohio State University.

216

participate in debate was swept aside long ago. Apprenticeship may still precede full partnership, but the increased volume and complexity of the problems with which the Congress is compelled to cope dictate more efficient use of the membership.[2]

Results from a study on norm learning reinforce Clapp's point: nonfreshman representatives did not consider apprenticeship as mandatory for newcomers and the newcomers themselves indicated low adherence to the norm. Support for the norm of apprenticeship declined among freshmen in the early months of their House service and those newcomers who thought it necessary to serve an apprenticeship talked in terms of a period of months, not years.[3]

Some Direct Evidence on the Changing Status of the Freshman

If the norm of apprenticeship has a more restricted denotation today than in earlier days, as suggested above, then the situation of the newcomer can be said to have improved. But this is indirect evidence and more direct evidence is available. Nonfreshmen were asked in a survey if, in their congressional experience, there had been a change in the status of freshmen.[4] Twenty-five representatives said that there had been no change, two did not know, and thirty-six asserted that there had been a change, unanimously described as an upgrading or improvement in the newcomer's status. Recent freshmen were commonly described as brighter, younger, more capable, and more aggressive. They were seen as participating earlier, being more effective, receiving better committee assignments, and being more vocal. Some common responses were:

Yes, I have observed a change . . . since I became a member of Congress thirteen years ago. For many years before I became a member of Congress, and even at the time I entered as a member of the freshman class in the 85th Congress, we often heard it said that "freshman members of the House should be seen and not heard." The fact of the matter is that this seemed to be pretty much the way things were until the early 60's. Since that time, many new members have aggressively moved forward introducing new programs and legislation which they promptly supported in what appears to be a far more vocal manner than was previously done. They have not been at all reluctant to let their voices be heard in the party caucuses and have even organized small informal groups within their respective party structures in an effort to become more effective in both legislative and policy matters.

• • •

I'm a fairly new person here, but even in my brief time it would seem to me that younger members are playing a more aggressive role in the work of the House, especially on the Republican side and especially in the 90th Club which has been the most aggressive group of freshmen in recent history. Almost from their arrival, they have talked on the floor, in committee, and in conference committee.

Note that the latter response refers to party differences, with Republican freshmen taking a more active role and being treated better by their senior party colleagues. In fact, as Table 1 demonstrates, Republican incumbents were far more likely to perceive a change in the status of the freshman, a result unchanged by a control for seniority.

The party differences in perceptions of a status change are striking and consistent. But even more significant are the responses to the item about party differences in the treatment of freshmen. Of the thirty-six Representatives who thought there had been an improvement in the status of the freshman, twenty-one perceived party differences with nineteen of the twenty-one claiming that the Republicans handled their first term members

TABLE 1

ATTITUDES TOWARD A STATUS CHANGE BY PARTY AND SENIORITY

	6 or fewer years of service			7 to 10 years of service			More than 10 years of service		
	Rep (14)	Dem (14)	All (28)	Rep (7)	Dem (7)	All (14)	Rep (11)	Dem (8)	All (19)
Status Change	64%	36%	50%	100%	29%	64%	82%	50%	68%
No Status Change	36%	64%	50%	0	71%	36%	18%	50%	32%

better. Even more noteworthy is that of the four Democrats who perceived both a status change and party differences, three said that the Republicans were fairer with their freshmen. A liberal Western Democrat commented that "the Democratic establishment treats freshmen shamefully, while the Republican leadership treats them astutely." There were fifteen incumbents who perceived a status change yet did not think there were any party differences. As one senior Republican said, "No, there really is no difference between the two parties. I sense the same thing happening within both the Democratic and Republican legislative organizations and party structures."

For those incumbents who thought there had been an improvement in the status of the freshman, the change could be one of participating earlier, of gaining better committee assignments, and so on. Hence, to gain comparability on a specific point, the incumbent congressmen were asked whether freshman committee assignments had improved. Four members did not know, three said that it depended on the caliber of the freshman and the specific political situation, twenty-eight said yes, and twenty-two no. Of the twenty-eight affirmative responses, nine volunteered the opinion that the improved committee assignments held only for Republicans; two of these nine were Democrats. As Table 2 reveals, there are marked differences by party in regards to a possible improvement in freshman committee assignments.

The interview responses strongly suggest that there has been an improvement in freshman committee assignments, a change more pronounced on the Republican side. While objective measures also indicate an improvement, they fail to uncover the party differences cited in the interview material. Before proceeding to these

TABLE 2

PERCEPTION OF IMPROVEMENT IN
FRESHMAN COMMITTEE ASSIGNMENTS BY PARTY

	Republicans(30)	Democrats(27)
Improvement	66%	30%
Don't Know, Depends	17%	7%
No Improvement	17%	63%

other data, I would like to offer some general comments about committee rankings and committee assignments.

If one examines the desirability of committee assignments over time, it simplifies matters greatly to assume that the prestige rankings of the committees have remained constant over that period. This assumption seems generally valid, although it appears that attitudes toward a few committees have shifted. For example, Education and Labor seems to be a far more desirable assignment today, at least for certain representatives. In the freshman interviews, it was commonly described as the committee where the action was; its subject matter was considered most relevant to contemporary domestic problems. Prestige rankings may also be very misleading in that a low prestige assignment may be very desirable to a freshman if the problems of his district are particularly related to the area of concern of that committee. Assignment to Merchant Marine and Fisheries or Interior and Insular Affairs may be very advantageous to a freshman from a coastal area or a Western district. Another problem with regard to committee assignments is the matter of vacancies and committee ratios. Perhaps instead of merely comparing freshman committee assignments for each party, one should make an allowance for the types of committees having vacancies which each party has to fill. This of course complicates the analysis, especially when the party ratios on the committees change substantially as they did in 1965 (the 89th Congress) after the 1964 Democratic landslide.[5] There will not be any specific adjustments for types of vacancies in the subsequent discussion, although comments about the kinds of openings on committees in the various Congresses will be offered.

One simple classification of committee prestige is the House's own categorization of exclusive, semiexclusive, and nonexclusive committees. I examined the committee assignments of the eight most recent freshman classes by party according to this three-fold classification.[6] The data do not indicate any striking differences between the two parties in committee assignments to freshmen. During this fourteen-year period, only nine freshmen were assigned to exclusive committees (seven to Appropriations and one each to Rules and to Ways and Means) and five of these were Republicans. Donald G. Tacheron and Morris K. Udall state that in the 1946–65 period, no newly elected member was assigned to Rules, only two to Ways and Means, and sixteen to Appropriations so that the frequency of freshman assignments to exclusive committees has remained relatively constant in the last two decades.[7] While Republican newcomers were slightly more likely to get the few exclusive assignments, they were also more likely to be assigned to the nonexclusive committees. One should note that Republican freshmen did worst (in the sense of being placed on nonexclusive committees) in the 89th Congress after their party's 1964 election debacle and did best in the 90th Congress, after the 1966 comeback, and in the 92d and 93d Congresses. Freshmen on both sides of the aisle have done best (in the sense of not being placed only on nonexclusive committees) in the four most recent Congresses; this is especially pronounced in the GOP during Gerald Ford's tenure as Minority Leader. From the 86th through the 88th Congresses, almost 30 per cent of Republican freshmen were assigned to nonexclusive committees only; the comparable figure since Ford became Minority Leader is under 10 per cent. Thus, these data appear to support the interview assertions about an improvement in freshman committee assignments, although the party differences are not as striking as suggested by the interview responses.

These results may be somewhat misleading since the exclusive, semiexclusive, and nonexclusive categorization is a crude one, especially in the middle category. Many observers see a substantial prestige difference between Foreign Affairs, Judiciary, and Armed Services on the one hand and Post Office and Civil Service, Public Works, and Science and Astronautics on the other, and yet all of these are semiexclusive committees. Hence, rather than simply relying upon the House's three-fold classification of committee desirability, prestige scores developed by Warren Miller and Donald Stokes were assigned to each committee. Then the mean prestige of the freshmen committee assignments for each party in the last eight Congresses was calculated. Where a member received two assignments, his committee's prestige level was the higher of the two.[8] The results are presented in Table 3.

Note again that each party's freshmen fared worst after their party had suffered an election defeat, the Republicans in the 89th

TABLE 3

MEAN PRESTIGE SCORES OF FRESHMAN COMMITTEE ASSIGNMENTS,
86th–93d CONGRESSES

Congress	Republican Mean	Democratic Mean
86th	3.19	3.02
87th	3.15	2.70
88th	3.06	3.00
89th	2.50	3.46
90th	3.29	3.71
91st	3.28	3.47
92d	3.48	3.80
93d	3.54	3.88

Congress and the Democrats in the 87th after losing numerous House seats while winning the Presidency in 1960. The main exception to this pattern was the Democratic freshman class in the 90th Congress, which overall received the third best committee assignments of all groups studied, even though the Democrats lost over forty seats in the 1966 congressional elections. This can probably be accounted for by the small number of Democratic freshmen that year (fourteen), which made it easy to find decent assignments for them. The party differences in Table 3 are not very large except for the 89th Congress; perhaps the most notable point is that Republican freshmen in the four most recent Congresses and Democratic newcomers in the five most recent ones have fared the best.

Thus, objective measures indicate some overall improvement in freshman committee assignments, but they do not uncover the party differences often cited in the interviews. In fact, the objective measures suggest that Democratic freshmen do slightly better than their Republican counterparts with respect to committee assignments, a conclusion just the opposite of that drawn from the interviews. There are a number of plausible explanations for this apparent discrepancy. When representatives view each party's committee selections, what may really be salient to them is the disposition of the assignments to the top three committees. And in this respect Republican freshmen have fared slightly better, perhaps creating the impression that, overall, GOP newcomers do better. It may be, however, that prestige scores are irrelevant to the whole argument. The alleged party differences in committee assignments might arise not from the fact that Republican freshmen automatically get more prestigious assignments, but because the GOP Committee on Committees is more attentive to the policy and re-election concerns of its freshmen.[9] Two incumbent representatives (a Democrat and a Republican) took essentially this line. They argued that the GOP was more attentive to the needs of its freshmen in distributing committee assignments, particularly because of the need for the GOP to build party strength if it hoped to become a majority.[10]

The interview material indicated that both Republican and Democratic freshmen in the 91st Congress were highly successful in obtaining a seat on their first or second committee choice, with Republicans slightly more successful in being assigned to their most preferred committee—nine of fifteen Republicans were successful compared to six of eleven Democrats. More important, both parties' freshmen expressed high levels of satisfaction with their assignments.[11] Charles S. Bullock's interviews with freshman members of the 92d Congress uncovered similar results. Newcomers in both parties were highly successful in getting at least one preferred committee assignment with GOP freshmen enjoying somewhat greater success—100 per cent for Republicans compared with 86 per cent success for Democrats.[12]

Party Differences in the Treatment of Freshmen

Since objective measures did not clearly confirm that Republican freshmen receive better committee assignments, the incumbents' perceptions of party differences in the treatment of freshmen still remain to be explained. I will argue that these perceptions are meaningful data reflecting the incumbents' experiences in Congress. That these perceptions are widespread is underscored by the fact that early in their tenure three freshmen (two Republicans and a Democrat) said they had heard that GOP newcomers were treated better. The existence of such perceptions may be important for the socialization of freshmen if it leads to changed expectations about the proper role and treatment of first term members. There appear to be six interrelated reasons why Republican newcomers are treated better by their party, or, more accurately, why the incumbent sample perceived such a situation.

1. *Leadership personality.* Probably the least important reason and certainly the one most difficult to collect systematic information about is leadership personality. A number of representatives commented that the personality of the GOP leaders, especially Gerry Ford, was far more conducive to an open, casual style of leadership. A Ford press aide (admittedly not an unbiased source) said:

> Ford is not an aggressive, flashy, noisy leader. Rather, he puts together a team and keeps harmony among them and gets them to work together. . . . It is inherent in his personality not to resent others' shining.

One prominent Democrat said that his own party's leadership (especially Rayburn and McCormack) tried to maintain an iron control and became uncomfortable if events got the slightest bit out of hand.

2. *Leadership policies.* A second source of party differences in the treatment of freshmen is leadership policies. Both Democrats and Republicans asserted that the GOP leadership had a specific policy of encouraging and assisting freshman to participate. A midwestern Republican remarked:

> The leadership, especially Gerry Ford, made a deliberate decision to upgrade the role and responsibilities of freshmen. Freshmen were assigned to most committees, freshmen were put on conference committees. The talents of the freshmen were utilized. This is a deliberate policy decision that is still operative.

In a similar vein, a Democratic member stated that the Republicans "have vigorous leadership that deliberately tries to recruit younger members, gets more of them, and then encourages them to be active." What are the reasons for these policy differences? One possible answer might be the personality traits of the respective leadership cited above, but a far more reasonable explanation is rooted in the recent internal political history of each party.

3. *Recent political history of each party.* Twice in recent years

the Republican Party has overthrown its Minority Leader in the House—the upset of Joseph Martin by Charles Halleck in 1959 following the disastrous (for the GOP) congressional elections of 1958 and the overthrow of Halleck by Gerald Ford in 1965 following the 1964 Goldwater debacle. And between these two major battles, there was an additional skirmish in which Ford defeated the Halleck-backed candidate for chairman of the Republican Conference. All of these contests were generally viewed as struggles between junior and senior elements of the party and not as ideological struggles. John Bibby and Roger Davidson described numerous sources of discontent among junior Republicans in 1963, including disappointment in the off-year 1962 congressional election in which the GOP made a net gain of only two seats, dissatisfaction with the party's image, especially as portrayed by the Ev-and-Charlie show, and criticism of the limited participation in party affairs allowed to junior Republicans.[13] On all these issues, Ford was the insurgent confronting the establishment candidate.

Congressional Quarterly described the 1965 Ford-Halleck contest for Minority Leader in similar terms.[14] Peabody asserted that a necessary (but not sufficient) condition of the 1965 contest was the Republican election disaster of 1964.[15] The 1964 election had two main consequences: It compounded the dissatisfaction of the younger Republicans and at the same time made the GOP a more junior party. Thus, Ford geared his campaign to these junior members and because of the 1964 election, the already young GOP became even more junior which increased the likelihood of a Ford victory.

Throughout this period, the only leadership change on the Democratic side occurred after the death of Sam Rayburn with John McCormack and Carl Albert moving up the House Democratic hierarchy. While there was a challenge to Albert's accession to the post of Majority Leader, it was withdrawn prior to the vote.[16] As Peabody has noted, recent leadership change in the Democratic Party has largely been uncontested, being more a matter of routine advancement.[17] Thus, the Democratic leadership, unlike its Republican counterpart, is predominantly a well-established, highly-tenured group.

The importance of Ford's 1965 triumph to a policy of better treatment for freshman Republicans was cited by three representatives in the incumbent sample. One Republican thought his party's leadership was more receptive to younger members because "Ford needed freshman votes to defeat Halleck and he has responded in turn." Ford's 1965 platform was described by two representatives as being geared primarily to the junior Republicans, and his subsequent actions were seen as fulfilling campaign promises to his supporters. But mere repayment of past favors does not explain why Ford and the GOP leadership are still more positively oriented to freshmen some years after the leadership struggles of 1963 and 1965. A major part of the explanation is to be found in the respective seniority distributions of the two parties.

4. *Seniority distributions of each party*. Table 4 presents the seniority levels for each party at the opening of the 91st Congress, the Congress during which the interviews reported in this paper were conducted.

Note that almost 70 per cent of the GOP are serving in their fifth term or less as opposed to only 50 per cent of the Democrats. More important is the fact that 21 per cent of the Democratic membership is composed of representatives with more than ten terms of service as compared to only 5.7 per cent for the Republicans.[18] And between 1965 and 1969, the Republican Party became

TABLE 4
SENIORITY LEVELS IN THE TWO PARTIES

Term of Service	Republicans (192)		Democrats (243)	
	%	Cumulative %	%	Cumulative %
1	9.4	9.4	7.8	7.8
2	25.0	34.4	7.0	14.8
3	12.0	46.4	16.9	31.7
4	12.5	58.9	9.5	41.2
5	10.9	69.8	9.1	50.3
6	5.7	75.5	11.1	61.4
7	5.2	80.7	2.9	64.3
8	2.1	82.8	6.6	70.9
9	7.3	90.1	6.2	77.1
10	4.2	94.3	2.1	79.2
More than 10	5.7	100.0	21.0	100.2

a more junior party and the Democrats a slightly more senior one.[19] Between 1969 and 1973, the differences between the parties at the most senior level (beyond ten terms) narrowed a bit, although it was still the case in 1973 that a substantially greater proportion of Democrats had achieved such lengthy tenure—18.8 per cent as compared with 7.3 per cent for Republicans.

The relatively junior composition of the GOP and particularly the large freshman Republican class of 1966 were salient to numerous congressmen. One Republican mentioned that the average age of nonincumbent GOP challengers in 1966 was substantially lower than in 1964. Three representatives (two Republicans and a Democrat) directly asserted that it was the huge size of the 1966 GOP freshman class that compelled the Republican leadership to be more attentive to and considerate of freshmen. A senior Republican noted that the Democratic House majority was a result of elections held more than ten years ago and that therefore the Republicans were more receptive to the ideas put forth by younger members.

5. *Majority vs. minority party status.* The question of majority vs. minority status also appears relevant to party differences in policies toward newcomers. A senior Republican, a member of his party's Committee on Committees, flatly declared that "the Republicans, out of power, make special concessions to freshmen, hoping to attract more Republican congressmen from the various areas." Another member explained that Minority Leader Ford actively recruited promising GOP stalwarts to become candidates for Congress using as an inducement the guarantee of full participation if elected. Should the Republican Party gain control of the House, there would likely be a more rapid loosening of the restrictions of junior members and a rapid demise of the traditional norm of apprenticeship. Committee leadership would rest in a much more junior group of representatives who have moved speedily up the committee hierarchies because of the Republican election disasters of 1958 and 1964. At this stage, the Republicans would not even be able to chair each committee with a member of more than ten terms' service. And House leadership would fall to a group of men associated with efforts to improve the situation of the newcomer.

6. *Administration control.* One of the comments often made about the GOP leadership under Ford was that it seldom pressured members, including freshmen, to toe the party line, a situation which contrasted sharply with that in the Democratic Party. Leadership in the GOP was seen as more open with even junior members being able to participate. One reason given for this situation was the easygoing personality of Gerry Ford. There may be some validity to these assertions, but one must question whether they are still appropriate for Republicans today.

The comments about Ford and the GOP leadership all referred to a period when the Democrats controlled the White House and the House Democratic leadership had the responsibility of promoting the administration program. This entailed enforcing a measure of party unity, especially among freshmen who *a priori* seem more susceptible to the blandishments and threats of the party leadership. No such responsibility befell the Republican leadership; hence there was little need to maintain party discipline, especially from 1964 to 1966 when the GOP was hopelessly outnumbered in the House. But today the Republican Party controls the White House and its congressional leadership is responsible for the President's program, despite being a minority in the House and Senate. Therefore, we might expect more strenuous efforts by Ford and other party leaders to hold the rank and file membership, particularly freshmen, in line. Unfortunately, our interviews were conducted over too short a period of time to yield much information about this, but there were comments suggesting that the Republican leadership had become more hard-nosed on such issues as the Elementary and Secondary Education Act and the raising of the debt ceiling, proposals strongly advocated by the administration.[20]

Forces Contributing to an Upgrading in the Status of the Freshman

Two types of evidence have been presented thus far to suggest that the situation of the newcomer has improved: Interview responses talked of an upgrading in the status of the freshman in general, while both interviews and objective data[21] demonstrated an improvement in freshman committee assignments. There are additional forces outside Congress that have contributed to the improvement in the newcomer's situation.

One factor affecting the situation of the newcomer is the expansion that the job of the representative has undergone. Constituency casework is heavier than ever before and the expansion of the federal government in the 1960's into such areas as education, poverty, medicare, and space has made the congressman an even more important link between constituency and government, particularly the national bureaucracy. A recurrent theme throughout the interviews was that the congressman had become an ombudsman. Many representatives either complained about or merely cited the heavier workload; they said they had more constituents with more problems and greater expectations. As one member said:

The job is far more demanding and exasperating today. The range of problems is so great; the number of people we represent has increased. It all generates a hell of a lot of work. People demand that you get home more frequently because of improved transportation. In the past, Congress would recess in July; now it's a full time job.

The obvious import of all this for freshman is that they will not be untouched by the increased work load. While heavy constituency demands may detract from the time the newcomer can devote to serious policy matters, such requests, many of which are far from routine, do get the newcomer actively involved in the legislative process, most importantly, the formulation and submission of bills and the development of a communications network with various legislative and executive personnel. A more intangible effect of the increased work load and the wider range of issues with which Congress deals was outlined by three representatives. They argued that the huge amount of work confronting the institution forced it to utilize all its members and to get freshmen into the mainstream of activity as quickly as possible.

A second factor contributing to greater participation by newcomers rests in the electoral properties of congressional districts. With the exception of vacancies resulting from the death or retirement of an incumbent and the creation of new districts by re-apportionment, turnover in House membership seems to be increasingly confined to a small subset of truly marginal districts. The position of the representative has become a career one with little voluntary departure from office except for reasons of age or Senate aspirations. And a House career is intimately related to incumbency from a safe district. As one member noted, "the 'senior safes' are frequently isolated or at least not buffeted by national political trends. . . . Meanwhile, younger new congressmen are being elected for the most part from highly competitive two-party districts." Thus, freshman congressmen, largely from marginal districts, are the members most vulnerable to re-election pressures and therefore the ones least able to afford to be inactive for two years. Participation becomes a matter of political survival. At the freshman seminars in 1959, Stewart Udall uttered a similar comment:

> I know there is a school of thought among our colleagues that new congressmen should be seen and not heard; but the truth of the matter is—as most of you newcomers know, since many of you are from what we call marginal districts—that unless you are heard in the next two years you may never be heard at all. You have to make your mark now, because where congressmen are concerned, there aren't the quick and the dead but the quick and the defeated.[22]

Closely related to the electoral characteristics of the district is the mode of recruitment of freshmen. Two representatives claimed that recruitment patterns have changed in recent years, a change that has in turn produced departures from traditional freshman behavior. A New York Democrat observed that "more and more freshman have come through the primary, rather than being hand-picked by political bosses, and are more politically aware and unwilling to abide by older rules." A Michigan Republican concurred:

> The old political machinery, both in cities and rural areas, that used to provide Congress with new members is breaking down. Both political parties are under increased pressure to reject so-called party hacks for candidates and to put up the best possible men in these competitive two-party districts. Thus, a new breed of man is

being elected to Congress—bright, young, combative, and in a hurry. The seniority structure of the House of Representatives works against the man in a hurry, and there is growing restlessness.

More systematic evidence is required in order to confirm the changes in recruitment patterns.

Many representatives described recent newcomers as younger,[23] abler, more intelligent, better educated, and more aggressive, with different reasons given for each of these changes. Two members referred to increases in congressional salaries as being responsible for attracting more qualified, talented men, a point echoed as far back as 1959 by Stewart Udall at the freshman seminars.[24] Another representative said that the higher educational levels in the population were being reflected in congressional membership, although it seems likely that freshman representatives have always been highly educated.

The final factor helping to bring about an improvement in the newcomer's situation can be classified under the heading of information dissemination developments within the House. Foremost among these are the seminars for freshman congressmen begun in 1958 under the auspices of then representative Stewart Udall. The seminars present a wide variety of information to the freshmen at the outset of their service. The topics covered at the 1963 seminars give an indication of the breadth of the subject matter: There were sessions on "House Office Organization and Operating Procedures," "Becoming an Effective and Creative Member of the House," "The Rules of the Legislative Road," and "Congress: Its Strengths and Weaknesses." The dean of a Northeastern delegation attributed the increased participation by freshmen directly to these seminars. Besides conveying technical information, the seminars also transmit encouragements to participate and warnings to be cautious, with the former far more prevalent. Additional seminars have been organized of late. Four freshman members of the 93d Congress have attended a month-long special course for House newcomers at the Kennedy Institute of Politics at Harvard. Should these various seminars expand in scope, one can envisage extraordinarily well-prepared freshman classes in the future.

Another development in the area of information dissemination that may help newcomers is the proposed computerization of much congressional activity. A number of bills proposing computerization have been submitted; their advocates assert that a wide range of information could be instantaneously available including immediate data on issues before Congress complete with committee and subcommittee votes, background data and cost estimates, information on all federal contracts, analyses of administration budget proposals, and much else.[25] While it is not entirely certain that computerization would benefit junior members of the House, evidently some senior members fear such a result. As *Congressional Quarterly* has noted:

> Some veteran committee chairmen are said to be reluctant to introduce ADP automatic data processing techniques in the House. They believe easy access to detailed information would tend to weaken the seniority system, making a diligent freshman Representative as knowledgeable on some subjects as his superiors in the hierarchy.[26]

Other information sources are available to the newcomer, a relatively minor one being the set of materials distributed to freshmen by the Legislative Reference Service. There are pamphlets on casework, cosponsorship of bills, House debate, and other topics. Finally, no freshman congressman today need have a staff of novices. There is now on Capitol Hill a floating, semipermanent pool of staff people from which the newcomer can hire. For example, one member of the 91st class got his executive secretary and administrative assistant from the office of a representative who had just retired, while another got almost his entire staff from the office of his home state senator who had retired. In fact, the rarest occurrence among the 91st Congress freshmen was a staff composed entirely of district people. An experienced staff can play a crucial role in the development of an effective legislator.

The implications of all these developments for the situation of the freshman are obvious. If the historically low status of the freshman has been due to a lack of information, then such developments will partially remedy the situation. No longer will senior representatives have a monopoly on information. It is probably just this result that prompted the original opposition to the freshman seminars and is presently generating opposition to the computerization of much of congressional business. An equalizing of the ability to gain information will undoubtedly encourage freshman representatives to participate more fully and more rapidly.

Conclusion

I have argued that the status of the freshman representative has improved and is still undergoing change. The need for a lengthy inactive apprenticeship no longer seems to be accepted; freshmen appear to be participating more frequently and earlier in their careers than the traditional description of the newcomer would lead one to expect. I further suggested that there were party differences in the handling of freshmen, with Republicans treating their newcomers better. Interview information seemed strongly to confirm this assertion, although more objective measures of committee assignments did not. The objective measures did suggest an improvement in the committee assignments given to freshmen. Yet while the preponderance of evidence pointed to an improvement in the position of the newcomer, the classical image of the freshman still remains with us. Why is this so?

A good part of the answer must rest in the lack of any thorough, systematic study of freshman congressmen; the public's chief source of information about this subject has been journalistic treatments, some of which strive less for accuracy than for sensationalism. These efforts often have as their focus the abuses suffered by a few newcomers, abuses which undoubtedly will always exist, and thus such efforts tend to perpetuate the classical description. Furthermore, because the traditional image is still the one given the widest circulation, particularly by some familiar adages, freshman members of the House most likely undergo a bit of anticipatory socialization about their "proper" role prior to entering the House; this also contributes to the maintenance of the old view—some first term representatives must actually unlearn the famous adages pertaining to them. Another reason for the persistency of the classical image is the recentness of the changes taking place, making them more difficult to identify. Also, the influence of House patriarchs who still believe in the classical image may be sufficient to maintain it. However, the fact that so many incumbent House members, the primary agents of socialization for freshman representatives, thought that there had been an upgrading in the newcomer's status strongly suggests that future freshman classes will be socialized in a milieu even more supportive of freshman activity and participation.

The changes discussed are not confined only to freshmen in the House. It is clear that the norm of apprenticeship has fallen into bad times in the Senate, especially since 1964. In his round table discussions with Senators, Randall B. Ripley found that the notion of the "Inner Club" or Senate establishment was rather unimportant to most Senators and was certainly not a source of significant dissatisfaction.[27] David E. Price has noted that current legislative literature has identified a certain kind of senator who has lately been more conspicuous—"activist in his legislative orientation, generally liberal, often low in seniority and representing a large or urban state, oriented to the media and national issues."[28] Nelson Polsby has written in a similar vein about the demise of the "Inner Club."[29]

The consequences of the newcomer's improved status for the legislative process are unclear. It is difficult to argue that the policy outputs of Congress will be substantially affected in a liberal or a conservative direction. More likely, the changes that do occur will come in the realm of congressional reform, in how the House processes legislation. While the most visible concern for congressional reform early in the 93d Congress has come from the Democratic side, the Republican House contingent may play a crucial role in reform, particularly if the junior GOP members can work in concert. The sizable influx of freshman Republicans in the 90th Congress has been repeated in the 93d. Forty-three of the 192 Republicans in the 93d Congress are newcomers, many of whom replaced ranking minority committee members and other influential Republicans. This suggests that junior Republicans remain in a strong bargaining position vis-à-vis their House leadership. On the Democratic side, the influx of freshmen has been less, but the concern with reform greater. The Hansen Committee (House

Democratic reform committee) has recommended, among other things, a "Johnson" rule for the House that would guarantee each freshman one major committee assignment. The end result of these reform efforts are uncertain, but some (at least marginal) improvement in the situation of junior members in general is indicated.

What can we finally conclude about the status of the freshman? It seems likely to continue to improve, perhaps more so on the Democratic side now with the greater efforts made by relatively junior Democrats to exercise influence in their party. The changes in the newcomer's status are reflected in the ways he has been addressed over time. Early in the century, he was commonly called a baby congressman. Then the term freshman came into prominence, but the freshman, less helpless than the baby, still had to undergo a rigorous initiation before becoming an active member of the House fraternity. By 1969, a neutral term without connotations of second class membership had become popular with the 91st class—first-term representative.

NOTES

1. Woodrow Wilson, *Congressional Government* (Cleveland and New York: World Publishing Company, 1967), pp. 59–60; Irwin N. Gertzog, "Frustration and Adaptation: The Adjustment of Minority Freshmen to the Congressional Experience," (paper presented at the 62d annual meeting of the American Political Science Association, New York City, September 6–10, 1966), p. 1.

The literature on the status of the freshman can be classified under the headings of academic, journalistic, and biographical/autobiographical with the latter branch presenting the least bleak description of the newcomer's situation, undoubtedly because of the exceptional congressional personages that are the subjects of such literature and a tendency on their part to recall the most pleasant aspects of their House service. Additional examples of academic literature include Richard F. Fenno, Jr., "The Freshman Congressman: His View of the House," in *Congressional Behavior*, ed. Nelson W. Polsby (New York: Random House, 1971), pp. 129–35; and Nelson W. Polsby, *Congress and the Presidency* (Englewood Cliffs, New Jersey: Prentice-Hall, 1964), pp. 47–48. Two examples of journalistic pieces are Larry L. King, "Inside Capitol Hill: How the House Really Works," *Harper's Magazine* (October 1968): 58–71; and Clem Miller, *Member of the House: Letters of a Congressman*, ed. John W. Baker (New York: Charles Scribner's Sons, 1962), pp.

63–64. Finally, examples of the biographical and autobiographical literature include Alben W. Barkley, *That Reminds Me* (Garden City, N.Y.: Doubleday, 1954), pp. 91–99; C. Wright Dorough, *Mr. Sam* (New York: Random House, 1962), p. 129; George W. Norris, *Fighting Liberal* (New York: Macmillan, 1945), p. 94; Joe Martin, *My First Fifty Years in Politics* (New York: McGraw-Hill, 1960), p. 236; Brooks Hays, *A Hotbed of Tranquility* (New York: Macmillan, 1968), p. 21; and Miller, *Member of the House*, pp. 55–56.

2. Clapp's evidence is incomplete because his round table participants tend to be disproportionately liberal and reformist. See Charles L. Clapp, *The Congressman: His Work as He Sees It* (Garden City, New York: Doubleday, 1963), pp. 12–13.

3. See Herbert B. Asher, "The Learning of Legislative Norms," *American Political Science Review* 67 (June 1973): 499–513. A two-part panel study of the freshman representatives in the 91st Congress was conducted with emphasis on the learning of norms and voting cues and attitudes toward the job of the representative. Of the 37 freshmen elected in November, 1968, 30 were interviewed in late January and February of 1969 and of these 30, 24 were reinterviewed in May of 1969. In addition, a sample of nonfreshman congressmen was also interviewed. The nonfreshmen were stratified by party, region, and seniority and proportionate random samples were selected from each stratum. The interviews obtained reflect Republican House membership quite well, while they underrepresent Democrats in general and senior Democrats in particular. The sample is highly representative in terms of the ideological positions of Democrats and Republicans as measured by ACA, ADA, and Conservative Coalition support and opposition scores.

The 91st freshman class is exceptional in a number of respects relevant to this study. The unusually low turnover in 1968 produced an unusually low proportion of freshman nonsuccessors, that is, representatives who succeeded members of the opposite party. The percentage of nonsuccessors in 1968 was 24 compared to 56, 28, 59, and 58 for the 1958, 1960, 1964, and 1966 elections, respectively. Nonsuccessors would appear to have a greater adjustment to make, particularly with respect to determining district preferences, and might be less confident and more uncertain in their actions. The fact that there were so few nonsuccessors in 1968 might give a misleading impression of the capabilities of freshman classes in general. The 91st class is also unique in that, compared with the preceding five classes, it has the highest proportion of members with previous state legislative experience and ranks at the top in mean years of state legislative service.

4. The exact question was: "In the years that you have been in Congress, have you noticed any change taking place in the status or role of the freshman representative? If so, please describe the change."

If the respondent thought there had been a change, he was then asked a series of probes: To what do you attribute the change? Do you think the change is permanent? Do you see any differences between the two parties in this matter? If so, please elaborate. Note that while the respondents were cued to think in terms of a status change, they were not cued to the direction of that change. Similarly, respondents were encouraged to think in terms of party differences, but not in terms of the nature of these differences.

5. It is interesting to note here that in the negotiations between the party leaderships concerning the realignment of party ratios on committees in 1965, the one point that Minority Leader Ford insisted upon and won was the enlargement of the Foreign Affairs Committee in order to allow the lowest ranking Republican to remain on it. With this concession, Ford was able to guarantee that no Republican would be dropped from a committee on which he had served in the 88th Congress. See *Congressional Quarterly Weekly Report* 23 (January 8, 1965): 36.

6. Where a member received two committee assignments, the more prestigious was considered.

7. Donald G. Tacheron and Morris K. Udall, *The Job of the Congressman* (Indianapolis and New York: Bobbs-Merrill, 1966), p. 153.

8. The ordering of the committees' prestige scores corresponds very closely to the figures one would obtain if one rank-ordered the committees according to the difference between transfers to and transfers from a committee. The actual scores ranged from zero to six with Internal Security, Veterans' Affairs, and Post Office and Civil Service at the low end and Rules, Ways and Means, and Appropriations at the high. Where a freshman received two committee assignments, it generally made little difference whether one took the more prestigious of the two committees or averaged the two as both assignments were usually to less prestigious committees. Only in the 92d Congress were there noticeable differences in the two procedures.

9. This is essentially the argument made by Bullock. See Charles S. Bullock III, "Initial Committee Assignments of the 92d Congress" (mimeographed, University of Georgia, 1972), p. 13.

10. Bullock has demonstrated that freshmen from marginal districts, presumably those with the greatest re-election worries, are not given preferential treatment in committee assignments. See Charles S. Bullock III, "Freshman Committee Assignments and Re-election in the United States House of Representatives," *American Political Science Review* 66 (September 1972): 996–1007.

11. In relying upon the freshman's statement of his preferred committee assignments, there is the danger that he may engage in rationalization, thereby bringing into congruence his preference and the assignment he actually received. There is no reason, however, to believe that the rationalization process would operate differentially across the parties; therefore, we can probably safely conclude that success rates of Republican and Democratic freshmen were quite similar.

12. Bullock, "Initial Committee Assignments of the 92d Congress," p. 13.

13. John Bibby and Roger Davidson, *On Capitol Hill: Studies in the Legislative Process* (New York: Holt, Rinehart and Winston, 1967), pp. 116–20. For additional information on the 1963 contest, see *Congressional Quarterly Weekly Report* 21 (February 8, 1963): 150.

14. *Congressional Quarterly Weekly Report* 23 (January 8, 1965): 34.

15. Robert L. Peabody, "Party Leadership Change in the United States House of Representatives," *American Political Science Review* 61 (September 1967): 686.

16. For an interesting discussion of the Albert-Bolling contest for Majority Leader, see Nelson W. Polsby, "Two Strategies of Influence: Choosing a Majority Leader, 1962," in *New Perspectives on the House of Representatives*, eds. Robert L. Peabody and Nelson W. Polsby (Chicago: Rand McNally 1963), pp. 237–70.

17. Peabody, "Party Leadership Change," pp. 675–93.

18. Since the beginning of the 91st Congress, the accident of death has served disproportionately to make the GOP House membership an even more junior contingent. In addition, the resignation of a number of Republicans to accept positions in the Nixon administration or to assume other elective offices has also led to a less senior Republican membership in the House. And the retirement of numerous senior Republicans at the end of the 92d Congress insured the maintenance of a relatively junior GOP.

19. In 1965, 66.4 per cent of the Republicans and 57.3 per cent of the Democrats were from the five most recent freshman classes; the comparable figures for 1969 were 69.8 and 50.3 per cent. This is of course largely due to the election in 1966 in which 46 new Republicans took office. A sizeable number of senior Republicans were defeated in 1964 and even though the GOP regained many of these seats in 1966, the winners were most often new candidates rather than the former incumbents. Even in the Congress preceding the 1964 election (the 88th), the Republicans were clearly the junior party. Of the 55 members serving beyond their tenth term, only 23.6 per cent were Republicans; the comparable percentages for the 89th and 91st Congresses were 17.6 (9 of 51) and 17.7 (11 of 62).

20. Interview data collected by John Kingdon which span the entire first session of the 91st Congress strongly suggest that control of the administration led the Republican House leadership to be more active in striving for party unity. One of Kingdon's respondents said that the GOP leadership had treated only one bill as a party matter in the second session of the 90th Congress, but that in the first session of the 91st, many bills were so treated. See John Kingdon, *Congressmen's Voting Decisions* (New York: Harper & Row, 1974).

21. One can imagine additional objective measures that might yield some information concerning the changing status of the freshman. A prime source for such measures is the *Congressional Record*. If the status of the freshman has improved, then recent newcomers should be participating in legislative activity more frequently and earlier in their career.

One rather sophisticated type of activity index might be the number of amendments and motions introduced by freshmen. These data could again be collected over time by paging through the *Record*, although interpreting any observed changes would pose problems because of the varying levels of legislative activity in the respective Congresses. Other possible indicators are the number of conference committees to which freshmen were assigned and the number of special assignments they received. These and other measures were calculated in the major project from which this paper is drawn for the first session of the 91st Congress. See Herbert B. Asher, *The Freshman Congressman: A Developmental Analysis* (Ph.D. diss., University of Michigan, 1970), pp. 61–62, 67–70, 162–65. The results showed a total of nine amendments and motions introduced by freshman Republicans compared to three for Democratic newcomers, one Republican appointment on a conference committee vs. four Democratic appointments, and eleven special appointments given to GOP freshmen vs. four for Democrats.

22. *School for Freshmen* (Washington, D.C.: Congressional Quarterly, Inc., 1959), p. 1. A limited printing, unofficial transcript of five orientation meetings held January 13 through January 21, 1959, for eighty-two new members of the House.

23. Age data collected to determine whether recent freshman classes were younger revealed no noteworthy differences. The median and mean ages of the freshman classes in the 86th through the 92d Congresses fluctuated very little; no trend was observable in the data. It was in 1966 (the 90th Congress) that both parties got their youngest group of freshmen in recent years. For Republicans this group constituted about a fourth of the total GOP membership, so that it is not surprising that many interview comments referred specifically to the young GOP 90th class.

24. *School for Freshman,* p. 15.

25. *Congressional Quarterly Weekly Report* 27 (April 11, 1969): 524.

26. *Ibid.,* p. 525.

27. Randall B. Ripley, *Power in the Senate* (New York: St. Martin's Press, 1969), p. 185.

28. David E. Price, "A Review of *Power in the Senate,*" *American Political Science Review* 64 (June 1970): 631.

29. Nelson W. Polsby, "Goodbye to the Senate's Inner Club," in this volume.

A TWENTIETH-CENTURY MEDIUM IN A NINETEENTH-CENTURY LEGISLATURE: THE EFFECTS OF TELEVISION ON THE AMERICAN CONGRESS

MICHAEL J. ROBINSON

People who should know better frequently *overestimate* the impact of television. Senator Edmund Muskie, himself a congressional victim of television journalism, has said that "television can determine the outcome of . . . each and every national issue,"[1] and David Garth, TV consultant for John Lindsay in 1970, once claimed that "nobody could be elected to major political office anymore without the effective use of television."[2] Garth and Muskie both seem to share the opinion that television is some sort of omnipotent force in American politics. But television is not an omnipotent medium in any phase of politics; and its impact on Congress, which is our concern here, has not been nearly as direct and revolutionary as a Muskie or a Garth would imply. Instead, it has been in some respects *indirect* and *evolutionary*, and in others virtually nonexistent.

The key to understanding TV in Congress lies in distinguishing the effects of television on congressional *behavior* from its effects on congressional *role*. In essence, *television has not substantially*

Michael J. Robinson is Assistant Professor of Political Science at The Catholic University of America.

*changed the behavior of the American Congress; but it has funda-
mentally altered the political role which Congress plays in determining public policy.* Stated differently, the members of Congress,
the leadership, and the committee chairmen all behave now much
as they did in 1946, before the development of television; but, as
an indirect consequence of television, the political significance of
that behavior—the significance of the congressional process—has
progressively declined.

In. keeping with this two-way thesis, the first section of this
essay explains why television has not appreciably altered congressional behavior. The second section shows how television has left
Congress with several new, if somewhat less than meaningful,
roles to play in the political process.

Television and Congressional Behavior

Generally, when network television beams in on an American
political institution, that institution changes. For example, network coverage of the national conventions has compelled both
parties to nominate during prime time (except in the case of
McGovern), and to limit the number and length of seconding
speeches.[3] But change occurs only in the operations of those institutions which permit television to cover the proceedings. This can
be stated as a First Law of videopolitics: Television alters the
behavior of institutions in direct proportion to the amount of
coverage provided or allowed; the greater the coverage, the more
conspicuous the changes. Consequently, television has not altered
the processes through which Congress operates because Congress
has so totally limited the scope of its coverage.

Television is prohibited from the floor of both the House and
Senate. But despite the fact that both houses have denied access
to the floor to both television and radio, the House and the Senate
have, historically, adopted different methods for dealing with the
electronic media.

Traditionally, the House has been the far more restrictive body.
Two direct rulings by House Speaker Sam Rayburn barred televi-

sion cameras from all House committee hearings in addition to deliberations on the floor. During Rayburn's tenure as Speaker, television was totally excluded from all House proceedings. In fact, from 1945 until 1970, the House leadership allowed electronic media to intrude during only four years (1947–48, 1954–55), the years in which the Republicans held a majority. In 1970, the House reorganized and loosened its restrictions slightly by permiting television coverage of open committee hearings. And in 1974, under the unique circumstances surrounding the Presidential impeachment proceedings, the House finally amended its rules to permit live television coverage of committee meetings as well as hearings. But a majority of the committee must still approve all requests by the networks, and coverage of floor proceedings remain prohibited.[4] Only on ceremonial occasions such as the State of the Union message—occasions during which the House is not functioning as a legislative organ—are cameras permitted.

The Senate also forbids electronic equipment within the chamber. Roger Mudd and his colleagues at ABC and NBC are habitually standing somewhat frustratedly on the west lawn of the Capitol, telling us what took place behind the Senate doors through which the TV cameras may not pass. But until the summer of 1974 the Senate had always been more cooperative with the networks and in some cases has encouraged their participation in Senate proceedings.

Estes Kefauver was the first senator to use live network television. Kefauver's committee investigations of organized crime in 1951 created the format that would be utilized by Joseph McCarthy's hearings on communism (1954), John McClellan's hearings on labor racketeering (1957), J. William Fulbright's hearings on the Vietnam war (1966), and, of course, the Ervin hearings on Watergate. But these Senate hearings, successful as they have been in making "stars" of the committee members, have not compelled the House or Senate to alter their basic policy, which denies significant access to the congressional process *per se* to our most pervasive medium. In fact, since 1970, the House and Senate have both killed in committee separate resolutions that would have compelled television stations to broadcast evening sessions of Congress during prime time. The 92d Congress was nearly as reluctant as the 81st Congress to utilize television as a vehicle for communicating *as an institution* to the public. And the 92d Congress not only refused to be televised in session, but also rejected a modest proposal to allow its leaders the chance to appear on television to speak for Congress.

There are three traditional explanations offered for this unchanging stand: (1) electronic equipment will interrupt proceedings; (2) electronic coverage will *influence the behavior of the members*, causing them to play to the cameras, that is, to act uncongressionally; (3) the public won't understand the dynamics of congressional deliberation.

None of these explanations is specious although the behavior of the House Judiciary Committee while on camera undercut most of the usual complaints. But the best explanation for Congressional camera shyness is politically more fundamental. In the beginning, the Democratic leadership seems to have believed that television represented a threat to the normal, or traditional, processes through which Congress has always operated. To admit television might make telegenic profile or glibness the key to congressional importance. And to be sure, in the Senate, where television has been able to intrude periodically, the handsome, articulate senators—the Percys, Tunneys, and Kennedys—have achieved a stature that their length of tenure (or, some would add, their competence) would not predict. Although there are other political explanations for Congress's reluctance to use television in any formal way, this one prevails. Television could, if admitted into its inner sanctums, produce for congressmen a new source of power *within* the institution, power not drawn from seniority or tradition or party loyalty but from television *savoir faire*.

In the House, where, as one senior Democrat told me, "Rayburn was opposed to television, violently opposed,"[5] this reasoning also persisted. The leadership in both houses apparently believed in our First Law of videopolitics and tried to keep the electronic media out in order to keep basic power relationships intact and to prevent institutional change. It worked. Within the confines of the Capitol, Congress behaves now much as it did when television first arrived. Outside the Capitol, however, there have been some modest and perceptible behavioral changes.

Television and Campaign Behavior

While Congress as an institution has restricted and sometimes prohibited the use of television, its members have not. Once the members leave the chambers, television becomes much more an accepted fact of life. Congressmen believe, after all, that if they avoid television outside the Capitol as systematically as they do inside, their political opponents will have an unfair electoral advantage. Given this belief, the leadership has never even attempted to limit the use of television beyond the perimeters of the Capitol, although the Campaign Spending Act of 1971 did restrict the use of television to a modest degree. The Congress, as an organization, "understands" about TV campaigns. Both houses have facilities for producing electronic communications and for conducting electronic campaigning. The House maintains six recording rooms —one for film, one for videotape, and four for radio—which members use; the Senate has six studios, too. Members use the facilities for making audio or audiovisual news reports; this entire service is subsidized by Congress. In 1973 a congressman was charged only twenty-five dollars for a five-minute film. Were it done by private organizations at union scale, the cost would be hundreds of dollars.

In 1971, during a three-month period, the members of the House made 101,000 minutes of radio recording, 172 hours of videotape, and 12 hours of film.[6] (Videotape is the preferred medium because the congressman and his staff can get instant replays and decide whether to retake the entire segment.) For the House member, the recording studio is, in theory, an important entity because House members are so widely unknown. But the television reports produced by the studios are not crucial because they are probably not very effective. In and near cities, where the competitive districts are found, local stations do not always carry these canned stories. The days when a congressman could take a government film, add his introduction, and peddle the whole thing as his own, belong to a simpler past. In any case, nobody has demonstrated the influence of these "TV" press releases on House elections.

Senators also use the congressional facilities to communicate with their constituents. Newton Minow, former Chairman of the FCC, reports that, in 1968, the radio and TV studio set up outside the Senate produced, on the average, "more than one interview every three weeks for each senator."[7] Robert Kennedy was considered a champion of the canned news item, whether produced at the Senate studio or within his own office. But senators, especially a Kennedy, are less in need of the recording studio. Senators, unlike representatives, can attract "real" television cameras—network television cameras—as a matter of course. The networks all show a much greater affinity for senators than House members and the Senate receives as much as ten times more news coverage than the House.[8] And it is the senators who have altered their behavior to suit television, not the members of the House.

This raises an important point. Television has not affected the behavior of House and Senate members equally. The truth is one cannot legitimately speak of the impact of television on congressional behavior, especially congressional *campaign* behavior, without making this fundamental distinction between the two houses.

In most cases neither the House member nor his (her) opponent relies on television to build a campaign or win an election. Representatives and challengers *try* to get themselves featured on network or local news shows. But in the minds of the network journalists, House people rarely merit network attention. The local stations are either unable to cover House members in Washington or unwilling to cover them extensively at home. The coverage provided by the stations and the networks must be, for the representative, painfully slight. The members want more than just the *free* exposure which news programs provide. The candidates also know that the public uses TV news programs as a political guide, believing them to be the best standard for evaluating candidates. House members would, for this reason, like to reach voters through television news. But they usually are denied the chance.

Of course House people have the option to utilize television in the traditional way—by buying time to advertise. But even in this single most controversial aspect of the House campaign—the hard-sell phase—television does not play much of a role. The acid test for this assertion comes in an analysis of the campaign expenditures for TV in House campaigns. In 1970, the single most expensive year for congressional campaigns on TV, House candidates spent an average of $5,725 for TV and radio combined. Even this figure is somewhat inflated because it reflects only those districts in which there were at least two candidates and at least one of those candidates made *some* expenditures for electronic communications. Stated more concretely, the average candidate for the House of Representatives invested as much in TV and radio as he or she would have spent buying a VW rallywagon.

Given that this runs contrary to the conventional wisdom about congressional television, one might ask why the candidates for the House who are locked out of news programming at the network and local level would also avoid television addresses, spots, and commercials. An administrative assistant to a fifth-term Democrat—a Democrat who used television in only one of his five campaigns—stated quite simply that "TV is too expensive for a House election."[9] Of course TV is always expensive—for everybody. But for the candidates in the House, the cost of television is an unusual extravagance. TV, as it stands now, is a rip-off for most congressional office seekers. All House campaigns are conducted through local stations (obviously, no candidate for a House seat will buy network time). But for most congressional candidates the local station has a potential audience that is usually too big to be useful. (Sometimes the potential audience is too small.) In the cities and suburbs a candidate's district is smaller than the station's signal. To buy time is to waste money. One congressman from Minnesota estimated that he would waste 70 cents in each dollar were he to campaign on TV, because 70 per cent of the adults receiving the local signal were not located within his district.[10]

In the most extreme case, New Jersey, a state which has *no* local VHF stations (regular commercial stations) each candidate would have to buy time in New York or Philadelphia. A congressman from Newark would pay to reach 20 million viewers, of which approximately one-half of one per cent would be potential supporters in his district! On the other hand, some candidates come from districts that are too big for TV. In Wyoming, a candidate would need to buy into several stations just to reach a hopelessly spread-out constituency.

Besides this poor fit between the power of the signal and size of district, there are other reasons for the lack of television usage among candidates for the House. House candidates suspect: that voters don't bother to listen to House campaigns; that in the general elections, voters simply vote "party"; and that, in the primaries, using television is media overkill. There is some evidence to support these suspicions. Social scientists have recently demonstrated that the impact of television campaigns on voters in congressional elections is, at best, modest.[11]

For all these reasons, television has had little effect on campaigns for the House. House candidates, especially incumbents, use television sparingly and reluctantly. And although challengers generally feel that TV is an important weapon against incumbents, the truth is that neither television nor any medium dispatches many incumbents; 95 per cent of the incumbents win in the House, TV or no. Television has done little to change the complexion of the House campaigns or the House membership.

The impact of television on Senate campaigns has been a different matter. Senators and their staffs believe that television is the most important medium for getting elected and for holding office. One study of the Senate, conducted as early as 1958, indicates just how quickly senators came to rely on television. Each of the senators was asked, "If you were to single out just one thing which you did during your most recent election, which would you say got the message across best?"[12] As Table 1 indicates, television was the pre-eminent medium, even then.

Senators and their challengers really do believe that television campaigning will work. And there is considerable evidence to support their beliefs. Consequently, television is the major expense for senators in both the primary and the general election. In 1970, candidates for the Senate spent an unprecedented $16 million on radio and TV.

TABLE 1

PERCEIVED BEST METHOD FOR GETTING MESSAGE ACROSS IN
ELECTION ACCORDING TO 96 U.S. SENATORS, 1958

Television	53%
Newspapers	38%
Radio	3%
Outdoor Advertising	3%
Direct Mail	3%
	100%

In Senate primaries especially, there are classic cases in which a TV campaign did make the difference. Howard Metzenbaum, a relatively unknown businessman who specializes in airport parking lots, spent $265,000 in the 1970 Ohio Democratic primary. John Glenn, who was familiar to virtually every Democratic voter in the State as the first American to orbit the earth, spent only $31,000—one-eighth the amount spent by Metzenbaum. Metzenbaum got the nomination; Glenn did not.

In that same year, Richard Ottinger spent $735,000 in the New York Democratic primary and took the senatorial nomination away from two more widely known Democrats, Ted Sorenson and Paul O'Dwyer. Together Sorenson and O'Dwyer spent approximately $125,000, about one-sixth as much as Ottinger. In both Ohio and New York, the senatorial nomination was clearly influenced by an extraordinary imbalance in TV campaigning.

One should point out, however, that both of these men, Metzenbaum and Ottinger, went on to outspend their opponents and still *lose* in the general elections. And, even in Senate races, television is not a certain path to victory. In 1970, in the general elections for Senate, the average loser outspent the average winner by $17,000. Nonetheless, there are individual cases in which an enormous advantage in media apparently did provide victory in the general election. In 1972, Senator John Tower outspent his opponent, Barefoot Sanders, by almost 2 to 1 in the Texas general election and won. His success in that election has been attributed to his television campaign.[13] In the same year, Charles Percy invested nearly three times as much in TV as his opponent, Roman Pucinski, and that difference has been regarded as the most important factor in Percy's victory.[14]

Of course, these cases do not prove that TV wins Senate elections. But the evidence is not simply anecdotal. Paul Dawson and James Zinser estimate, after considering the advantage of incumbency and the percentage of the vote traditionally captured by each party in the state, that *in Senate races* TV and radio made winners out of marginal losers in a majority of cases.[15]

Why is this true? Why does television have this much power over who sits in the Senate? Again the answer lies in the congruity between a senator's constituency, and the television audience served by his state's local station or stations. Senators represent an entire state; one wastes less money reaching viewers in a race for the Senate because most all of the viewers are in the constituency. Besides that, stations (and networks) regard senators as important enough to elicit viewer interest. News coverage will publicize the Senate candidate and, in effect, underwrite the campaign. The candidate can use the local stations within the state to reach the actual constituency. And at the local and state level, the Senate candidate crosses the line between that which makes good copy and that which does not. The Senate candidate makes it both ways. Local television meets the candidate's needs; the Senate candidate meets the needs of local TV.

There are explicit differences between the ways in which candidates for the two houses have attempted to adjust to an electronic mode of campaigning. Candidates for the House recognize the advantages of television campaigns and television coverage. But free television coverage—TV news coverage—is not easy for them to come by, a predicament that is even more disturbing to them in comparison with the amount of coverage received by candidates for the Senate. In 1964 *Broadcasting* magazine questioned 117 incumbent members of the House and 30 from the Senate. *Broadcasting* found that 38 per cent of the senators felt that the local stations absorb the costs of televised communication within the district, but only 13 per cent of the House members felt the same way.[16]

House candidates and incumbents recognize this incongruity between their needs and the needs of the stations. And although House candidates do not foresake television, they keep it in perspective. In 1964, the *Broadcasting* survey found that 70 per cent of the senators used television and radio regularly in campaigning; only 59 per cent of the House members did so. This again over-estimates the use of television by House members, because most of the expenditures for electronic campaigning made by candidates for the House go into radio, not TV. Another survey conducted among House members in 1964 found that 10 per cent of those responding simply rejected television as a medium of communication and stated frankly that it was better suited for statewide—senatorial—elections.[17]

The opinions expressed by candidates for House and Senate are clearly reflected in the way these candidates conduct their campaigns. I have used dollars and cents to compare behavior of House candidates and Senate candidates in 1970, the last non-presidential campaign year for which we have figures.

In 1970, a year described as an orgy of TV spending, in almost one-fifth of the contested districts for the House there was no money whatever spent for radio or TV.[18] But in every Senate race there was money for TV. And, on the average, the candidate for the Senate spent three times as much per voter as the candidate for the House. Significantly, the Senate campaign in 1970 cost more than three times as much as all the House campaigns in absolute dollars, despite the fact that there were more than ten times as many candidates for the House!

TABLE 2

TV AND RADIO USE IN HOUSE AND SENATE CAMPAIGNS, 1970

	House	Senate
Percentage of constituencies in which TV and radio used at all	81% (435)	100% (35)
Percentage of all campaign funds expended on radio and TV	18.5%*	29.2%*
Average cost per voter of media campaign	6¢** (388)	17¢** (35)
Average cost of radio/TV	$5,725**	$132,150**
Overall cost	$6.1 million	$16.0 million

* Figures from 1972 in this case.
** Figures taken from Dawson and Zinser, "Broadcast Expenditures," p. 401.

All this variation between the candidates for House and Senate has a rational explanation, at least in one sense. The data from 1970 indicate that the relationship between TV campaign spending and winning is more than five times as great in the Senate than in the House. In other words, statistically speaking, outspending one's opponent in the Senate is five times more important in getting votes than outspending one's opponent in the House. According to Paul Dawson and James Zinser, most of the House candidates who won in 1970 would have won without TV and radio. But this was not true in the Senate; most of the winners would have lost.[19] The congressional election of 1972 provides a vivid case for this thesis. In that election, the Senate's four biggest TV spenders all won. And among the ten most costly Senate races, nine of the candidates who spent more on TV and radio won. But of the top ten spenders in 1972 in the House, seven lost![20]

Obviously, it is impossible to extrapolate from these cases in 1972 without examining each case individually. One must consider incumbency, the general makeup of the district, personalities, and even the level of the public's familiarity with the candidates before the campaign began. The 1970 data noted above take all these things into account and the conclusion still remains: Television has more influence over the conduct of senatorial campaigns because television has more influence over the voters in Senate elections. And this is true for two reasons: Senate candidates can spend enough on TV to make a real difference and Senate candidates get a considerable amount of free news time on TV. In essence, television is frustration for the House candidate but inspiration for the Senate candidate.

The development of the TV campaign may, as a consequence, have had an important *indirect* impact on the relationship between the House and Senate—one that has yet to be considered here or elsewhere. Having tried the inordinately expensive television campaign and having tried unsuccessfully to get local or national TV coverage for himself during the campaign, the House member may well realize that TV is a big bust for him and his colleagues. Assuming that the House member recognizes the Senator's advantage in attracting and utilizing television, one might well argue that the greatest, most important outcome of congressional TV campaigns has been an increase in the traditional institutional jealousy that House members feel toward the Senate. In other words, attempts at television campaigning may only serve to make House members more hostile toward senators. And this increased hostility from one house toward the other may reduce the capacity of both houses to perform their traditional *role* in policy formulation.

Granted, to this point we have ignored the question of congressional role, but we must consider that question now. For the effects of public affairs television on congressional roles, indirect as they may be, are, I suggest, the most important effects of all.

Television and Changing Congressional Roles

We began this report with a First Law of television's effect on institutions—the more coverage, the greater the impact on the behavior of the institution. Now we must formulate a Second Law of videopolitics to explain the impact of television on public perceptions of basic congressional roles. Second Law: Television alters the popularly perceived importance of institutions and individuals in direct proportion to the amount of coverage provided—the greater the coverage, the more important the institution and its members appear to be.

This Second Law of videopolitics helps explain three important changes in Congressional roles since the fifties.

1. *The changing status of House and Senate.* That the Senate is the more prestigious body is hardly debatable. It has always been that way. Nobody voluntarily leaves the Senate to run for the House, whereas the opposite path is well traveled: Of our present 100 senators 39 once sat in the House.

But television has made the inequality even more glaring, an inequality that has implications for the roles each house plays in making policy. Perhaps the most conspicuous single case of the Senate's greater command of television coverage occurred in 1973, during the confirmation hearings of Gerald Ford. The Senate Rules Committee and the House Judiciary Committee both held jurisdiction. Both had the same theoretical role to play in deciding Ford's fate and both committees decided to grant the networks permission to cover the hearings live. But the networks chose to televise the Senate hearings, and *not* to televise the hearings in the House. The hearings in the House were merely filmed and the edited film was shown briefly on the evening news programs.[21] An aide to the House Judiciary Committee confessed to me that this decision by the networks was an unpopular one with many of the members of the committee.[22]

One might argue that television merely reflects the reality of differences in status between the Senate and House. The senator does sit four notches ahead of the representative according to official U.S. protocol. But this is not quite right. Television, after all, does not focus as much on the House Speaker as it does on several "prominent" Senators, despite the fact that the Speaker of the House is at least six notches ahead of those same Senators according to the same official U.S. protocol. All this "excessive" coverage of the Senate *increases* the difference in status between the two houses.

This increase in senatorial status (which is just another way of saying change in senatorial role) can be explained by a historical factor—the idiosyncratic notions of Sam Rayburn, who did everything he could to exclude television from the House during TV's formative years. During these growing years of TV journalism, the Senate, on the other hand, granted the new medium access to its hearings and opportunities to film its members. Perhaps television journalists focus on the Senate today because they focused there first. But this interpretation is shallow. Television journalism relies on the Senate for the same reasons senators rely on TV campaigns. Network television and the Senate, as institutions, fit together much more comfortably than television and the House. As such, television has widened the gap between the perceived importance of the House and the Senate, and of the representative and the senator.

This widening gap between the status of House and Senate has not gone unnoticed, especially in the House. As early as 1961, one member openly challenged the ruling by Sam Rayburn that committee hearings in the House could not be televised. Congressman George Meader (R-Mich.) told the House:

> So it seems to me that . . . it is in the interest of the members of the House of Representatives to use these modern media. . . . The Senate of the United States has never had a ban on the telecasting of their committee hearings. . . . But we in the House have a thick curtain between us and the people . . . [The people] are not aware . . . of the good work that is done . . . in the House. *The effect of this blackout is to downgrade the House of Representatives.* [Italics added.][23]

Again, the effect of television is greater intercameral jealousy and animosity. But this change in perceived status may also mean that the House and the Senate will, in time, behave even more differently as institutions than they do now—the House maintaining its traditional role and the Senate playing for the cameras. In fact, one can already see this change beginning to take place.

2. *The changing role of the Senate.* Television confers status on senators because television spotlights them. Television spotlights them because they meet the needs of the networks and affiliates better than anyone else, except the President. As Edward Epstein suggests in *News from Nowhere,* a brilliant interpretation of the behavior of network news departments, the senators are almost perfect—they are few in number, national in scope, and, above all, they work in Washington, where the camera crews are.[24] Given that senators allow coverage of hearings, they make nearly perfect TV copy. Too nearly perfect, perhaps.

Television focuses on senators so directly and intensely that television has made the Senate the *mother of Presidents.* What we have is a symbiotic relationship, a TV-Senate alliance. The senators get coverage and stature; the networks get to cover, in self-fulfilling prophecy, the "Presidential contenders." If one examines the changing path to the White House since the coming of television, the influence of the networks becomes clear. Between 1900 and 1960 only two of the thirty major party nominees for President came from the Senate—a paltry 7 per cent. Since 1960 *all* our Presidential nominees have been senators before entering Vice-Presidential or Presidential politics. (Johnson and Nixon were senators before becoming Vice-President.) The governor's mansion no longer leads to the White House, as it did for 150 years. Network television precludes gubernatorial recruitment because governors are too far out in the sticks. The networks are in Washington. The governors do not get coverage; senators do. And, now that television has made the appearance of success in primaries the *sine qua non* of Presidential nomination, it is far more imperative for the candidate to get network coverage than experience in state administration. The tendency to nominate politicians from big states has diminished too. Since 1960, half of the major nominees have come from small states. Size of state doesn't matter any more; a senator is a senator.

This is not to say that senators do not make good Presidents. The point is that, due to the logistics of network coverage, a seat in the Senate is almost a necessary condition for nomination. The system eliminates an enormous number of political leaders from Presidential competition. Tom McCall sits in Oregon; Dan Evans sits in Washington State, both hoping for a spot on the *Today* show. But Howard Baker, Scoop Jackson, and Charles Percy all work in Washington, D.C., near the networks. McCall and Evans get left out. (Reagan and Rockefeller work near major stations owned by the networks.) All this is a function of the Second Law of videopolitics, not of national politics. Baker, Jackson, and Percy become a public item because they are in a good location very close to ABC, NBC, and CBS bureaus. That the networks have turned the Senate into our Presidential incubator is only a little more obvious than it is unjustified.

3. *Television journalism and the role of the American national legislature.* At this point we must reunite the two houses and consider the general impact of television journalism on the role played by the entire legislature in the policy process. To do this we must consider the impact of both the *type* of television coverage given Congress and the *extent* of coverage given Congress.

The House and Senate have, until recently, allowed the electronic media access only to public hearings. This limitation has forced the networks to adopt a type of coverage which is based upon an artificial image of Congress as the Grand Inquisitor. Edward Epstein calls it "Congress—An Investigative Agency."[25] The other roles which Congress plays or should play—policy writer, policy innovator, and so forth—are largely ignored by the television networks because the networks cannot cover these functions. Consequently, Congress has a TV image, based solely on congressional hearings and impeachment proceedings. This image may have several important consequences for public policy, none of which, admittedly, have yet to be demonstrated empirically. The public may come to regard Congress as something it does not wish to be—either an effete sounding board in which senators and leaders of interest groups argue and debate policy or as a President-baiter—or, Congress may acquiesce to these roles assigned it by the media and abdicate its traditional role in policymaking. These are not *inherently* evil scenarios, and they are, I repeat, speculations. But it would be more than ironic if the future roles for Congress were the mere side-effects of the organizational needs of television—organizational needs which require heroes and plot.

The Second Law of videopolitics predicts that the more coverage an institution secures, the greater its public stature and the more significant its role. As the most recent study on Presidential television demonstates vividly, the Presidency secures far more coverage than the House and Senate combined. And, predictably, the Presidency secures its media advantage for precisely the same reason that the Senate has upstaged the House: The Presidency does not just make good TV copy—it is the ultimate TV copy. The Presidency is stationary, singular, national, human, and Washington-based. The Presidency, as TV institution, overwhelms both houses of Congress combined.

What is perhaps equally important is that television has been especially helpful to Presidents in securing popular support for some of their most important decisions. Television not only enhances the President's role as chief policy-maker, it also sustains him whenever he announces these decisions in prime time appearances. In 1970, Louis Harris compared the level of support for Presidential initiatives in foreign policy before and after Presidential network appearances in defense of each of those initiatives. In every case, the level of support for the President's decision increased, often dramatically, in the period following the televised appeal. (See Table 3.) Following the Cambodian incursion in

April of 1970 and President Nixon's prime time explanation of that incursion, the level of support for the President increased by a multiple of seven![26] Only the Watergate scandals reversed the general trend in which the President makes his case on television and gains public support as a matter of course. And even as late as August of 1973, former President Nixon found that, despite increasingly damaging Watergate evidence, a prime-time appeal in which he proclaimed his innocence could work to his considerable advantage.[27]

But the issue is larger than these specific instances of increased public support. The basic issue is the effect of general exposure on the public perception of the President's role in the policy-making process. Television may contribute to the notion that the President is both the Great Legislator and the ultimate policy-maker.

Is all this inevitable? Probably. Even had the House and Senate agreed in the 1950's to admit TV, it is quite likely that the *inherent* advantages for the networks in a Presidential focus would have insured Presidential ascendency as a public institution,

TABLE 3

LEVELS OF PUBLIC SUPPORT BEFORE AND AFTER
PRESIDENTIAL APPEARANCES ON NETWORK TELEVISION

Date and Event	Percentage Supporting Policy	
	Before	After
Kennedy announces nuclear test ban treaty July 26, 1963	73	81
Johnson explains Gulf of Tonkin incident in Vietnam August 1, 1965	42	72
Johnson announces resumption of bombing on Vietnam January 31, 1966	61	73
Nixon announces policy of phased troop withdrawals May 14, 1969	49	67
Nixon plea for support of his Vietnam policy November 3, 1969	46	51
Nixon announces Cambodian strike by U.S. troops April 30, 1970	7	50
Nixon announces withdrawal of troops from Cambodia May 27, 1970	47	56

Watergate notwithstanding. However, ironically, the Congress helped speed the process. By burying its head, Congress *saved* its method of operation, but it also gave the Presidency a head start in using television as a vehicle for concentrating political and institutional power. Congress may have perpetuated its nineteenth-century procedures by keeping the media out. But, in the long run, because Congress and the Presidency are on a political seesaw, in which one's loss of power is the other's gain, to have stayed the same procedurally meant to have fallen behind politically. Again, all this may have been, to some degree, inevitable. There are, of course, several other explanations for the post-Depression erosion of congressional authority. But Congress has *facilitated* the process by keeping its doors closed and avoiding the pain of reforming and retooling. In short, television did not change the congressional role in policy-making directly. It changed the political process all over Capitol Hill, leaving Congress cosmetically the same, in conduct, but fundamentally different in role.

Conclusions

Several attempts have been made to force Congress to acquiesce and admit cameras to all its proceedings. Senator Hugh Scott and Congressman William Springer have sponsored resolutions that would not only allow TV coverage of congressional deliberations, but *compel* the stations to broadcast these proceedings. Senator Fulbright has also sponsored a resolution that would provide time for a congressional response to a Presidential address, or, in the absence of a Presidential address, provide for a regular airing of congressional opinion on prime time TV. All of these reforms are bent on increasing the extent to which Congress is televised, and hence, the significance of congressional activity. Are these reforms worthwhile?

I think the issue is still unsettled. If the networks and the stations did come to the Capitol, that *might* increase public regard for Congress; our Second Law predicts it. But unless Congress changes its procedures, this is doubtful. Visitors to the galleries of the House and Senate are rarely impressed with the congressional process. Of course TV might insure the changes that would make the congressional process look better than it does now to the visiting public.

But there is a more fundamental problem than this. Congress may not be able to put itself together to meet the scrutiny of television. Perhaps the congressional process is unsuited for video presentation, and the leadership was right from the start. Virtually every other democracy in the world gave in decades ago and made its legislature subordinate to the executive branch and the organizational leaders of the major political parties. So, it is not unreasonable to argue that the congressional system which exists today is, at base, a nineteenth-century system that cannot withstand the exposure of twentieth-century media. But to allow television into Congress will, at least, force changes (remember the First Law of videopolitics) that might make Congress a more *modern* organization, one more capable of coping with a Presidency that has enormous inherent advantages in gaining attention from media. Until we develop a more meaningful party system—and television doesn't help in this instance either—Congress is the only institution that can stand beside or in opposition to the Presidency, when opposition is warranted. I therefore believe that Congress should risk the changes that the intrusion of television will demand.

During the impeachment proceedings in the House of Representatives, the House, under intense pressure, did change the rules. Thanks to Richard Nixon, television may now come to Congressional committee meetings. But, despite the lopsidedness of the vote—346 to 40—the Speaker and the leadership were not terribly sure that the House was doing the right thing. As it turned out, the decision was a wise one. The Committee on the Judiciary, whose impeachment hearings provoked the revision of the rules, did a fine job in presenting its case to the public. And, as if to support my recommendations, the Gallup organization found that between April and August of 1974, public approval scores for Congress increased by eighteen percentage points. Gallup attributed the bulk of the increase to the televised debate among the members of the Judiciary Committee.[28]

But despite the revision of the rules and despite the exemplary behavior of the Judiciary Committee, the prospects for a full revision of the rules and a real change in policy toward the networks are not bright. Traditions, as well as rules, change slowly on Capitol Hill. Much of the old aversion to television still exists, especially among the leadership. One should remember that the House and the Senate, once off the hook with impeachment, dropped the whole issue of whether to permit or require network coverage of floor debate.

One thing is, however, relatively certain: Television journalism will, for some time to come, continue to grow as our first political medium. If television focuses more on the Presidency, after the Nixon debacle, the Presidency will grow too. As it stands now, as the Presidency grows, Congress withers. Consequently, Congress can only hope that the pain which will surely exist for the members and the leadership in converting to a TV mode of behavior—a modern mode of behavior—will invigorate Congress enough to cope with the networks, the public, and even the executive branch.

NOTES

1. Hearings on S.J. Res. 209 before Senate Committee on Commerce, subcommittee for Communications, 91st Cong., 2d sess., no. 91-74 (1970), p. 53.

2. *CBS Reports*, "Television in Politics," Mike Wallace, Fall, 1970.

3. Robert MacNeil, *The People Machine* (New York: Harper & Row, 1968), chapter 2.

4. See *Congressional Record*, July 22, 1974, pp. H6803–H6814.

5. Personal conversation with one of the Democratic committee chairmen, January 24, 1974.

6. Newton Minow, John Martin, and Lee Mitchell, *Presidential Television* (New York: Basic Books, 1973), p. 114.

7. *Ibid.*, p. 115.

8. I used the summaries in Edith Efron's *The News Twisters* to compute this figure. I counted references about Senators and House members that were made during the seven weeks preceding the 1968 election. I did *not* include references about Humphrey or Muskie in this tabulation. See Efron's *The News Twisters* (Los Angeles: Nash, 1971).

9. Personal interview, January 18, 1974.

10. *Ibid.*

11. Paul Dawson and James Zinser, "Broadcast Expenditures and Electoral

Outcomes in the 1970 Congressional Elections," *Public Opinion Quarterly* (Fall, 1971): 398–402.

12. Cited in Edward Chester, *Radio, Television, and American Politics* (New York: Sheed and Ward, 1969), p. 106.

13. *Congressional Quarterly Weekly Report* (December 1, 1973): 3130.

14. *Ibid.*

15. Dawson and Zinser, "Broadcast Expenditures," p. 400.

16. "How Congressmen Use Radio–TV," *Broadcasting* (March 16, 1964): 66.

17. Bernard Rubin, *Political Television* (Belmont, Calif.: Wadsworth, 1967), pp. 128–29.

18. Computed from Wayne Kelley, *Dollar Politics* (Washington, D.C.: Congressional Quarterly, Inc., 1971), p. 19.

19. Dawson and Zinser, "Broadcast Expenditures," p. 400.

20. *Congressional Quarterly Weekly Report* 31 (September 22, 1973): 2517. These figures do not represent television expenditures only but all general expenditures.

21. Michael Robinson, "A Congressional Attempt at Daytime Political Education: The Impact of the Televised Watergate Hearings," *Journal of Communication* (Spring, 1974).

22. Personal conversation, January 25, 1974.

23. *Congressional Record*, Proceedings and Debates of the 87th Congress, 1st Sess., vol. 107, part 2 (February 23, 1961): 2613.

24. Edward J. Epstein, *News From Nowhere* (New York: Random House, 1973), pp. 251–52.

25. *Ibid.*

26. Louis Harris data from Harris Survey, September 3, 1970. Cited in *Congress and Mass Communications: An Institutional Perspective*, Joint Committee on Governmental Operations, Congressional Reference Service (Washington, D.C.: Government Printing Office, 1974), p. 18.

27. Michael Robinson, "A Congressional Attempt at Daytime Political Education: The Impact of the Televised Watergate Hearings," *op. cit.*, p. 23.

28. Cited in *Congressional Quarterly Weekly Report*, Aug. 31, 1974, p. 2365.

V. Looking to the Future

In the preceding sections, our analyses of congressional change have examined the dynamics of reform and the reasons behind Congress's institutional framework. In this final section, we become more prescriptive. What, in other words, can and should be done to make Congress better? As Richard Fenno points out, the definition of "better" can change with the political climate; it has at different times meant a Congress submissive before executive initiatives and a Congress asserting itself against Presidential encroachment upon legislative prerogatives. The latter definition is more *au courant* and the three articles in this section are concerned with revitalizing Congress as an independent first branch of government.

As one might guess, discussions of congressional reform generally center in two areas, the two areas in Congress where power has been historically vested: the committee system and the party leadership. A third possible area for reform, the legislature's floor procedures, is less often considered (the record teller vote struggle was an exception). The heavy emphases in the readings here on seniority and committee reforms and on leadership change reflect their importance as power centers in Congress.

As we have seen, turn-of-the-century dominance by party leadership in Congress was replaced throughout most of the twentieth century with decentralized, committee-concentrated power, which is basically a *negative* power. Decentralization takes away much of the ability to formulate and implement new, large-scale policies, but it places a veto power in the hands of many along the legislative trail. In a Congress whose committees were dominated by Southern conservatives from the mid-1940's on, this power to block legislative initiatives was enhanced. In the late 1950's and

1960's, when a great deal of sweeping social and civil rights legislation was proposed and then rejected by Congress, it is not surprising that a great number of voices were raised against the "obstructionist" Congress, the "sapless" branch,[1] the "deadlock of democracy."[2] Particularly during the Kennedy years, when committee chairmen were at their zenith of influence, and Democratic congressional leaders had limited success in achieving any party unity, the lack of leadership power in Congress was widely decried. In the Nixon years, the desire for congressional power has had a different focus, but still remains strong.

In an essay written for Time Inc.'s fiftieth anniversary symposium, Charles O. Jones goes beyond an amorphous appeal for leadership to develop some specific proposals to give party leaders more capability to shape legislative policy while still remaining free of "Cannonism." Among other things, Jones clearly recognizes that television attention in contemporary America is synonymous with power, and he outlines ways to heighten the media focus on congressional leaders.

Richard F. Fenno, Jr., in another essay sponsored by Time, makes several other points about congressional power and congressional reform, which provide a valuable counterpoint to Jones's thesis. Fenno has two focuses in his essay: First, while we criticize Congress, we continue to re-elect our congressmen an astonishing percentage of the time. Indeed, "individual legislators run *for* Congress by running *against* Congress"—i.e., criticizing the institution. This strategy, arising from concern with one's re-election as a priority (compared with policy-making or internal influence) reinforces the public's negative judgments about Congress.

This leads Fenno to his second major point: Legislators' priorities are reflected in their committees, and if we are concerned about congressional performance we should focus in on individual committees and on individual members, and forgo "broken branch" type generalizations. He concludes with a caveat often missed by reformers. "It is the members who run Congress. And we get pretty much the kind of Congress they want. We shall get a different kind of Congress when we elect different kinds of congressmen." Mere institutional change, in other words, will not necessarily transform the legislature.

Donald M. Fraser (D-Minn.) and Iric Nathanson start from a somewhat different, "inside" perspective; unlike political scientists Jones and Fenno, they are directly involved as participants in the congressional process. They focus on the specifics of reform, aiming at the area where most current congressional power resides— the committee system. A series of provocative reforms are proposed to make committees more representative, less autocratic, and more responsive to party caucuses, and to streamline the policy process. Cutting down the number of committees, rotating assignments and chairmanships, and combining authorization and appropriations processes are the essential steps they propose. These far-reaching reforms are unlikely to be accepted in the foreseeable future. But the reader should ask himself or herself what impact these reforms would really have on Congress. And second, what kinds of reforms would better improve congressional processes and outputs?

SOMEBODY MUST BE TRUSTED:
AN ESSAY ON LEADERSHIP
OF THE U.S. CONGRESS

CHARLES O. JONES

As the nation prepares for two and possibly four more years of divided government, the matter of who will lead Congress becomes paramount. President Nixon will be inaugurated on Jan. 20, understandably confident that an overwhelming majority of Americans approves of the substance and style of his leadership. Yet the 93d Congress will convene with the Democrats continuing in the majority in both houses and actually having increased their margin in the Senate. No election in history better illustrates the eccentricity and the miracle of American politics. Like Dr. Doolittle's magnificent "Pushmi-Pullyu," the political system seems headed in both directions at once. If both halves are healthy, movement can occur only through cooperation and coordination. But the "Pushmi" Congress does not appear strong enough to withstand the independent movement of the "Pullyu" President. I will argue for more effective congressional leadership as a remedy, cautioning against unrealistic reform proposals.

Originally written as part of an editorial project by the editors of Time Inc., entitled "The Role of Congress: A Study of the Legislative Branch," and presented for discussion at the Racquet Club, Chicago, Illinois, December 5, 1972. Charles O. Jones is Maurice Falk Professor of Political Science at the University of Pittsburgh.

265

In his classic commentary on *Congressional Government*, Woodrow Wilson concluded that:

> If there be one principle clearer than another, it is this: that in any business, whether of government or of mere merchandising, *somebody must be trusted*, in order that when things go wrong it may be quite plain who should be punished. . . . The best rulers are always those to whom great power is intrusted in such a manner as to make them feel that they will surely be abundantly honored and recompensed for a just and patriotic use of it, and to make them know that nothing can shield them from full retribution for every abuse of it.[1]

Wilson's words reflect one variant of our political wants and needs. We do want "responsible leaders." Most Americans would probably agree with Wilson that "power and strict accountability for its use are the essential constituents of good government." On the other hand, Americans have consistently distrusted political leaders. We have seldom been willing to provide our leaders with enough authority to facilitate strict and unambiguous accountability. So while agreeing with Wilson that "somebody must be trusted," we support a political system based more on the operating principle of Inspector Clouseau (Peter Sellers' many-thumbed French police inspector): "I trust no one; I suspect everyone." The founding fathers sought to institutionalize the Clouseau principle, believing, with Lord Acton, that:

> Power tends to corrupt and absolute power corrupts absolutely. Great men are almost always bad men, even when they exercise influence and not authority; still more when you super-add the tendency or the certainty of corruption by authority. There is no worse heresy than that the office sanctifies the holder of it. . . .[2]

Whether or not we can agree that the framers made a fundamental error in building a system on distrust, it is a fact that our national political institutions developed within the basic guidelines established in 1787. What those men might do in a rewrite is anybody's guess; what their work has become is everybody's reality.

Being neither a revolutionary nor a dilettante, I propose here to focus more on reality than what might have been. And though that declaration sounds commonplace, many, if not most congressional reform proposals offered by journalists, political activists and some of my colleagues bear little relationship to how and why Congress organizes and does its work. To have any chance of approval and ultimate success, leadership reform in Congress has to be *contextually appropriate*. Every proposal should be tested by whether it is consistent with the power and functions of the American Congress. Those designed primarily to establish a parliamentary system in an American setting should be rejected out of hand as contextually unsuitable.

What is the political context in which congressional leaders must live and work? It is surely shaped by the following realities:

1. The Constitution diffuses responsibility, thus confusing accountability of leaders.
2. Americans still don't much like powerful leaders.
3. "Congress" is not a single institution—it is composed of two very different chambers.
4. Members of Congress are unlikely to support any change viewed as a threat to their careers.
5. Representatives, senators, and the President may be expected to respond to different interests in different ways.
6. The nature of modern issues, demands, and problems makes necessary a highly specialized organization in Congress.
7. Political parties have limited bases of support nationally and almost no sanctions available for use by congressional leaders.
8. The President gets more national attention than Congress and is the principal source of the congressional agenda.

One other political reality deserves emphasis in any essay on the strategy of reform. *Congress can be changed but it reforms itself.* Whatever is suggested here or elsewhere amounts to very little unless Congress or congressional parties can be convinced of the need to make improvements.

Some of these realities act as barriers to reform. Others set limits within which change is possible. Taken together they suggest that planning institutional change or seeking to redistribute power nationally involve very complex processes requiring much more patience and understanding than most reformers have demonstrated in the past. That does not mean change is impossible. Many changes have obviously taken place in national political institutions. Thus, for example, Woodrow Wilson was concerned that "the predominant and controlling force, the centre and the source of all motive and of all regulative power, is Congress."[3] He would be quite astonished to read Sir Denis Brogan's recent analysis that "the office of President of the United States has become the great overshadowing force in the American political system,"[4] to hear several observers refer to the presidency as the "American monarchy,"[5] and to learn that many liberals want to re-establish the primacy of Congress.

No, changes in power have clearly occurred in the past. Indeed, the shift in power from Congress to the presidency has caused concern, particularly since it has come with the cooperation of a Congress seemingly unable to meet the complex demands of a technetronic society frequently at war. Adaptive change over time is not excluded by the constitutional and political context. What is restricted is planned short-run change leading to comprehensive, rational distribution of power and responsibility. In fact, the restrictions are so great as to preclude that type of change and I suggest, therefore, that we not pursue it. A rather more fruitful line of inquiry is to identify those changes that are contextually appropriate and yet are likely to get the job done.

What is the job to be done? What is it we want out of Congress? I hope I speak for most Americans when I say that Congress should be the first branch of government. It was, after all, treated first in the Constitution. The House of Representatives was the only national political institution originally elected by "the People of the several States." It should continue to be the most public of our institutions—*the place of access*, of contact with the people. The Senate was intended to be *the place of debate and deliberation*, somewhat detached from public contact and, according to Hamilton,

> less apt to be tainted by the spirit of faction, and more out of the reach of those occasional ill-humors, or temporary prejudices and propensities, which, in smaller societies, frequently contaminate the

public councils, beget injustice and oppression of a part of the community, and engender schemes which, though they gratify a momentary inclination or desire, terminate in general distress, dissatisfaction, and disgust.[6]

Providing for access and debate is not enough, however. There must be a means of bringing the processes of information gathering, investigation and deliberation to a conclusion if people's needs are to be met. I have selected my words carefully here. Reaching conclusions is a more comprehensive process than simply passing laws. It includes identifying and defining problems, setting priorities, determining policy, and seeing to it that policy is administered as Congress intended. These are legitimate legislative functions. When they are delegated to the executive and the bureaucracy, Congress is weakened and therefore democracy is threatened. In the words of Theodore J. Lowi, we get "policy without law."[7]

Access, debate, conclusions—those functions constitute my short list of what ought to be happening in Congress. Of these, it is primarily the function of leadership *to see to it that conclusions are reached in Congress*. But conclusions about what? The President is, of course, the single most important source of items for the congressional agenda and he may be expected to try and get his program enacted into law. No one questions that the President has every right to exert this type of influence in Congress. At issue is the extent of that influence and whether Congress should have independent capacity to generate proposals and/or modify the President's program. My own view on that issue is unequivocal. The President's influence should be limited and his program modified by the Congress's own sources of information and support. I take it as given, therefore, that congressional leaders have an important role to play independently of the President.

Now one other point has to be emphasized before criticizing congressional leadership and discussing reasonable, feasible change. We have had strong leadership in Congress in the past—particularly in the House of Representatives. Indeed, the current diffusion of leadership among senior committee chairmen, so debilitating for centralizing responsibility in party leaders, can be traced to the backlash in Congress to the tyrannical reign of Speaker Joe

Cannon in the House and the strong hand of Senator Nelson W. Aldrich in the Senate during the first decade of this century. Speaker Cannon wielded impressive authority—rewarding his friends and harshly punishing his enemies. He did it by emphasizing the political party appeal. A journalist of that era, George Rothwell Brown, describes how it worked:

> The party appeal . . . was the most powerful psychological factor in the House, and the leadership not only made use of this, but over-capitalized it, until in the end the man of independent spirit and liberalized mind who sought to strike out for himself along new pathways of action, and to explore the uncharted seas of experimental legislation, was terrorized by having brought against him the allegation of party disloyalty. The mass tendency in the House was to preserve instinctively the party system upon which its great power as the champion of free institutions against the autocracy of the Executive was dependent; the individual instinct was to destroy it, as something hampering to free will.[8]

Individual instinct won out, of course, and rather than simply changing party leaders, the House effectively destroyed the basis of party leadership. Committee chairmen then emerged with independent authority as seniority emerged as a major determinant of congressional leadership.

I would guess that returning to Cannonism or Aldrichism is not a viable option in the search for effective and trusted leadership in Congress. Thus, in rejecting that alternative, I am finally able to put the central question for this essay: *How can congressional leaders get their respective chambers to reach conclusions without being tyrannical or thwarting the processes of access and debate?* I propose only to begin analysis of that most difficult question by recommending a style or basis of change both inside and outside Congress.

What Should Happen in Congress

The problem with the present leadership structure in Congress is that it facilitates access and debate but not conclusions. There is no way to knock heads together and say: "Enough is enough!

Find out what you want to do and do it!" Whatever other fine qualities they may have, the current stable of party leaders in Congress do not strike one as aggressive head-knockers. For example, when Senate Majority Leader Mike Mansfield was called upon in 1963 to "behave like a leader" he responded:

> I shall not don any Mandarin's robes or any skin other than that to which I am accustomed in order that I may look like a majority leader or sound like a majority leader—however a majority leader is supposed to look or sound. I am what I am and no title, political face-lifter, or imagemaker can alter it. . . . I do my best to be courteous, decent, and understanding of others and sometimes fail at it. But it is for the Senate to decide whether these characteristics are incompatible with the leadership.[9]

The Senate has not, to date, made any such decision. Mansfield is completing twelve years as majority floor leader—a record for floor leader in either party. . . .

A political activist would be climbing the walls if forced to spend a week observing the leadership techniques of Senator Mansfield or Speaker of the House Carl Albert. But, of course, given the political context, an activist leader would be ignored. Senator Mansfield's "soft-sell" may not meet any of the commonly accepted standards of leadership, but it apparently has been acceptable to Senate Democrats to date. Should he decide tomorrow to do a turn-about and try to move the Senate he will find very little authority to back him up and even fewer sanctions to employ when powerful senators watch in wry amusement.

The trick then is to provide some incentives, some rewards for increasing the authority and changing the expectations of congressional party leaders. Reform proposals should be evaluated in terms of whether and how the members will benefit. Does this smack of compromise? It certainly does. And I see nothing wrong with that. Compromise is not a mode of decision-making developed to "bug" the moralists of this nation. It is well suited to the constitutional and political context within which Congress operates. So many limits have been imposed on institutions and their leaders that every major decision has to be arrived at through bargaining and accommodation. Thus, any change so fundamental as increasing the authority of party leaders must be accomplished by reassurance and guarantees either that the new arrangement will have payoffs for the members or that maintaining existing patterns will hurt them. *Failure to acknowledge this basic fact of political life in proposing change assures that the proposal will simply be dropped into the bottomless well of good intentions.*

I am not prepared at this time to support specific changes inside Congress to accomplish the goals I have outlined. This clearly requires careful study, involving the members themselves. I can, however, list possible changes to be evaluated by the test of improving the congressional capability for reaching conclusions and the test of political feasibility (e.g., whether members can be convinced of the benefits):

1. Provide for more formal nomination and campaign procedures in electing party leaders.

2. Increase the authority of party leaders to control legislative production in Congress, including methods by which legislation can be acted on in committees (e.g., careful monitoring of committee progress on major legislation; authority to withdraw legislation from a committee).

3. Require an end-of-session review of the legislative record of party leaders before a joint caucus of party members from both houses. Such a session should provide for debate of the record and be open to the press and the public.

4. Commission a study of the efficiency and effectiveness of the existing party structure in each house—directed by an independent agent but including members of both parties and both houses.

5. Expand the Congressional Research Service and the Office of Legislative Counsel; establish Offices of Congressional Committee Organization and Administration; and reduce the size of existing committee staffs.

6. Review the existing research capabilities for congressional political parties, possibly increase staff available for that purpose, make party leaders directly responsible for use of research staff, and require periodic reporting by party leaders in caucus.

I emphasize again that these are not reform proposals as such. If any strike a responsive chord, however, then each should be thoroughly evaluated for its effect on access, debate, and reaching conclusions. I am stressing reform strategy here—a first order of business in making change.

What Should Happen Outside Congress

Congress is basically not a self-starting institution. If the President is not actively and aggressively pursuing a program, the Congress is unlikely to initiate a program of its own, regardless of the pressure of issues. The same holds for initiating congressional reform. New members, fresh from having slain the dragon, and middle-aged members, wilted from the frustrations of heavy processes, may agree on the need for change but lack the influence, backing, communication, knowledge, or sagacity to get the ball rolling. Creating a climate of support for change among the general public *outside* Congress may overcome the resistance to change inherent in existing processes and structures. In a period of unexcelled communications technology, surely greater attention to Congress can have an impact—both in improving congressional capabilities and in providing leaders with the support necessary to counteract the centrifugal tendencies of congressional power.

In this sphere, of course, one does not depend solely on Congress to act. Rather an effort can be made to generate pressure for reform. "Congress can be changed," after all—both over time as a result of changes in society and hopefully in response to public concern that Congress is losing power. After all, both postwar Legislative Reorganization acts, 1946 and 1970, were enacted following a period of presidential dominance.

The television networks, and magazines and newspapers with national circulation, are particularly potent vehicles for creating a climate of support for and trust in party leaders. But first they must devote more sympathetic and constructive attention to Congress. I propose that the media buck the trends, or at least dam up the swift current of attentiveness to the President and his court. I acknowledge the self-sacrifice called for in that request —understanding that the media, too, "can be changed, but reform themselves." But what better time to accept such a challenge? . . . A period of consolidation is the perfect time to analyze the role of Congress. When government is reorganizing to do the job better, copy with "grab" is difficult to come by. The media, therefore, have nothing to lose by expanding their coverage of Congress and even taking the initiative in developing national support for strong and effective leadership in the national legislature.

One important caveat must be entered at this point. It will hurt rather than help the cause for the media to criticize only (though criticize they must) or submit to the understandable temptation to sensationalize, to be preoccupied with a few ethical lapses of members. An effort must be made to accentuate the positive, to feature those less newsworthy legislators seeking responsible change or those unexciting reports so necessary as the basis of that change. That will require initiative and careful planning. . . . And hopefully, where others have accentuated the negative, someone in the media will seek to turn the criticism into positive recommendation for change.

A number of specific recommendations come to mind for creating a climate of support for stronger and more effective leadership in Congress. Most of these are designed to monitor what goes on there, as well as encourage evaluation of performance by the public, journalists, and the members themselves. An attentive press can act both as a means of support for party leaders in their efforts to get Congress to reach conclusions, and as a source of criticism to prevent the autocracy characteristic of Cannonism:

1. Expand coverage of the election of party leaders in Congress —including background on candidates, the campaign and how members voted. . . .

2. Evaluate the performance of party leaders in Congress, taking account of problems with recalcitrant members or difficult committee chairmen.

3. Expand coverage of the nominating process for congressional candidates, including the financing of campaigns.

4. Develop special features on Congress—television specials, cover stories, possibly even a separate publication on Congress (less comprehensive, more popular, and more willing to evaluate than either the *Congressional Quarterly Weekly Report* or *The National Journal*).

5. Conduct year-end reviews of party performance in each house (based on careful research conducted by competent scholars of Congress).

6. Trace the development of specific legislation—showing not only what the President requested but the ways in which congressional leaders (both party and committee leaders) were involved.

7. Take special note of the fantastic array of public documents on Congress—possibly featuring a particularly important set of committee hearings and then judging the extent to which the findings resulted in legislation.

8. Maintain the expanded coverage over time. Changing institutions requires patience—consolidating the changes demands even more. Little will be accomplished if Congress is again treated as a second-class institution by the media.

One could continue this list almost indefinitely. The point has been made, however. Congress deserves more constructive attention than it has been getting. Any institution is shaped by expectations. Being told that Congress is a second-class institution, unable to do its job, naturally reduces our expectations of what is possible in that institution. Eventually, first-rate people decline association with Congress and reality soon coincides with prophesy. Since what happens outside Congress is absolutely vital for what happens within, the media should become an active partner in evaluating, improving, and maintaining that most public of our national political institutions.

Concluding Observations

Congress does not need more power—it has more than any other legislature in the world. It does need to find ways in which it can use its power effectively in the post-industrial society, however. Party leaders can play an important role in achieving that goal but only if given commensurate measures of responsibility and accountability. Woodrow Wilson saw this as a matter of trust; I agree. And yet Americans are accustomed to withholding trust—relying rather on mutual suspicion and doubt in government. This pattern in politics has become anomalous in view of the fact that the technological era has made American individualists very dependent. We have come to trust technology implicitly —insisting on very few checks and balances to prevent horrendous excesses. I am not arguing for such a high degree of trust in congressional leaders, but I am promoting enough so that we can legitimately hold them accountable for what they do, or fail to do. I do not expect many to argue this point—the problem is how to develop that confidence in a political system accustomed to operating on the principles of Inspector Clouseau.

NOTES

1. Woodrow Wilson, *Congressional Government* (Boston: Houghton Mifflin, 1885), pp. 283–84.

2. Lord Acton, *Essays on Freedom and Power* (Glencoe, Illinois: The Free Press, 1948), p. 364.

3. Wilson, *Congressional Government*, p. 11.

4. Sir Denis Brogan, "U.S. Presidency: As Powerful as Caesar in Rome?", *The Christian Science Monitor* (November 3, 1972): 9.

5. See, for example, George E. Reedy, *The Twilight of the Presidency* (New York: World Publishing Co., 1970).

6. *The Federalist* (New York: Modern Library edition, 1937), p. 167.

7. Theodore J. Lowi, *The End of Liberalism* (New York: W. W. Norton & Co., 1969).

8. George Rothwell Brown, *The Leadership of Congress* (Indianapolis: Bobbs-Merrill, 1922), p. 124.

9. *Congressional Record*, 88th Cong., 1st Sess., November 27, 1963, pp. 21758–59.

IF, AS RALPH NADER SAYS, CONGRESS IS "THE BROKEN BRANCH," HOW COME WE LOVE OUR CONGRESSMEN SO MUCH?

RICHARD F. FENNO, JR.

Off and on during the past two years, I accompanied ten members of the House of Representatives as they traveled around in their home districts. In every one of those districts I heard a common theme, one that I had not expected. Invariably, the representative I was with—young or old, liberal or conservative, Northerner, Southerner, Easterner, or Westerner, Democrat or Republican— was described as "the best congressman in the United States." Having heard it so often, I now accept the description as fact. I am even prepared to believe the same thing (though I cannot claim to have heard it with my own ears) of the members of the Senate. Each of our 435 representatives and 100 senators is, indeed, "the best congressman in the United States." Which is to say that each enjoys a great deal of support and approbation among his or her constituents. Judging by the election returns, this isn't much of an exaggeration. In the recent election, 96 per cent of all House incumbents who ran were re-elected; and 85 per

Originally written as part of an editorial project by the editors of Time Inc., entitled "The Role of Congress: A Study of the Legislative Branch," and presented for discussion at the Harvard Club, Boston, Massachusetts, December 12, 1972. Richard F. Fenno, Jr., is Professor of Political Science at the University of Rochester and author of several books on Congress.

cent of all Senate incumbents who ran were re-elected. These convincing figures are close to the average re-election rates of incumbents for the past ten elections. We do, it appears, love our congressmen.

On the other hand, it seems equally clear that we do not love our Congress. Louis Harris reported in 1970 that only one-quarter of the electorate gave Congress a positive rating on its job performance—while nearly two-thirds expressed themselves negatively on the subject. And we would not be here tonight if there were not considerable concern—dramatized recently by the critical Nader project—for the performance of Congress as an institution. On the evidence, we seem to approve of our legislators a good deal more than we do our legislature. And therein hangs something of a puzzle. If our congressmen are so good, how can our Congress be so bad? If it is the individuals that make up the institution, why should there be such a disparity in our judgments? What follows are a few reflections on this puzzle.

A first answer is that we apply different standards of judgment, those that we apply to the individual being less demanding than those we apply to the institution. For the individual, our standard is one of representativeness—of personal style and policy views. Stylistically, we ask that our legislator display a sense of identity with us so that we, in turn, can identify with him or her—via personal visits to the district, concern for local projects and individual "cases," and media contact of all sorts, for example. On the policy side, we ask only that his general policy stance does not get too frequently out of line with ours. And, if he should become a national leader in some policy area of interest to us, so much the better. These standards are admittedly vague. But because they are locally defined and locally applied, they are consistent and manageable enough so that legislators can devise rules of thumb to meet them. What is more, by their performance they help shape the standards, thereby making them easier to meet. Thus they win constituent recognition as "the best in the United States." And thus they establish the core relationship for a representative democracy.

For the institution, however, our standards emphasize efforts to solve national problems—a far less tractable task than the one we (and he) set for the individual. Given the inevitable existence of unsolved problems, we are destined to be unhappy with congressional performance. The individual legislator knows when he has met our standards of representativeness; he is re-elected. But no such definitive measure of legislative success exists. And, precisely because Congress is the most familiar and most human of our national institutions, lacking the distant majesty of the Presidency and the Court, it is the easy and natural target of our criticism. We have met our problem solvers, and they are us.

Furthermore, such standards as we do use for judging the institutional performance of Congress are applied inconsistently. In 1963, when public dissatisfaction was as great as in 1970, Congress was criticized for being obstructionist, dilatory and insufficiently cooperative with regard to the Kennedy programs. Two years later, Congress got its highest performance rating of the decade when it cooperated completely with the executive in rushing the Great Society program into law. But by the late 1960's and early 1970's the standard of judgment had changed radically —from cooperation to counterbalance in Congressional relations with the Executive. Whereas, in 1963, Harris had found "little in the way of public response to the time-honored claim that the Legislative Branch is . . . the guardian against excessive Executive power," by 1968 he found that three-quarters of the electorate wanted Congress to act as the watchdog of the Executive and not to cooperate so readily with it. The easy passage of the Tonkin Resolution reflects the cooperative standards set in the earlier period; its repeal reflects the counterbalancing standards of the recent period. Today we are concerned about Ralph Nader's "broken branch" which, we hear, has lost—and must reclaim from the Executive—its prerogatives in areas such as war-making and spending control. To some degree, then, our judgments on Congress are negative because we change our minds frequently concerning the kind of Congress we want. A Congress whose main job is to cooperate with the Executive would look quite different from one whose main job is to counterbalance the Executive.

Beneath the differences in our standards of judgment, however, lies a deeper dynamic of the political system. Senators and representatives, for their own reasons, spend a good deal more of their time and energy polishing and worrying about their individual performance than they do working at the institution's performance. Though it is, of course, true that their individual activity is related to institutional activity, their first-order concerns are individual, not institutional. Foremost is their desire for re-election. Most members of Congress like their job, want to keep it, and know that there are people back home who want to take it away from them. So they work long and hard at winning re-election. Even those who are safest want election margins large enough to discourage opposition back home and/or to help them float further political ambitions. No matter what other personal goals representatives and senators wish to accomplish—increased influence in Washington and helping to make good public policy are the most common—re-election is a necessary means to those ends.

We cannot criticize these priorities—not in a representative system. If we believe the representative should mirror constituency opinion, we must acknowledge that it requires considerable effort for him to find out what should be mirrored. If we believe a representative should be free to vote his judgment, he will have to cultivate his constituents assiduously before they will trust him with such freedom. Either way we will look favorably on his efforts. We come to love our legislators, in the *second* place, because they so ardently sue for our affections.

As a courtship technique, moreover, they re-enforce our unfavorable judgments about the institution. Every representative with whom I traveled criticized the Congress and portrayed himself, by contrast, as a fighter against its manifest evils. Members run *for* Congress by running *against* Congress. They refurbish their individual reputations as "the best congressman in the United States" by attacking the collective reputation of the Congress of the United States. Small wonder the voters feel so much more warmly disposed and so much less fickle toward the individuals than toward the institution.

One case in point: the House decision to grant President Nixon a spending ceiling plus authority to cut previously appropriated funds to maintain that ceiling. One-half the representatives I was with blasted the House for being so spineless that it gave away its power of the purse to the President. The other half blasted the

House for being so spineless in exercising its power of the purse that the President had been forced to act. Both groups spoke to supportive audiences; and each man enhanced his individual reputation by attacking the institution. Only by raising both questions, however, could one see the whole picture. Once the President forced the issue, how come the House didn't stand up to him and protect its crucial institutional power over the purse strings? On the other hand, if economic experts agreed that a spending ceiling was called for, how come the House didn't enact it and make the necessary budget cuts in the first place? The answer to the first question lies in the proximity of their re-election battles, which re-enforced the tendency of all representatives to think in individualistic rather than institutional terms. The answer to the second question lies in the total absence of institutional machinery whereby the House (or, indeed, Congress) can make overall spending decisions.

Mention of the institutional mechanisms of Congress leads us to a *third* explanation for our prevailing pattern of judgments. When members of Congress think institutionally—as, of course they must—they think in terms of a structure that will be most congenial to the pursuit of their individual concerns—for re-election, for influence, or for policy. Since each individual has been independently designated "the best in the United States," each has an equal status and an equal claim to influence within the structure. For these reasons, the members naturally think in terms of a very fragmented, decentralized institution, providing a maximum of opportunity for individual performance, individual influence, and individual credit.

The 100-member Senate more completely fits this description than the 435-member House. The smaller body permits a more freewheeling and creative individualism. But both chambers tend strongly in this direction, and representatives as well as senators chafe against centralizing mechanisms. Neither body is organized in hierarchical—or even in well-coordinated—patterns of decision-making. Agreements are reached by some fairly subtle forms of mutual adjustment—by negotiation, bargaining, and compromise. And interpersonal relations—of respect, confidence, trust—are crucial building blocks. The members of Congress, in pursuit of

their individual desires, have thus created an institution that is
internally quite complex. Its structure and processes are, therefore,
very difficult to grasp from the outside.

In order to play out some aspects of the original puzzle, however, we must make the effort. And the committee system, the
epitome of fragmentation and decentralization, is a good place to
start. The performance of Congress as an institution is very largely
the performance of its committees. The Nader project's "broken
branch" description is mostly a committee-centered description because that is where the countervailing combination of congressional expertise and political skill resides. To strengthen Congress
means to strengthen its committees. To love Congress means to
love its committees. Certainly when we have not loved our Congress, we have heaped our displeasure upon its committees. The
major legislative reorganizations, of 1946 and 1970, were committee-centered reforms—centering on committee jurisdictions,
committee democracy, and committee staff support. Other continuing criticisms—of the seniority rule for selecting committee
chairmen, for example—have centered on the committees.

Like Congress as a whole, committees must be understood first
in terms of what they do for the individual member. To begin
with, committees are relatively more important to the individual
House member than to the individual senator. The representative's
career inside Congress is very closely tied to his committee. For
the only way such a large body can function is to divide into
highly specialized and independent committees. Policy-making
activity funnels through these committees; so does the legislative
activity and influence of the individual legislator. While the
Senate has a set of committees paralleling those of the House, a
committee assignment is nowhere near as constraining for the
career of the individual senator. The Senate is more loosely organized, senators sit on many more committees and subcommittees
than representatives, and they have easy access to the work of
committees of which they are not members. Senators, too, can
command and utilize national publicity to gain influence beyond
the confines of their committee. Whereas House committees act
as funnels for individual activity, Senate committees act as facili-
tators of individual activity. The difference in functions is con-

siderable—which is why committee chairmen are a good deal more important in the House than in the Senate and why the first modifications of the seniority rule should have come in the House rather than the Senate. My examples will come from the House.

Given the great importance of his committee to the career of the House member, it follows that we will want to know how each committee can affect such careers. . . .

Where a committee's members are especially interested in pyramiding their individual influence, they will act so as to maintain the influence of their committee (and, hence, their personal influence) within the House. They will adopt procedures that enhance the operating independence of the committee. They will work hard to remain relatively independent of the Executive Branch. And they will try to underpin that independence with such resources as specialized expertise, internal cohesion, and the respect of their House colleagues. Ways and Means and Appropriations are committees of this sort. By contrast, where a committee's members are especially interested in getting in on nationally controversial policy action, they will not be much concerned about the independent influence of their committee. They will want to ally themselves closely with any and all groups outside the committee who share their policy views. They want to help enact what they individually regard as good public policy; and if that means ratifying policies shaped elsewhere—in the Executive Branch particularly—so be it. And, since their institutional independence is not a value for them, they make no special effort to acquire such underpinnings as expertise, cohesion, or chamber respect. Education and Labor and Foreign Affairs are committees of this sort.

These two types of committees display quite different strengths in their performance. Those of the first type are especially influential. Ways and Means probably makes a greater independent contribution to policy-making than any other House committee. Appropriations probably exerts a more influential overview of executive branch activities than any other House committee. The price they pay, however, is a certain decrease in their responsiveness to noncommittee forces—as complaints about the closed rule on tax bills and executive hearings on appropriations bills will attest. Committees of the second type are especially responsive to noncommittee forces and provide easy conduits for outside influence in policy-making. Education and Labor was probably more receptive to President Johnson's Great Society policies than any other House committee; it successfully passed the largest part of that program. Foreign Affairs has probably remained as thoroughly responsive to Executive Branch policies, in foreign aid for instance, as any House committee. The price they pay, however, is a certain decrease in their influence—as complaints about the rubber-stamp Education and Labor Committee and about the impotent Foreign Affairs Committee will attest. In terms of the earlier discussions of institutional performance standards, our hopes for a cooperative Congress lie more with the latter type of committee; our hopes for a counterbalancing Congress lie more with the former.

So, committees differ. And they differ to an important degree according to the desires of their members. This ought to make us wary of blanket descriptions. Within the House, Foreign Affairs may look like a broken branch, but Ways and Means does not. And, across chambers, Senate Foreign Relations (where member incentives are stronger) is a good deal more potent than House Foreign Affairs. With the two Appropriations committees, the reverse is the case. It is not just that "the broken branch" is an undiscriminating, hence inaccurate, description. It is also that blanket descriptions lead to blanket prescriptions. And it just might be that the wisest course of congressional reform would be to identify existing nodes of committee strength and nourish them rather than to prescribe, as we usually do, reforms in equal dosages for all committees.

One lesson of the analysis should be that member incentives must exist to support any kind of committee activity. Where incentives vary, it may be silly to prescribe the same functions and resources for all committees. The Reorganization Act of 1946 mandated all committees to exercise "continuous watchfulness" over the executive branch—in the absence of any supporting incentive system. We have gotten overview activity only where random individuals have found an incentive for doing so—not by most committees and certainly not continuously. Similarly, I suspect that our current interest in exhorting all committees to acquire more information with which to combat the executive may be misplaced. Information is relatively easy to come by— and some committees have a lot of it. What is hard to come by is the incentive to use it, not to mention the time and the trust necessary to make it useful. I am not suggesting a set of reforms but rather a somewhat different strategy of committee reforms— less wholesale, more retail.

Since the best-known target of wholesale committee reform is the seniority rule, it deserves special comment. If our attacks on the rule have any substance to them, if they are anything other than symbolic, the complaint must be that some or all committee chairmen are not doing a good job. But we can only find out whether this is so by conducting a committee-by-committee examination. Paradoxically, our discussions of the seniority rule tend to steer us away from such a retail examination by mounting very broad, across-the-board kinds of arguments against chairmen as a class—arguments about their old age, their conservatism, their national unrepresentativeness. Such arguments produce great cartoon copy, easy editorial broadsides, and sitting-duck targets for our congressmen on the stump. But we ought not to let the arguments themselves, nor the Pavlovian public reactions induced by our cartoonists, editorial writers, and representatives, pass for good institutional analysis. Rather, they have diverted us from that task.

More crucial to a committee's performance than the selection of its chairman is his working relationship with the other committee members. Does he agree with his members on the functions of the committee? Does he act to facilitate the achievement of their individual concerns? Do they approve of his performance as chairman? Where there is real disagreement between chairman and members, close analysis may lead us to fault the members and not the chairman. If so, we should be focusing our criticisms on the members. If the fault lies with the chairman, a majority of the members have the power to bring him to heel. They need not kill the king; they can constitutionalize the monarchy. While outsiders have been crying "off with his head," the members of several committees have been quietly and effectively constitutionalizing the monarchy. Education and Labor, Post Office, and Interior are recent examples where dissatisfied committee majorities have subjected their chairmen to majority control. Where this has not been done, it is probably due to member satisfaction, member timidity, member disinterest, or member incompetence. And the time we spend railing against the seniority rule might be better spent finding out, for each congressional committee, just which of these is the case. If, as a final possibility, a chairman and his members are united in opposition to the majority part or to the rest of us, the seniority rule is not the problem. More to the point, as I suspect is usually the case, the reasons and the ways individual members get sorted onto the various committees is the critical factor. In sum, I am not saying that the seniority rule is a good thing. I am saying that, for committee performance, it is not a very important thing.

What has all this got to do with the original puzzle—that we love our congressmen so much more than our Congress? We began with a few explanatory guesses. Our standards of judgment for individual performance are more easily met; the individual member works harder winning approval for himself than for his institution; and Congress is a complex institution, difficult for us to understand. The more we try to understand Congress—as we did briefly with the committee system—the more we are forced to peel back the institutional layers until we reach the individual member. At that point, it becomes hard to separate, as we normally do, our judgments about congressmen and Congress. The more we come to see institutional performance as influenced by the desires of the individual member, the more the original puzzle ought to resolve itself. For as the independence of our judgments decreases, the disparity between them ought to grow smaller. But if we are to hold this perspective on Congress, we shall need to understand the close individual-institution relationship—chamber by chamber, party by party, committee by committee, legislator by legislator.

This is not counsel of despair. It is a counsel of sharper focus and a more discriminating eye. It counsels the mass media, for example, to forego "broken branch" type generalizations about Congress in favor of examining a committee in depth, or to forego broad criticism of the seniority rule for a close look at a committee chairman. It counsels the rest of us to focus more on the individual member and to fix the terms of our dialogue with him more aggressively. It counsels us to fix terms that will force him to think more institutionally and which will hold him more accountable for the performance of the institution. "Who Runs Congress," asks the title of the Nader report, "the President, Big Business or You?" From the perspective of this paper, it is none of these. It is the members who run Congress. And we get pretty much the kind of Congress they want. We shall get a different kind of Congress when we elect different kinds of congressmen or when we start applying different standards of judgment to old congressmen. Whether or not we ought to have a different kind of Congress is still another, much larger, puzzle.

REBUILDING THE HOUSE
OF REPRESENTATIVES

DONALD M. FRASER and IRIC NATHANSON

A group of political scientists once described the twentieth century as an antiparliamentary era—a time when legislatures in many countries have become "walking corpses," surviving in form but not in political vitality.[1]

After viewing recent events in Washington, more than a few skeptics maintain that the U.S. House of Representatives has already joined the ranks of the living dead.

In 1973, the House sat by helplessly while President Nixon vastly increased his executive powers. Even as he struggled to save his presidency, Mr. Nixon impounded appropriated funds, dismantled congressionally authorized programs and greatly expanded the definition of executive privilege. With one notable exception, all presidential vetoes were sustained in the House.[2] Only a massive outpouring of public concern finally moved the lower body to face the constitutional crisis provoked by the Watergate scandals.

Hopefully, the next Congress, the 94th, will assert its authority more effectively. The new House's response to the larger national issues will depend in large part on political judgments made by its individual members. But the next House will be more than a loose collection of men and women who meet together at noon every

Donald M. Fraser is a Democratic congressman from Minnesota. Iric Nathanson is a staff assistant to Representative Fraser.

288

day in the U.S. Capitol. Its decisions, as a collective body, will be shaped by an elaborate institutional structure whose original parts were first put in place 185 years ago. From time to time, this structure has been repaired, but it is now creaky and rusty with age. Its output is clearly not equal to the demands placed on it during these difficult times.

In the following article, we outline some ways in which the organizational machinery of the House can be overhauled. We make four basic proposals:

1. The number of standing committees should be reduced to less than ten. Each new legislative unit should have jurisdiction over a broad range of related issues.

2. The federal budget period should be extended to two years.

3. The Appropriations Committee should be abolished and its responsibilities transferred to the newly enlarged program committees.

4. Committee memberships and chairmanships should rotate on an eight-year cycle.

Restructuring the Committee System

Our antiquated committee system with its 21 standing committees and 126 subcommittees forces House members to concern themselves with bits and pieces of policy questions. Jurisdiction over the same issue is often divided between more than a dozen different House groups. Eighteen subcommittees, for example, deal with education matters in one way or another.

The existing system was designed to handle problems of an earlier era. One group of 37 House members looks after the merchant marine and fisheries. Another group of 27 oversees the post office and the federal civil service. Yet no single committee has primary responsibility for environmental or energy matters. When new issues arise, competing committees often must wage jurisdictional battles with each other before the House can get on with the job of legislating.

We would like to see extensive committee reorganization. The number of House legislative units should be cut by nearly two-thirds if committees are to deal effectively with the larger issues facing the country. We hesitate to come up with detailed jurisdictional recommendations for these broad-ranged committees, however, because this is an exceedingly complicated task. The Select Committee on Committees, chaired by Rep. Richard Bolling (D-Mo.), spent nearly a year working up its more modest plan.

Professor Robert Peabody and others have already developed useful models which conform to our standards. Under the Peabody plan, the House would be organized into eight major legislative subgroups.[3] A human resources committee, for example, would pull together education, health, and welfare programs under the same jurisdictional umbrella. Similarly, a natural resources committee would handle agriculture, land use, pollution control, and related issues.

By estabishing large committees with 50 or more members, we would in effect be creating mini-Houses. Each new unit would have authority over a broad range of related issues. Subcommittees would be elevated in importance, much as they are today in the Appropriations Committee. Party caucuses on the committee level would become more significant, gaining more responsibility for establishing agendas and setting priorities.

The full House with its 435 members is an unwieldy body. Many of its responsibilities might be handled more adequately on the committee level. Take the question of jurisdictions, for example. Any major jurisdictional realignment of the House requires a major political effort by congressional reformers. It is much simpler for a committee to reorder the jurisdictions of its subcommittees. We have seen a considerable amount of realignment within committees recently—District of Columbia and Appropriations are two examples—but almost none between full committees in the last 27 years. More significant debates could occur in the larger committees, constituting an effective review of bills drafted by subcommittees. The committees could also consolidate the smaller bills, thus giving the full House more time to adequately consider the most important or controversial measures.

Extending the Budget Period

The present annual cycle of appropriations works to the detriment of Congress and the agencies whose spending levels are established through this process. The House Appropriations subcommittees barely have time to digest the Administration's budget requests before they are called upon to start reporting out bills. This time pressure in part accounts for the fact that spending measures are rarely approved before the start of a new fiscal year.

A two-year appropriations cycle, with a budget submitted well in advance of the start of the new fiscal year, would do much to relieve this legislative logjam.[4] It would also give House members time to thoroughly examine the ongoing operations of federal agencies. The most effective legislative oversight now occurs during budget review time at the start of each new session. But some Appropriations subcommittees must rush through hundreds of programs within a four-month period. Obviously each program receives less than a thoroughgoing examination under the current system.

A two-year budget cycle would also give agencies the time they need to plan and operate new programs. An agency administrator hardly has time now to implement a new congressional directive before he is faced with the prospect of a budget justification for the next fiscal year.

There is nothing sacred about a one-year appropriation. Many states budget on a two-year cycle with no apparent loss of public control over state spending.

Consolidating Authorizations and Appropriations

The authorization-appropriations split exemplifies the fragmentation that affects the policy-making process in Congress generally. The Appropriations Committee, through its control of the purse strings, can and does counteract the policy initiatives developed by the authorizing committees. Even the federal budget itself is not handled in a consistent way. Funding for highways, social security, veterans, and a variety of other programs—more than half the domestic budget—is outside the jurisdiction of the Appropriations Committee. The House has moved to deal with this problem through the Budget Control and Impoundment Act, H.R. 7130, voted on late in the 1973 session. The budget bill would bring so-called back door spending under the control of the Appropriations Committee by 1978.

This new legislation also attempts to integrate the budget process through the use of an overall spending target set by Congress before the House Appropriations Committee begins its deliberations. Subceiling targets for separate functional categories are also established. If aggregate appropriations result in spending figures higher than the initial targets, then either cuts are made or taxes raised to cover the spending increases. This plan, while it contains some useful innovations, does not consolidate the appropriations and authorization process, a step we feel should be taken. Alice Rivlin, Charles Schultze, and others have proposed the same kind of structural change.[5]

Under our committee reorganization plan outlined earlier, each of the new program committees could have two separate staffs. One would handle legislative oversight and budget review. It would be charged with the responsibility for determining whether programs were meeting the goals laid out for them. The second staff would be involved in long-range policy planning, feeding its work into the development of authorizing legislation. The House member himself would provide the link between the processes.

Even under this new system, we would be left with the need to establish overall spending priorities. This is not a problem that can be handled structurally, however, as the budget bill seeks to do. More can be done to clarify priority issues and give them visibility but their resolution must come through the political process.

Rotating Committee Memberships

Committees now have great difficulty maintaining an objective detachment from the programs and agencies they oversee. Often they become, in the words of one House member, either "grave-yards" or "unrestrained promotional agencies" for their jurisdic-tional matters.[6] We feel this problem can best be handled by limiting the length of time a congressman can serve on any one committee. Eight years might be adequate.

Some will maintain that rotating membership denies House members the opportunity to become experts in their subject mat-ter areas. But we should remember that congressmen are policy-makers, not technicians. We shouldn't expect a legislator to spend twenty years studying health care, for example, before he or she is qualified to make a political judgment about the need for a na-tional health insurance system. Rotating committee membership, in fact, could give senior members of the House the broader view of public issues they need to develop more effective public policy.

Under our plan, of course, the seniority system would have to be modified since no one House member would have more than eight years seniority on his or her committee. We suggest that full committee chairmen be nominated by the Democratic Policy and Steering Committee, when the Democrats control the House, with election to follow by the Democratic caucus. Subcommittee chair-manships, in turn, could be determined by party caucuses on the committee level.

This new committee membership arrangement could help solve the ongoing problem of jurisdictional realignment in the House. Until some way can be found to pry loose the vested interests en-crusted in the current committee system, any major reorganization of committee jurisdictions is likely to involve an enormous politi-cal struggle. Even rotation is not guaranteed to break up trouble-some pockets of vested interest. But, as the legislative players keep changing places, the House will be a much less rigid institu-tion than it has been in the past.

Structural reforms are clearly no substitute for political leader-ship and political will. No amount of institutional tinkering will force the House to confront the major issues of the time, if the basic motivation is lacking. But if the will to act is there, organi-zational arrangements can impede or facilitate the development of more adequate public policy.

We cannot enable the House to make the right decisions. We

can, at least, make sure the decision-making equipment is in good working order, ready and waiting to be used.

NOTES

1. Roger H. Davidson, David Kovenock, and Michael K. O'Leary, *Congress in Crisis: Politics and Congressional Reform*, (Belmont, Calif.: Wadsworth Publishing Co., 1966), p. 163.

2. On November 7, 1973, by a vote of 284 to 135 the House overrode President Nixon's veto of the War Powers Resolution, H.J. Res. 542.

3. See Robert L. Peabody, "House Leadership, Party Caucuses and the Committee Structure," Working Papers on House Committee Organization and Operation, 93d Cong., 1st Sess., June, 1973.

4. Consideration of biennial appropriations would be facilitated by the Bolling Committee recommendation to shift the start of the fiscal year from July 1 to October 1.

5. See Alice M. Rivlin and Charles L. Schultze, "Shaping the Budget, A Way Out of Chaos," *Washington Post Outlook* (September 9, 1973): C 1.

6. Statement of Hon. Bill Frenzel, A Representative in Congress from the State of Minnesota, Hearings Before the Select Committee on Committees, 93d Cong., 1st Sess., Part 2, Vol. 1, page 373.

BIBLIOGRAPHY

The Bibliography contains a sampling of sources on Congress, organized in five sections to correspond generally to the five parts of this book. Some sources provide background reading on particular aspects of the history or behavior of Congress; others explore further the nature of its evolution and reform. These selections are not intended to be all-encompassing or comprehensive, but will, hopefully, be of use to those who wish to engage in additional study of these topics.

I. History

ALEXANDER, DEALVA STANWOOD. *History and Procedures of the House of Representatives.* Boston: Houghton Mifflin, 1916.

GALLOWAY, GEORGE. *History of the House of Representatives.* N.Y.: Thomas Y. Crowell, 1961.

HASBROUCK, PAUL D. *Party Government in the House of Representatives.* New York: Macmillan, 1927.

HAYNES, GEORGE H. *The Senate of the United States.* 2 vols. Boston: Houghton Mifflin, 1938.

HINCKLEY, BARBARA. *Stability and Change in Congress.* N.Y.: Harper & Row, 1971.

MacNEIL, NEIL. *Forge of Democracy.* N.Y.: David McKay, 1963.

POLSBY, NELSON W. "The Institutionalization of the U.S. House of Representatives." *American Political Science Review (APSR)* 62 (1968):144–68.

PRICE, H. DOUGLAS. "The Congressional Career: Then and Now." In NELSON POLSBY, ed., *Congressional Behavior.* N.Y.: Random House, 1972.

ROTHMAN, DAVID. *Politics and Power: The United States Senate, 1896–1901.* Cambridge, Mass.: Harvard University Press, 1966.

WILSON, WOODROW. *Congressional Government.* N.Y.: Meridian Books, 1956.

WITMER, RICHARD T. "The Aging of the House." *Political Science Quarterly* 79 (1964):526–41.

YOUNG, JAMES S. *The Washington Community, 1800–1828.* N.Y.: Columbia University Press, 1966.

II. *Congressional Committees*

ABRAM, MICHAEL, and COOPER, JOSEPH. "The Rise of Seniority in the House of Representatives." *Polity* 1 (1968):52–85.

FENNO, RICHARD F., JR. *Congressmen in Committees.* Boston: Little, Brown, 1973.

———. *The Power of the Purse.* Boston: Little, Brown, 1966.

GOODWIN, GEORGE, JR. *The Little Legislatures: Committees of Congress.* Amherst: University of Massachusetts Press, 1970.

JONES, CHARLES O. "The Agriculture Committee and the Problem of Representation." In PEABODY and POLSBY, *New Perspectives.*

MANLEY, JOHN F. *The Politics of Finance: The House Committee on Ways and Means.* Boston: Little, Brown, 1970.

MASTERS, NICHOLAS A. "House Committee Assignments." *APSR* 55 (1961):345–57. Reprinted in PEABODY and POLSBY, *New Perspectives.*

MORROW, WILLIAM L. *Congressional Committees.* N.Y.: Charles Scribner's Sons, 1969.

PEABODY, ROBERT L., and POLSBY, NELSON W., eds. *New Perspectives on the House of Representatives.* Chicago: Rand McNally, 1963.

POLSBY, NELSON W.; GALLAGHER, MIRIAM; and RUNDQUIST, BARRY S. "The Growth of the Seniority System in the U.S. House of Representatives." *APSR* 63 (1969):787–807.

PRICE, DAVID E. *Who Makes the Laws?* Cambridge: Schenkman, 1972.

ROHDE, DAVID W., and SHEPSLE, KENNETH A. "Democratic Committee Assignments in the U.S. House of Representatives." *APSR* 67 (1973):889–905.

WOLFINGER, RAYMOND E., and HOLLINGER, JOAN HEIFETZ. "Safe Seats, Seniority and Future Power in Congress." In WOLFINGER, ed., *Readings on Congress.* Englewood Cliffs, N.J.: Prentice-Hall, 1971.

III. *Leadership*

BOLLING, RICHARD. *Power in the House.* N.Y.: E. P. Dutton, 1968.

EVANS, ROWLAND, and NOVAK, ROBERT. *LBJ: The Exercise of Power.* N.Y.: New American Library, 1966.

FENNO, RICHARD F., JR. "The Internal Distribution of Influence: The House." In TRUMAN, DAVID, *The Congress and America's Future.*

FROMAN, LEWIS A., JR., and RIPLEY, RANDALL B. "Conditions for Party Leadership." *APSR* 59 (1965):52–63.

HUITT, RALPH K. "Democratic Party Leadership in the Senate." *APSR* 55 (1961):333–44.

————. "The Internal Distribution of Influence: The Senate." In TRUMAN, *Congress and America's Future.*

JONES, CHARLES O. *Minority Party Leadership in Congress.* Boston: Little, Brown, 1971.

PEABODY, ROBERT L. "Party Leadership Change in the U.S. House of Representatives." *APSR* 61 (1967):675–93. Reprinted in PEABODY and POLSBY, *New Perspectives,* 2d ed.

————. *Leadership in Congress: Stability, Succession and Change.* Boston: Little, Brown, forthcoming.

PEABODY, ROBERT L., and POLSBY, NELSON W., eds. *New Perspectives on the House of Representatives.* 2d ed. Chicago: Rand McNally, 1969.

POLSBY, NELSON W. "Two Strategies of Influence: Choosing a Majority Leader, 1962." In PEABODY and POLSBY, *New Perspectives,* 2d ed.

RIPLEY, RANDALL B. *Majority Party Leadership in Congress.* Boston: Little, Brown, 1969.

————. *Party Leaders in the House of Representatives.* Washington, D.C.: Brookings Institution, 1967.

————. *Power in the Senate.* N.Y.: St. Martin's Press, 1969.

TRUMAN, DAVID, ed. *The Congress and America's Future.* 2d ed. Englewood Cliffs, N.J.: Prentice-Hall, 1973.

IV. *Rules, Norms, and Roles*

ASHER, HERBERT B. "The Learning of Legislative Norms." *APSR* 67 (1973):499–513.

DAVIDSON, ROGER. *The Role of the Congressman.* N.Y.: Pegasus, 1969.

FROMAN, LEWIS A., JR. *The Congressional Process.* Boston: Little, Brown, 1967.

HUITT, RALPH K. "The Outsider in the Senate: An Alternative Role." *APSR* 55 (1961):566–75.

MATTHEWS, DONALD R. *U.S. Senators and Their World.* N.Y.: Random House, 1960.

MILLER, CLEM. *Member of the House: Letters of a Congressman.* N.Y.: Charles Scribner's Sons, 1962.

ORNSTEIN, NORMAN J., and ROHDE, DAVID W. "The Strategy of Reform: Recorded Teller Voting in the House of Representatives." Paper presented at the 1974 Annual Meeting of the Midwest Political Science Association, Chicago, April 25–27, 1974.

PREWITT, KENNETH; EULAU, HEINZ; and ZISK, BETTY H. "Political Socialization and Political Roles." *Public Opinion Quarterly* 30 (1966–67): 569–82.

PRICE, CHARLES M., and BELL, CHARLES G. "The Rules of the Game:

Political Fact or Academic Fancy?" *Journal of Politics* 32 (1970): 839–55.

SALOMA, JOHN S. *Congress and the New Politics.* Boston: Little, Brown, 1966.

SMITH, T. V. *The Legislative Way of Life.* Chicago: University of Chicago Press, 1940.

WAHLKE, JOHN, et al. *The Legislative System.* N.Y.: John Wiley & Sons, 1962.

V. Congressional Reform

BIBBY, JOHN, and DAVIDSON, ROGER. "Inertia and Change: The 1970 Legislative Reorganization Act," in *On Capitol Hill.* 2d ed. Hinsdale, Ill.: Dryden, 1972.

BOLLING, RICHARD. *House Out of Order.* N.Y.: Dutton, 1966.

CLARK, JOSEPH S. *Congress: The Sapless Branch.* N.Y.: Harper & Row, 1964.

———, ed. *Congressional Reform.* N.Y.: Thomas Y. Crowell, 1965.

DAVIDSON, ROGER; KOVENOCK, DAVID; and O'LEARY, MICHAEL. *Congress in Crisis: Politics and Congressional Reform.* Belmont, Calif.: Wadsworth, 1966.

MCINNIS, MARY, ed. *We Propose: A Modern Congress.* N.Y.: McGraw-Hill, 1966.

ORNSTEIN, NORMAN J., ed. "Changing Congress: The Committee System." *The Annals of the American Academy of Political and Social Science* 411 (January, 1974).

U.S., Congress, House, Select Committee on Committees, *Committee Organization in the House*, 93d Congress, 1st sess., 1973, 3 vols., 7 parts.